The Timetable of
COMPUTERS

OCTAL DECIMAL BINARY

The Timetable of COMPUTERS

Second Edition

A Chronology of the Most Important People
and Events in the History of Computers

DONALD D. SPENCER, Ph.D.

CAMELOT PUBLISHING COMPANY
Ormond Beach, Florida

DEDICATION
Mary Francis Aumiller

Published by
CAMELOT PUBLISHING COMPANY
P.O. Box 1357
Ormond Beach, FL 32175

Library of Congress Cataloging-in-Publication Data

Spencer, Donald D.
    The timetable of computers : a chronology of the most important people and events in the history of computers / Donald D. Spencer. -- 2nd ed.
      p. cm.
    Includes bibliographical references and index.
    ISBN 0-89218-346-2
    1. Computers--History.   I. Title
QA76.17.S65 1999
004'.09--dc21   98-34757
                                          CIP

PREFACE

The computer has evolved naturally through the centuries from early counting devices like the abacus. But today, instead of manipulating beads on a wire, we rely on electronic impulses to accomplish the same goals. Like the telephone, television, the automobile, and the airplane, the computer has transformed our world. In this book we will look at the history of computing, from primitive calculating methods to modern microcomputers.

The Timetable of COMPUTERS is an illustrated chronology of the most important events in computing from early days to the present. This book tells what happened, and who made it happen. The book is a work that allows the reader to comprehend the events that have taken place in computing. In a manner that is both fascinating and accessible, it charts the progress to date and documents the remarkable achievements of the men and women of computing, computer science and related areas.

Illustrations and photographs are used throughout the book to highlight specific computers and computing events and to portray some of the people who made important contributions to computing. The comprehensive index will allow the book to be used for general and particular reference. It is hoped that this book will prove a useful guide through the many centuries of computing development.

The book is an indispensable reference work for everyone interested in the history of computing, computers, computer science and information processing. As a guideline to the development of computing and computers, **The Timetable of COMPUTERS** will be invaluable to computer science teachers, students, writers, researchers, and others. Follow Donald Spencer's computing guidelines for an entertaining and informative trip through the history of computing.

TABLE OF CONTENTS

3000 BC

Clay tablets with grooves to hold pebbles or other small objects for counting are designed in the Tigris-Euphrates Valley.

2000 BC

The abacus originates in Egypt, almost a millennium before it reaches the Orient.

Stonehenge

Stonehenge astronomical observatory is built in England.

1800 BC

Babylonian mathematician develops algorithms to resolve numerical problems.

530 BC

By arranging simple gnomons (carpenters' square units) and pebbles a certain way, Pythagoras was able to free mathematicians from "Egyptian geometry." This marks the beginning of modern mathematics.

450 BC

Stones used as counters are used by the Greeks. This form of abacus will later be adopted by the Romans and developed into the medieval European counting board.

105 BC

Mathematician Heron founds the first college of technology at Alexandria.

100

Paper is invented in China.

200

Chinese mathematicians use the saun-pan, a "computing tray," while the Japanese use a similar device, a soroban.

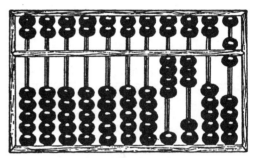

abacus

300

The abacus reaches Europe.

524

Roman philosopher Boethius attempts to replace the abacus with a device that uses fewer counters. His invention is not extensively used, and he is beheaded when he falls out of favor with the Goth King.

595

Decimal reckoning appears in India.

600

Book printing starts in China.

The use of the abacus dominates European computing.

1000

Pope Sylvester II, known as monk Gerbert of Aurillac (France, 938-1003), devises another, more efficient abacus, which is not widely accepted. He also creates the idea of mechanizing algorithms. A computer program is the translation of an algorithm into a well defined computer language.

1200

Hindu-Arabic numerals are introduced into Europe.

1202

Leonardo of Pisa (Fibonacci) publishes a book called *Liber Abaci* (The Book of the Abacus), which does not deal with the abacus at all but is designed to show how the new Hindu-Arabic numerals can be used for calculation.

1300

The abacus is firmly entrenched in Chinese society.

1398

The first known use of the word "computer" is by a scribe named Trevisa who writes of "compotystes... departed by twelve mones, in six even and sixe odde," a reference to maintaining the calendar.

1450

A calibrated instrument known as a quadrant is developed in Europe for taking sights and measuring distances.

Johann Gutenberg

1456

Johann Gutenberg (1396-1468) first to print using movable type.

1489

The + and - symbols come into use.

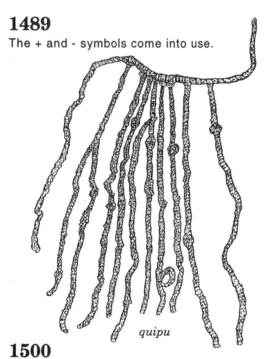

quipu

1500

The quipu is used extensively by Incas.

1502

The first watch is invented.

1606

Developing military technology gives rise to the need for instruments to calculate a gun's trajectory. This need is met by several inventors, including Galileo in Padua, who designs a mechanism called a "sector."

1608

The telescope is accidentally invented by Dutch spectacle maker Hans Lippershey.

1614

John Napier's *Merifice Logarithmorum Canonis discripto*, one of the great papers in the history of science, is published. It introduces logarithms and contains ninety pages of tables.

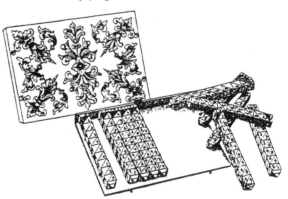

Napier's bones

1617

Scottish nobleman John Napier devises a set of numbering rods, known as "Napier's bones," to ease the pains of calculations. These sticks make multiplication and division easier by being, in essence, movable multiplication tables. They will directly influence the invention of the slide rule and some of the calculating machines that will follow.

1621

William Oughtred (1575-1660), an English mathematician, invents a circular slide rule that translates Napier's logarithms onto a set of rotating scales. The device is considered to be one of the earliest analog computing devices. Oughtred calls his device the "Circles of Proportion."

1623

Wilhelm Schickard (1592-1635), at the University of Heidelberg in Germany, designs and begins to build a calculating machine that incorporates Napier's bones onto cylinders that can be rotated to perform calculations. It accomplishes multiplication and division by converting numbers to logarithms, adding or subtracting them, and converting them back. The machine is destroyed in a fire before completion. It is the first known description of an adding machine. Schickard dies of the plague shortly thereafter.

1624

Henry Briggs computes common logarithm tables to 14 decimal places.

1628

Adrian Vlacq publishes the first complete set of modern logarithms.

1631

English mathematician William Oughtred (1575-1660) proposes the symbol "X" for multiplication.

1637

In his *Discourse on Method*, Rene Descartes conceives of a machine that can "utter words" or "cry that it is hurt." He only knows of clockwork figures, primitive when compared with modern computers, but he conjectures that, however clever the machine, it will never be able to hold a conversation with a human being.

Pascaline—Pascal's adding machine

1642

French mathematician, Blaise Pascal develops the first workable automatic calculator—the *Pascaline*. Similar to calculators used until a few decades ago, the machine arranges the digits of a number in wheels. When each wheel makes a complete revolution, it in turn shifts its neighboring wheel one-tenth of a revolution, totaling each digit counted. On top of the box are windows through which one can view the totals. The machine can add and subtract.

1654

Robert Bissaker develops the first slide rule with a sliding stock.

1666

Sir Thomas Morland (1625-1695) uses a series of disks to replace Napier's bones and develops an operational multiplier.

Gaspard Schott of Germany creates an Organum Mathematicum, a mathematical mechanical aid that expands upon "Napier's bones."

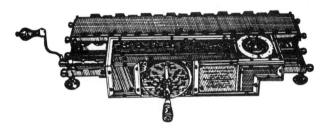

Leibniz's calculator

1673

German philosopher Gottfried Leibniz (1646-1716) builds a mechanical calculating machine that can multiply and divide as well as add and subtract. The machine uses a cylinder with stepped teeth, now known as the Leibniz wheel. It is the first general-purpose calculating device able to meet the needs of mathematicians.

1679

Gottfried Leibniz helps perfect the binary number system.

1709

The Italian Giovanni Poleni builds a calculating machine that will accept instructions by a setting of various levers. The machine then automatically goes through the prescribed sequence. Wind it up, and you can automatically compute the four fundamental arithmetic operations to three figures.

1710

On February 14, the Watt patent is issued for a duplicating machine.

1725

Basile Bouchon uses a perforated tape to control the weaving of ornamental patterns in silk. This idea will be refined over the years by a number of inventors, including Joseph Marie Jacquard and Charles Babbage.

Lepine's adding machine is built.

1726

Jonathan Swift describes a machine that will automatically write books in Gulliver's Travels.

1728

M. Falcon, a French engineer, develops a loom that is operated by perforated cards.

1735

John Harrison's chronometer refines the clock to a precision instrument.

1738

Jacques de Vaucanson (1709-82) exhibits a mechanical copper duck that flaps its wings, swims, drinks, pecks, and smooths its feathers with its beak. This is the first example of a machine built to imitate natural animation—a robotic duck.

1745

Jacques de Vaucanson uses holes punched in metal drums (and later in cards) to control textile looms.

Benjamin Franklin

1752

Benjamin Franklin, in Philadelphia, erects lightning rods after having found, through his famous kite experiment in 1751, that lightning is a form of electricity.

1769

Baron von Kempelen of Presburg, Hungary, tours Europe to exhibit a chess playing "machine" whose cabinet actually conceals a human chess master.

1770

Hahn introduces the first dependable four-process calculator (using the Leibniz cylinder).

1777

Charles Mahon (1753-1816) invents a "logic demonstrator." A simple, pocket-sized instrument, it can solve traditional syllogisms, numerical problems in logical form, and also elementary questions of probability.

1786

Galvani becomes the first person to identify electric current.

J.H. Muller publishes an idea for an automatic difference engine.

1800

Counting boards were widely used in Europe between 1200 and 1800.

The first wet battery is developed.

Jacquard's textile loom

1801

Frenchman Joseph M. Jacquard (1752-1834) invents the first successful machine to operate from punched cards—a textile loom. This machine is used to weave intricate designs into cloth. Jacquard introduces automation and becomes the forefather of the punched card system. By 1812 11,000 looms had been sold in France, and some 1,000 more in the rest of Europe.

1814

J.M. Hermann designs a special-purpose analog computer called the "Planimeter."

1820

Danish physicist Hans Christian Oersted discovers the relationship between electric current and magnetism.

Charles Xavier Thomas (1785-1870) of France designs a calculator which is said to be the first to perform all four mathematical functions correctly. This calculator, called the "arithmometer," will win a medal at the International Exhibition in London in 1862. Over the next 30 years, approximately 1500 arithmometers are manufactured.

1821

Michael Faraday, widely recognized as the father of electricity, reports his discovery of electromagnetic rotation and builds the first two motors powered by electricity.

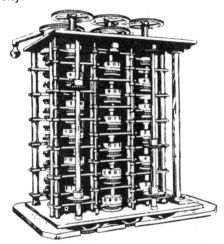

Difference Engine

1822

Endowed with a passion for accuracy, Englishman Charles Babbage (1791-1871) successfully designs a Difference Engine to calculate logarithmic tables. Babbage spends more than 6,000 pounds of the government's money and draws from an inheritance of his own as well, but the machine is never built.

1831

Michael Faraday, the son of an English blacksmith, builds the first electrical generator.

1833

Charles Babbage has a new idea for a calculating machine. In striving to improve the design of his Difference Engine, he develops the outline for the first general-purpose computer, the Analytical Engine. This machine is never completed but involves brilliant parallels to modern computers. Augusta Ada Byron (1815-1853), a skilled mathematician and close friend of Babbage, works closely with

Babbage and proposes the idea that it will be possible to program the Analytical Engine with a single set of cards for recurring sets of instructions. Thus, the Analytical Engine is the world's first computer and it can be programmed to solve a wide variety of logical and computational problems. This machine will be the standard by which future calculating machines will be measured.

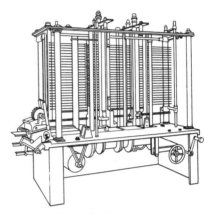

Analytical Engine

1835

Joseph Henry invents the electrical relay, a means of transmitting electrical impulses over distances that serve as the basis of the telegraph.

Roschenschold publishes the discovery that an electric current will flow only one way through some solids—the basis of the solid state or semiconductor diode as a device for controlling electron flow.

1837

Samuel Morse patents his version of the telegraph, which sends letters in codes consisting of dots and dashes.

Augusta Ada Byran

1842

Lord Byron's daughter, Augusta Ada Byron, documents the work of Charles Babbage, becoming the first programmer. She also inspires Babbage, a man badly in need of inspiration, to continue his work. Augusta Ada, for whom the ADA programming language is named, dies of cancer at age 36.

1843

British clock maker Alexander Bain patents the basic concept of sending an image electrically. He uses punched paper tape to send telegraph messages, greatly improving the speed of transmission.

1850

Amedee Mannheim designs the logarithmic slide rule, which will dominate mechanical calculation for the next 100 years.

D.D. Parmalee develops the first key-driven calculator. A patent is issued on February 5.

1851

Victor Schilt exhibits a key-driven adding machine at the Crystal Palace Exposition in London, England. The Exposition promotes the application of science to technology and focuses world attention on British progress in both fields.

1852

A Frenchman named Martin Corteuile patents an organ that is programmable. The upright Steinway will be made in 1860 and will use a roll of programmed paper.

George Boole

1854

English mathematician George Boole (1815-1864) creates Boolean algebra and lays the groundwork for Information Theory. Boole's theory of logic, based on the three operators "and," "or," and "not," reduces logic to a simple form of algebra so that many arguments can be handled as simply as mathematical formulas.

An electric telegraph is installed between London and Paris.

1855

The first practical programmed computer is built by Swedish engineer George Scheutz of Stockholm, Sweden, and exhibited at the Paris Exposition. Based on the principles expounded by Charles Babbage, but of simpler construction, Scheutz's calculating engine can compute to four orders of difference, and print out answers accurate to eight places of decimals. Scheutz's Difference Engine is the world's first printing calculator.

1855

Heinrich Geissler Igelshieb develops his mercury pump, used to produce the first good vacuum tubes. These will lead to the development of cathode rays and eventually to the discovery of the electron.

1859

England's Registrar's office uses the Scheutz Difference Engine for calculating actuarial tables to predict life expectancy. This is the first use of the new technology by a government agency.

1860

In Sweden, Martin Wiberg builds a Difference Engine and uses it to prepare a set of interest tables for publication. The machine is also used in the preparation of logarithmic and trigonometric tables that will appear in 1875.

1861

New York and San Francisco are connected by a telegraph line.

1863

Thomas Edison discovers the thermionic emission which is the basis of the vacuum tube.

1865

Abbé Caselli introduces the first commercial facsimile system between Paris and Lyons, France.

1866

Cyrus West Field lays the first successful transalantic cable across the Atlantic Ocean, stretching from Ireland to Newfoundland.

1867

In the June issue, the computer keyboard's predecessor, the typewriter, is first described in *Scientific American*.

American logician Charles Sanders Peirce notices that George Boole's two-valued logic lends itself readily to a description in terms of electrical switching circuits. Peirce's discovery will lie dormant until the mid-1930s when Claude Shannon at MIT, John Atanasoff at Iowa State College, and the German engineer Konrad Zuse will independently demonstrate that binary numbers and Boolean algebra are both ideally suited for computer design. That is, an appropriate electric circuit of switches can simulate both arithmetic and logic.

1869

William Jevons (1835-1882) sees Boole's algebraic logic as the greatest advance since Aristotle. His machine, called Jevons' Logical Piano which uses a logical alphabet of four terms, is built to perform operations on Boolean principles.

C.L. Sholes patents the first practical mechanical typewriter. Four years later Sholes will sell his improved machine and it will become Remington Rand's No. 1 mechanical typewriter.

Charles Babbage

1871

Charles Babbage dies before the Analytical Engine is completed. On October 23, Babbage's obituary appears in the *Times* of London. He left more than 400 square feet of drawings for his Analytical Engine. By the time Babbage died, all the ingredients to make the electronic computer had been discovered.

1874

W.T. Odhner (1845-1905), a Swedish engineer, patents a "pinwheel" method for adding any digit from 1 to 9, now known as the "Odhner wheel." Odhner machines are widely used until the introduction of the electronic calculator in about 1960.

Emile Baudot perfects a system called the multiplex telegraph, which allows up to eight telegraph messages to share a single telegraph line. It is the first electronic communication device to use a typewriter-style keyboard, a tradition that continues to this day.

1875

Frank Stephen Baldwin invents the first practical reversible four-process calculator in the United States.

The Tanaka Seizousyo company is founded in Japan. The company, which manufactures telegraphic equipment, later merges with the Shibaura Seisaku-sho company to form Tokyo Shibarura Denki. The name of this company will later be shortened to Toshiba, a worldwide manufacturer of many items, including computer products.

A breakthrough in the calculating machine industry happens when the first properly constructed variable toothed gear is made.

1876

William Thomson (Lord Kelvin) shows that machines can be programmed to perform mathematical calculations.

The telephone is invented by Alexander Graham Bell. His patent (U.S. Patent 174, 465) is the most lucrative patent ever granted.

1877

The microphone is invented.

1878

On September 10, a patent is issued for Ramon Verea's direct multiplication and division machine.

James Ritty develops the first cash register. The machine sells poorly and he later sells the business.

Thomas Edison, in a letter to a friend, uses "bug" in its context long before the term is used with computers.

Arthur Burkhardt makes improvements on the machine made by Charles Thomas, and founds the calculating machine industry in Germany.

1879

William Thomson (Lord Kelvin), a nineteenth-century scientist, builds a "tide predictor." A mechanical system of drums, cables, and dials, it shows that differential equations, which deal with relationships among variables, can be solved by machine. The tide predictor is one of the earliest special-purpose analog computers.

Thomas Alva Edison invents the first incandescent light bulb that can burn for a significant length of time.

1880

Emile Baudot's punched paper tape telegraph code is introduced.

1881

Only five years after Alexander Graham Bell patented the telephone, Kibataro Oki sets up a company to manufacture telephones in Japan. Oki Electric will later become a communications company and a major electronics manufacturer including computer chips and equipment.

American Allan Marquand builds a machine which can handle propositional logic problems.

E. Thacher, a New York inventor, patents a huge cylindrical rule.

1882

The following comment is contained in a letter written by Lord Rayleigh in England: "Yesterday, I had the opportunity of seeing the telephone which everyone has been talking about. The extraordinary part of it is its simplicity. A good workman could make the whole thing in an hour or two. I held a conversation with Mr. Preece from the top to the bottom of the house with it and it certainly is a wonderful instrument, though I suppose not likely to come much into practical use."

1883

Astronomer John Couch Adams devises a method of solving differential equations. This computational technique will be used by Francis Bashforth to improve the accuracy of ballistic tables.

Initially a discovery by Thomas Edison, the vacuum tube forms the building block for the entire electronics industry. Because Edison is trying at the time to create a better light bulb, he doesn't pay much attention to the potential value of the tube within the bulb.

1884

Thomas Edison invents the electric light bulb. It consists of a carbon filament (modern bulbs use tungsten wire) enclosed in a vacuum inside a glass bulb. An electric current flowing through the filament causes the filament to heat up and glow.

John Henry Patterson purchases the Ritty cash register patents and the National Manufacturing Company of Dayton, OH, and renames it National Cash Register Company (NCR). NCR will go on to become a major manufacturer of computers and terminals.

Felt's calculating machine

Dorr Eugene Felt (1862-1930) designs a calculating machine that is the forerunner of today's key-driven calculators. His initial machine, called Felt's "macaroni box," is made from meat skewers, elastic bands, staples, and a large wooden macaroni box. Felt will finish a perfected model, called the Comptometer, in 1885.

1885

Boston is connected to New York by telephone.

The first computing scale is patented by Julius E. Pitrat of Gallipolis, Ohio. His patents are bought by Edward Canby and Orange O. Ozias, businessmen in Dayton, Ohio, who incorporate the Computing Scale Company in 1891. This company will become part of the Computing-Tabulating-Recording (C-T-R) Company and eventually the IBM Corporation.

1886

Another inventor driven by the drudgery of manual calculation, William Burroughs (1857-1898), an American bank clerk, develops the first commercially successful mechanical adding machine. His company is the forerunner of Burroughs Corporation, now part of Unisys Corporation.

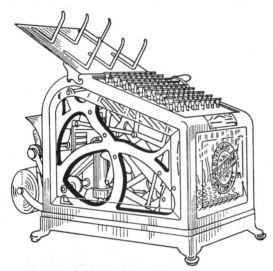

Burrough's adding machine
Ottmar Mergenthaler invents the Linotype machine, which produces complete lines of metal type.

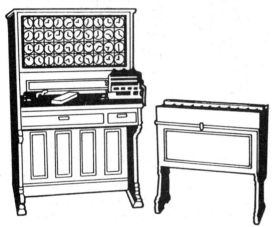

Hollerith's tabulator

1887

Herman Hollerith (1860-1929), a statistician with the U.S. Census Bureau, develops a punched card machine to take the census figures of the United States for 1890. After completing the census, Hollerith starts the Tabulating Machine Company (TMC). Over the years through acquisitions and mergers, TMC will grow to become the IBM Corporation.

Leon Bollee of France invents the first machine to successfully perform multiplication by the direct method instead of by repeated addition.

1888

On August 21, a patent is issued for William S. Burroughs' calculating machine. This machine is later modified to include subtraction and printing. It is the world's first dependable key-driven calculator and will soon win widespread acceptance.

Willard Bundy, a jeweler in Auburn, New York, devises a mechanical time recorder. The next year, his brother Harlow organizes the Bundy Manufacturing Company to produce time recorders. The company later relocates to Endicott, New York as the International Time Recording Company which, in 1911, becomes part of the Computing-Tabulating-Recording (C-T-R) Company and eventually the IBM Corporation.

1889

Dorr Felt produces the Comptograph, a practical adding and listing machine.

Charles Babbage's son, Henry, builds a working model of the mill portion of the Analytic Engine. The mill is used to compute multiples of π.

Leon Bollee, at the age of eighteen , wins a gold medal at the Paris Exposition for his "multiplier." Bollee will invent other calculators and office machines, but in his mature years he will be chiefly interested in designing, building, and racing automobiles. He later founds LeMans, the famous French racetrack, and built racing cars of advanced design.

Troncet develops a pocket type of calculator which performs both addition and subtraction.

1890

Handling the information needed to run a business—inventory, billing, sales figures, profit and loss statements—has been done by clerks, by hand. But now the growing size of businesses is straining the capacity of manual systems. Businesses are looking for a fast, accurate form of mechanical tabulation.

Facing the prospect that the current census will take more than ten years to compile manually, the U.S. Census Bureau uses Herman Hollerith's invention, the first electromechanical punched card tabulator. Hollerith's tabulator is the first machine that uses punched cards for data processing.

Otto Schaffler in Vienna used machines based on Hollerith's design to tabulate the Austrian census.

The cover and the main article in the August 30 issue of *Scientific American* discusses Herman Hollerith's punched card system. The cover shows scenes from the 1890 U.S. population census.

1891

Henri Genaille's and Edouard Lucas' rulers, similar to "Napier's bones," are marketed.

1893

Chess playing machine is envisioned by Ambrose Bierce in his short story *Moxon's Master*.

Otto Steiger (1858-1923), of Zurich, Germany, develops a machine that is, in effect, an automated version of Gottfried Leibniz's machine. Between 1894 and 1935, over 4,500 calculators are sold under the name "Millionaire" for scientific calculations. The Millionaire is used by government agencies and scientists, especially astronomers, well into the 20th century.

1894

William S. Burroughs produces the first practical adding machine for business purposes.

Variable-toothed gear is invented by Odhner and Baldwin and becomes the basis for the Monroe calculator.

1895

Herman Hollerith goes to Moscow to sell his tabulating equipment to the Russians, who have never taken a general census. Hollerith sells them the equipment for tabulating the results of their census in 1897.

John Gore, a life insurance actuary, worn out by long hours of calculation, designs a perforating machine and a card sorter. The machines, built with the help of his engineer brother-in-law, will be used well into the 1930s.

1896

W. Jordan reprints the sine and cosine tables from the three hundred year old *Opus Palatinum*. This is early evidence that the introduction of machines has revived the necessity for natural tables.

After adding a sorting machine to his tabulator and seeing the census calculated in just three years, Hollerith decides it is time to go into business for himself. He forms the Tabulating Machine Company, one of the three firms which later became the IBM Corporation.

1897

J.J. Thomson discovers the flow of electrons from a filament to a positively charged electrode and names it the Edison effect. With this property of electron flow, the study of electricity branches out into electronics.

1898

A.A. Michelson, working with Samuel W. Stratton, designs an eighty element harmonic analyzer to study light waves.

1899

NEC is founded as a joint venture between AT&T and a group of Japanese investors. In 1932, NEC will become a wholly Japanese managed company. NEC will go on to become a major chip and computer equipment manufacturer.

Charles H. Duell, U.S. commissioner of patents, who urges the abolishment of the patent office says, "Everything that can be invented has been invented."

1900

Mechanical calculators start to become commonplace.

The entire civilized world is connected by telegraph.

The earliest known example of a complex mechanical analog computer is found in a sunken ship off the Greek island of Antikythera near Crete. The device could "calculate and display" astronomical positions. The ship it was found in sank about 65 BC.

1901

Guglielmo Marconi in Newfoundland receives the first transatlantic telegraphic radio transmission.

1902

Thomas Edison studies the concept of sending images electrically and newspapers begin sending photographs.

1903

Yugoslavian Nikola Tesla, who worked for Thomas Edison, patents electrical logic circuits called gates or switches. Tesla's patents prefigured the relay, the vacuum tube, and the transistor. Tesla, the wild man of electronics, was born in 1856 and came to America in 1884. Tesla loved the power of electricity and dreamed of a world filled with electric light.

1904

Arthur Korn develops a scanner to send photographs by telegraph.

1905

William S. Burroughs' company, the American Arithmometer Company, changes its name to the Burroughs Adding Machine Company. In 1953 the company will become the Burroughs Corporation. Later it will become Unisys Corporation.

The thermionic emission phenomenon is used by John Ambrose Fleming in the construction of the diode vacuum tube.

The first Japanese punched card machine is designed and constructed by Kawaguchi. Japan's second machine will be designed by Takahashi of the Electrotechnical Laboratory in 1920. Ten units of this machine are produced for use in the first census of Japan. All of these machines will be destroyed by the famous earthquake of 1921 in Kanto.

1906

On October 25, Lee DeForest and R. von Lieben invent the first triode vacuum tube. The tube can be used not only to receive signals, but also to amplify them. These two principles, the diode and the amplifier, are used in all manner of electronics. Vacuum tubes will later be replaced by transistors, which are smaller and more efficient.

1907

James Powers develops punched card equipment using mechanical, instead of electrical, sensing devices. His machines will eventually be sold by the Remington Rand Corporation and be major competition to the tabulating system developed by Herman Hollerith.

1908

In Ireland, Percy Ludgate proposes a new design for an analytical engine.

In the 30-year period prior to 1908, five national censuses had been carried out on Hollerith's Tabulating Machines, the American of 1890 and 1900, the Austrian of 1890 and 1900, and the Russian of 1895.

1909

Charles F. Dettering develops the first accounting machine for the National Cash Register Company.

Author L. Frank Baum shares the turn of the century optimism about machines as a positive force. An admired (but not beloved) character in his famous Oz series is Tik-tok, the clockwork copper man who "was sure to do exactly what he was wound to do, at all time and in all circumstances."

1910

James Powers develops a die-set device capable of punching all of the holes in a 20-column card simul-

taneously. His patents will later form the backbone of Remington Rand Corporation.

Tik-tok from Frank Baum's Oz series

Hollerith's company sues the Census Bureau, claiming that machines developed for the agency by James Powers infringe on his patents. The suit is disposed of without significant action.

Principia Mathematica, a book by Bertrand Russell and Albert North Whitehead presents the idea that logic is the foundation of all mathematics. Twenty-seven years later, in 1937, Claude E. Shannon shows that the methods of symbolic "true or false" logic described by Russell and Whitehead can have practical application to the design of electrical switching circuits.

There are 7,635,400 telephones in use.

1911

The company previously formed by Herman Hollerith (Tabulating Machine Company) merges with the Computing Scale Company and the International Time Recording Company to become the Computing-Tabulating-Recording (C-T-R) Company. C-T-R is the beginning of what will become the IBM Corporation.

James Powers forms the Powers Accounting Machine Company. His company eventually becomes Remington Rand Corporation, Sperry Rand Corporation, and finally Unisys Corporation.

1912

The Institute of Radio Engineers (IRE) is formed.

1913

Henry A. Wallace, an agriculture professor at Iowa State University, develops methods and shortcuts in computing correlations with calculating machines.

Printing tabulators that print only numbers come into use.

Watson's THINK slogan

1914

Thomas J. Watson, Sr. is hired by Herman Hollerith's company, now the Computing-Tabulating-Recording Company (C-T-R), with 1,300 employees. The company resulted from the merger of the original Tabulating Machine Company with the International Time Recording Company, and the Computing Scale Company. Watson, Sr. formerly worked for the National Cash Register Company, where he coined his legendary THINK slogan.

Jay R. Monroe introduces the Monroe Calculator which incorporates previous designs by Frank Baldwin. The Monroe Calculator is the first keyboard rotary machine to attain commercial success.

Lenardo Torres y Quevedo, (1852-1936) a Spanish researcher, publishes detailed plans for the construction of a digital calculating machine using electromechanical design principles. Arithmetic problems are typed in on a typewriter, and the arithmometer causes the typewriter to type out the answers. At about the same time, Torres also built what is considered to be the first decision-making automatic machine—a chess playing machine. Playing an end game with a rook and king against a human opponent's king, the machine would checkmate.

Scientific American hails the arrival of "a great brass brain," a tide predictor designed for the U.S. Coast and Geodetic Survey by E.G. Fischer and R.A. Harris.

1915

The first North American transatlantic telephone call is made between Thomas A. Watson in San Francisco and Alexander Graham Bell in New York.

1917

Aberdeen Proving Ground develops mathematical techniques for computing and printing firing tables for new types of advanced ordnance used in World War I.

1918

H. Abraham and E. Block invent the electronic swing, or multivibrator circuit which clears the way for the use of vacuum tubes in computers. The circuit, which instead of producing wave-like vibrations induces the bouncing of waves between two unstable points, will prove invaluable in computer technology.

The Victor Adding Machine Company is founded. The first product is the Victor 110, a keyboard adding machine designed by Oliver David Johantgen. Forty years in the future they will have produced 1,500,000 adding machines.

1919

American physicists W.H. Eccles and R.W. Jordan invent the flip-flop electronic switching circuit. The circuit "flips" and "flops" from one stable state to another and is the heart of the high-speed electronic counting system which will become the key function of the digital computers of the future.

Early versions of the Enigma cipher machine is built in Europe.

The first radio transmission of a voice across the Atlantic ocean takes place.

1920

The term "robots" is first used in Czechoslovakian dramatist Karel Capek's play R.U.R. (Rossum's Universal Robots). Capek extracts the now-common name for automation from "robota," the Czech word for work. The humanoid mechanical servants in his drama rebel and destroy their human masters. The word, robot, becomes a synonym for the remote-controlled mechanical "men" built in the 1920s and 1930s.

The IBM Corporation sells at least 15 different makes of coffee grinders.

Smathers invents the mechanical-electrical typewriter.

In Spain, Leonardo Torres y Quevedo builds several algebraic equation solvers since 1893, each increasingly sophisticated. In 1920 Torres constructed an electromagnetic calculating machine that was driven by operands typed on a typewriter and delivered its results using the same device.

Electromechanical machines come into general use.

Ben D. Wood pioneers the use of technology to perform research on statistical data. To help him, the IBM Corporation modifies a commercial translator.

Radio broadcasting begins in Pittsburgh, Pennsylvania, at station KDKA.

1921

Radio Shack opens its first store in Boston, Massachusetts. The company later becomes part of the Tandy Corporation and an early manufacture of popular microcomputers.

1923

Vladimir Kosma Zworykin, the father of television, gives the first demonstration of an electronic television-camera tube, using a mechanical transmitting device.

Thomas J. Watson, Sr.

1924

Thomas J. Watson, Sr. rises to president and CEO of his company, changing the name to International Business Machines Corporation (IBM Corporation). The original name of the company was Computing-Tabulating-Recording Company (C-T-R). Ironically, Watson knows more about salesmanship than about his company's product line.

IBM Corporation develops the Carroll Press, a printing cylinder that is used to manufacturer punched cards commercially at high speed. The fast rotary press helps meet the industry's need for billions of punched cards annually.

1925

IBM Corporation begins selling punch card equipment in Japan.

Vannevar Bush and colleagues at Massachusetts Institute of Technology start building a large-scale analog calculator, the differential analyzer. Though mostly mechanical, the calculator will have electric motors that store number values as voltages in its thermionic tubes. The differential analyzer will be the first analog computer.

IBM Corporation introduces the IBM 080 card sorter which can process 400 punched cards per minute.

Formal establishment of AT&T's Bell Laboratories, a research company that will produce many discoveries in the computer area.

1926

On October 8, the Lilienfeld patent is filed for the solid crystal amplifier.

Mechanical people appear in the movies in Fritz Lang's silent film, *Metropolis*.

Early versions of the Hagelin and German *Enigma* cipher machines appear.

The first commercial transatlantic telephone service opens.

1927

Powers Accounting Machine Company, through a series of consolidations, becomes the Tabulating Machine Division of Remington Rand Corporation, which later becomes Sperry Rand Corporation and then Unisys Corporation.

The *New York Times* describes the earliest type of CRT display, the television. The article questions the commercial viability of such a product. This is the first public mention of TV.

J.A. O'Neill patents magnetic coated tape.

1928

Leslie John Comrie of England utilizes Herman Hollerith's electromechanical devices for computing the predicted motion of the moon over a 65-year interval. His work will help foster the use of computing machines in conjunction with scientific research.

Russian immigrant Vladimir Kosma Zworykin at RCA Corporation receives a patent for a color television system.

The German Enigma machine encodes the first message for transmission.

IBM Corporation adopts the 80-column punched card, the standard for the next 50 years. The increased data capacity of a punched card from 45 to 80 columns of information paves the way for a new series of machines to be introduced in the early 1930s—machines that not only can add and subtract but can also perform full-scale accounting operations.

British astronomer Leslie John Comrie uses punched card machinery to compute moon orbits. He was the most influential champion of the calculating machine's use in science.

John von Neumann presents the minimax theorem, which will be widely used in game-playing programs.

Gustav Tauschek of Austria patents an electromagnetic drum storage device.

Paul V. Galvin founds the Galvin Manufacturing Corporation in Chicago, Illinois. The company manufactures battery eliminators, which allow radios to run on normal household current.

1929

The use of tabulating machinery grew so quickly that Russia is reported to be the third largest user, following the United States and Germany.

The number of telephones in the United States totals 20 million—more than twice as many as in the whole of the rest of the world.

Remote access to computing facilities have early beginnings. Edward Rogal installs point-of-sale recorders in Kaufmann's department store in Pittsburgh, with each recorder connected by wire to a central keypunch facility, the purpose being to control credit authorization and inventory by recording unit transaction data at the time it occurs.

The first person to make use of punched card machines in scientific computation is L.J. Comrie in England. He produces a classic paper titled *Brown's Tables of the Motion of the Moon*.

The sales of radio sets reach $900 million, up from $60 million seven years earlier.

1931

The IBM Corporation introduces its accounting machines in Japan.

Compagnie Machines Bull is founded in France to produce and sell punch card equipment. In 1950 the company decides to build a big computer. The Gamma 3 will be introduced in 1953, but it will be a fiasco. Later, with a license agreement with RCA, Bull will sell and produce the RCA 301 computer.

1932

Physiologist Walter B. Cannon views the animal body as a self-regulating machine. Cannon's ideas are well known to Norbert Wiener. In fact, Cannon's *Wisdom of the Body* may be read as sort of an introduction to Wiener's *Cybernetics*, which will be published in 1948. The essential idea is that homeostatic behavior in animals may be viewed in the same terms as goal-seeking mechanical automata.

Derrick Henry Lehmer builds the Photoelectric Number Sieve, a specialized machine useful only for finding prime numbers and for finding the factors of composite integers.

The first computer tune is "Daisy" at Bell Laboratories. HAL will also sing it while having his memory banks unplugged in the 1968 film *2001: A Space Odyssey*.

First use of a totalisator board to record racetrack bets.

The RCA Corporation demonstrates a television receiver with a cathode ray picture tube. The following year Russian immigrant Vladimir Kosma Zworykin produces a cathode ray tube, called the iconoscope, that makes high-quality television almost a reality.

Cambridge physics professor C.E. Wynn-Williams is the first to use large-scale electronic counters for constructing a binary counter to keep track of events in experiments.

1933

The IBM Corporation's first educational building and an engineering laboratory are constructed in Endicott, New York.

Vannevar Bush (1890-1974) and his associates at the Massachusetts Institute of Technology develop and place in operation the first analog computer to solve differential equations. Called a differential analyzer, it is mechanical, and uses differential gears whose angular rotation indicates quantities.

Wallace J. Eckert (1902-1971) links together several different IBM punched-card accounting machines. To run these machines as a unit, Eckert makes a mechanical program that controls a plug cable relay box. His unique arrangement of machines is the forerunner of scientific computing at Columbia University.

H.W. Dudley builds the first electric speech machine, the Voder (Voice Demonstrator).

IBM Corporation enters the electric typewriter business when it purchases Electromatic Typewriters, Inc. The first IBM electric typewriter will be put on the market in 1935.

A Totalisator machine is installed at a racetrack near Chicago, Illinois.

Vannevar Bush

IBM Corporation introduces the IBM 031 keypunch. It is one of the first machines to permit punching of letters as well as numbers into cards.

British physicist Douglas R. Hartree is the first to use an automatic calculator for problems in atomic theory. He builds, with Arthur Porter, a model of Vannevar Bush's differential analyzer. Based on the success of the model, Hartree directs the construction of a full-scale differential analyzer the following year at the University of Manchester.

1934

The IBM Corporation introduces the IBM 405 tabulator which can add or subtract 150 punched cards per minute.

The Communications Act of 1934 creates the Federal communications Commission (FCC), the agency that will regulate interstate and international communications, including telecommunications.

1935

At last users are convinced that the electric typewriter, available in some form since 1902, is safe to use. This change of heart is largely the result of the IBM Corporation's investment of more than a million dollars in their new model.

The Burroughs Adding Machine Company's product line includes 450 standard models of manual and electric calculators, bookkeeping machines, and typewriters.

IBM Corporation introduces the IBM 601 multiplying card punch.

Alan Turing

1936

Alan M. Turing (1912-1954), an English logician, proves mathematically that it is possible to build a digital computing machine that can solve virtually any mathematical problem which can be formulated in a clearly-defined manner. He publishes a paper outlining the theory of mathematical logic that illustrates computer design. The paper "On Computable Numbers" is published on November 12. By showing that simple computing machines can be instructed to simulate any more complicated machines, he provides a basis for the development of automatic programming.

In Germany, Konrad Zuse, a mechanical engineer, designs the Z1 computer, with keyboard input, mechanical switches and a row of light bulbs to flash answers. This is the first machine to use floating-point binary arithmetic.

First large IBM installation at the Social Security Administration, where punched-card equipment perform over 120 million postings per year.

Konrad Zuse

Church's Thesis and a similar proposal by Emil Post are later considered conceptually identical to the concept of a Turing machine.

Benjamin Burack, a psychologist at Roosevelt College in Chicago, Illinois, constructs the first electrical logic machine.

George Stibitz

1937

While working at his kitchen table one evening, Bell Laboratory mathematician George Stibitz hooks together some batteries, lights, and wires according to the principles of Boolean logic. By connecting several logic gates in a particular arrangement, he

creates a circuit that can add binary numbers. This circuitry, called a binary adder, is the basic building block of all modern computers. Stibitz's adder demonstrates the feasibility of mechanizing binary arithmetic.

The IBM 077 collator is developed for the Social Security program. The Social Security agency punched cards from the records sent in by employers all over the country. Ida Fuller of Ludlow, Vermont, receives the nation's first Social Security benefit check.

ASIS is founded.

Engineer Howard Aiken begins work on digital computers. By 1944 he produces the Automatic Sequence Controlled Calculator (ASCC, also called the Harvard Mark I). It will be the most popular calculator ever to use rotating electromechanical components.

Claude Shannon

1938

American mathematician Claude Shannon shows how an abstract algebraic system can be applied to logical problems. This will lead, a decade later, to his "information theory" which presents communication in terms of statistics and information in terms of measured quantities, and will bring about a fundamentally new approach to computer programming. Shannon shows how Boolean algebra can be used to analyze computer circuits.

American engineer, Doug T. Ross, constructs the first machine able to "learn" from experience. The machine, based on the principle of feedback memory, can find its way out of a maze by trial and error. Later, more refined versions will become computer-controlled industrial robots, capable of adjusting their actions to adapt to new situations.

G.A. Philbrick develops the first electronic analog computer. It is used primarily for military purposes.

In Germany, Helmut Schreyer receives his doctoral degree in engineering for demonstrating how electronic vacuum tubes can be used as basic units for ultra-high-speed digital computers.

The photocopying process is patented by Chester F. Carlson. In nine years, Xerox copy machines will become available.

William Hewlett and David Packard, doing graduate work at Stanford University, their alma mater, find the perfect place to live: a house in Palo Alto with an apartment for Packard and his wife Lucille, a cottage on the grounds for Hewlett, and, most important, an 18 by 12 by 8 foot garage. In their garage workshop they begin making audio oscillators and other electronic devices. This is the beginning of their company—the Hewlett-Packard Company. They name their company with a coin toss. Hewlett wins the toss, and his name is used first. The company will go on to become one of the major computer manufacturers. Fifty years later the garage will be declared a historic landmark as the birthplace of Silicon Valley. It is originally painted brown, with green doors and eaves.

1939

Konrad Zuse completes his Z2 machine.

World War II starts in Europe. Alan Turing's ideas will play a key role in British efforts to break the Germans' Enigma code machine.

Atanasoff-Berry Computer (ABC)

Iowa State College professor John V. Atanasoff designs a prototype for the ABC (Atanasoff-Berry Computer) with the help of graduate student Clifford Berry. The design is said to be the first working model of the electronic digital computer. It is the first machine to use vacuum tubes for the logic circuits. Atanasoff discovers the four basic principles for a digital computer in an interesting epiphany on a dark and cold winter night; he jumps in his car in front of his Iowa house to think things over for a bit and ends up in an Illinois roadhouse four hours later, with all the details worked out in his mind. In 1973 a judge rules the ABC is the first automatic digital computer.

Elektro and Sparko button

In the Westinghouse exhibit at the New York's World's Fair, Elektro and Sparko, a robot man and dog, demonstrate the art of robotics. Elektro's 26 actions include smoking cigarettes, counting up to 10 on his fingers and reciting a speech. Sparko can set up, beg, bark and wag his tail.

The Complex Number Calculator (Model 1 relay computer), one of the first electrical digital computers built of relays, is built at Bell Laboratories by George Stibitz. Controlled manually via keyboard, this machine is used for engineering calculations.

The first Radio Shack catalog is published.

1940

A British team creates Robinson, an electromechanical relay computer. This machine is later replaced with Colossus, a computer that uses electronic tubes.

In January, Dickinson files a patent for electronic storage element.

Claude Shannon releases his first paper on communications theory.

At Bell Laboratories, George Stibitz is able to enter data on a teletypewriter located at Dartmouth College in Hanover, New Hampshire and connected by wire to his Complex Number Calculator in New York, receiving replies by wire at Dartmouth. This remote processing experiment, creates the first terminal.

On August 27, the first color TV broadcast.

In 1937, Adolf Hitler bestowed upon Thomas J. Watson, Sr., CEO of the IBM Corporation, the Order of Merit of the German Eagle with Star, and assured him, "There is to be no war." Three years later, Watson severs diplomatic relations with Hitler by sending back his medal. Hitler retaliates by forbidding Watson to ever set foot on German soil. In Basel, after the war, Watson has the last word, gleefully walking across the bridge to Germany and back.

Parkinson sketches the M-9 robot.

Zuse's Z3 relay computer

1941

Konrad Zuse builds the Z3 electromechanical relay computer. Its program is entered on punched film. The Z3 has a 64-word memory and a 3 second multiplication time.

When World War II starts, IBM puts all company facilities at the disposal of the government. More than five thousand accounting machines are used in Washington to keep track of men and materials. Other machines are installed in mobile units that follow U.S. troops overseas. Among wartime products made by the IBM Corporation are naval and aircraft fire control instruments, Browning automatic rifles, .30 caliber carbines, bombsights, and aircraft supercharger impellers.

William Hewlett, cofounder of Hewlett-Packard Company, is drafted into the Army Signal Corps, and David Packard is left to run the company.

The first direct application of computer technology to weaponry (antiaircraft gun director system) occurs.

The IBM 040 unit converts telegraph paper tape directly into punched cards. It is the first machine to do so.

1942

On August 25, Morton and Flory patent is filed for a storage device.

On December 2, the first nuclear reactor operates.

J. Presper Eckert and John Mauchly, of the University of Pennsylvania's Moore School, propose an electronic version of the Vannevar Bush differential analyzer for the Army, which would operate digitally instead of by analog means. The proposal will lead to the development of the ENIAC.

Substituting the radio industry's vacuum tubes for relays, IBM Corporation engineers build an experimental multiplier (IBM Vacuum Tube Multiplier). It can calculate thousands of times faster than electromechanical machines.

Vannevar Bush completes his second model of the analog calculator, subsequently used to help devise artillery firing tables for the U.S. Government.

John Mauchly writes *The Use of High Speed Vacuum Tube Devices for Calculating.*

German computer designer Konrad Zuse and his sometime associate Helmut Schreyer, an Austrian electrical engineer, propose constructing a radical kind of computer. The two men want to redesign the Zuse Z3 computer so that it uses vacuum tubes rather than electromechanical relay switches. Their proposal is turned down. It is still early in the war, and Adolph Hitler feels so certain of quick victory that he orders an embargo on all but short-term scientific research.

1943

In February, a patent is issued for printed wiring.

Colossus

Great Britain's Colossus decoding machine gives the Allies a direct line to the German high command. The machine works fast enough to test all possible code combinations before the information becomes outdated, and accurately decodes the crucial German Enigma messages until the end of World War II. Colossus, an electronic computer designed by Alan Turing, has over 20,000 vacuum tubes, occupies two floors, and can do four mathematical functions: addition, subtraction, multiplication, and division. Although it is, in theory, a powerful general-purpose computer, the Colossus is dedicated solely to code breaking and will be classified until well after the end of World War II. Only one piece of this computer exists today.

IBM Corporation develops a top-secret IBM computer that decodes intercepted radio messages for the U.S. during World War II. The machines are essentially hot-rodded commercial IBM punch-card machines with special relay calculators. Some of the work done with the computer: it decodes messages sent by German spies about U-boat schedules; it helps the U.S. learn of a Japanese plan to send fake radio messages from the Aleutian Islands after they had been abandoned in an effort to forestall an invasion of U.S. forces; and it helps find out that Japanese leaders approached Russian leader Josef Stalin with a peace plan, which Stalin rebuffed.

Grace Murray Hopper works with Howard Aiken on the Harvard Mark I. At Harvard University, she starts a distinguished career in the computer industry by being the first programmer for the Mark I.

Emil Post defines computation based on generalized grammar rules. These rules eventually become the basis for transformational grammars in linguistics and rule-based expert systems in computer science.

The IBM Corporation makes the W2 Form a reality. It provides the government with the equipment to track withholding pay.

J. Presper Eckert

John W. Mauchly and J. Presper Eckert, two scientists from the University of Pennsylvania, sign a contract with the Ballistic Research Laboratory to develop ENIAC (Electronic Numerical Integrator And Calculator), the first large-scale electronic digital computer. ENIAC is completed three years later. By means of electronics, it brings speed to the world of computers. It is used to calculate ballistic trajectories.

An analog flight simulator project called "Project Whirlwind" is developed at the Massachusetts Institute of Technology. Two years later the project will be switched from analog to digital electronics.

1944

The Colossus Mark II computer is built in England.

The IBM Corporation produces the Pluggable Sequence Relay Calculator for the U.S. Army.

An important application of computer technology to weaponry in World War II is the M-9. During the defense of Antwerp, the M-9 enables Allied Forces to shoot down 4,672 out of 4,883 V-1 rockets.

IBM Corporation engineers, after eight years of research, develop the first typewriter to have proportional spacing.

John W. Mauchly

Automatic Sequence Controlled Calculator

Howard Aiken of Harvard University, collaborating with IBM engineers, completes the ASCC (Automatic Sequence Controlled Calculator). The ASCC is used until 1948 to produce math tables day and night. The ASCC is also known as the Harvard Mark I. The ASCC is the largest electromechanical calculator ever built. It has 3,300 relays and weighs 5 tons. It can multiply two 23-digit numbers in six seconds. The ASCC is patterned after Charles Babbage's Analytical Engine. Numbers are stored on "registers" containing sets of wheels. Each wheel rotates according to its number and is controlled by a telephone relay. Punched paper tape carries the instructions.

The U.S. Army asks the Moore School at the University of Pennsylvania to build a more powerful calculator than ENIAC, which is still under construction. A year later John von Neumann responds with a complete logical design for a machine to be called the EDVAC (Electronic Discrete Variable Automatic Calculator). Von Neumann's report is titled *First Draft of a Report on the EDVAC.*

First documented use of the word "bug" in relation to computers is in Bob Campbell's April 17th entry in the Log Book for the Mark I computer at Harvard University. Thomas Edison in 1878 was the first person to use the word "bug" in its context.

1945

In wartime Germany, unable to obtain material for circuits to control his computers, Konrad Zuse creates Plankalkul, a high-level programming language for both numerical and non-numerical problems. The language is never implemented.

Alan Turing gives a clear exposition of nested subroutines whose calling sequences are based on a pushdown stack, floating point arithmetic, and remote use of a computer over a telephone line.

The Pilot ACE (Automatic Computing Engine) is designed by Alan Turing at the National Physical Laboratory in Middlesex, England. ACE has a storage capacity of 512 words, an adding time of 32 microseconds, and a multiplication time of 1 millisecond. ACE is adapted for commercial development by the English Electric Company.

Science fiction writer Arthur C. Clarke proposes the use of geostationary satellites for communications between distant parts of the Earth. He thus lays the intellectual foundation for nearly all modern space communications systems.

Whirlwind, an experimental computer, is started at the Massachusetts Institute of Technology and it eventually yields the first magnetic core memory.

Only one model of this 16-bit computer is ever produced; it will operate from 1950 to 1959.

Teleregister Corporation develops and installs a reservation system called Reservisor for American Airlines. This system is later replaced by the SABRE computerized reservation system.

The Electronic Journalism Research Society is founded.

Vannevar Bush's article, "As We May Think," appears in *Atlantic Monthly*, foreseeing the use of hypertext and predicts the development of personal computers.

IBM President, Thomas J. Watson, Sr., orders the firm's Endicott, New York laboratory to develop a successor to the Harvard Mark 1. This leads to the development of the Scientific Sequence Electronic Calculator (SSEC) in 1947. The research becomes the springboard for future IBM systems.

IBM, with sales of $142 million, ranks 94th among the top 100 corporations in the United States. Some four decades later, in 1984, revenues of $46 billion catapults the company into sixth position among the 500 leading industrial firms in America.

Konrad Zuse completes the Z4 electromechanical programmable calculator. Wernher von Braun helped Zuse escape from Berlin, Germany with this machine hidden in a wagon. Zuse went into hiding in the Swiss Alps. He later did work for the IBM Corporation and Remington Rand (now Unisys Corporation), and sold his interests to the German computer firm Siemens.

1946

Vacuum tube machines can multiply two 10-digit numbers in 1/40 of a second.

On June 28, John von Neumann, with Arthur W. Burks and Herman H. Goldstine, publishes *Preliminary Discussion of the Logical Design of an Electronic Computing Instrument.* This is a crucial document in the history of computer science. It describes how a program is a sequence of numbers stored in the computer's memory.

Computerized Monte Carlo techniques are developed in conjunction with early nuclear weapons research by Stanislaw Ulam and John von Neumann.

Time is money—Chicago has the first drive-in bank. Fifty years in the future, almost all banks will have drive-in facilities and computer-controlled automatic tellers.

ENIAC

J. Presper Eckert, John Mauchly and a team of fifty engineers complete the Electronic Numerical Integrator And Calculator (ENIAC), the first large-scale, electronic digital computer, at the University of Pennsylvania's Moore School. Weighing 30 tons, and covering 1500 square feet, ENIAC operates at 357 multiplications per second. Sponsored by the U.S. Army, the $500,000 project is aimed at designing a computer for the rapid calculation of military ballistic tables. It is programmed by externally set plugs and switches and, therefore, is not considered a true stored program computer. ENIAC is widely used for scientific calculation until it is retired in the early 1950s.

IBM Corporation introduces the IBM 603 Calculator, the first production line vacuum tube machine, it helps write an end to electromechanical data processing.

International Standards Organization (ISO), an international organization that sets standards, is founded.

John von Neumann begins the influential IAS project at Princeton University which has the goal of developing a digital computer.

Herman H. Goldstine invents flowcharts.

Howard Vollum starts Tektronix after World War II to build oscilloscopes.

Warren Weaver and Andrew Booth propose natural language translation by machine.

John Tukey is the first person to use the term "bit" for binary digit.

The first of the two Bell Laboratories' Model V computers is completed. The second machine is built the following year.

1947

At the University of Pennsylvania, John von Neumann designs and builds the EDVAC (Electronic Discrete Variable Automatic Calculator) for the U.S. Government's Ballistic Research Laboratory. It is the first machine capable of storing a flexible program which can be changed without revising the computer circuits. The EDVAC is not completed until 1952.

The selectron vacuum tube is introduced at the RCA Laboratories. This is one of the earliest electronic tube binary memory units. It becomes part of a new calculator at the Institute of Advanced Studies in Princeton, New Jersey, which is capable of multiplying "any great number in about a hundred millionths of a second."

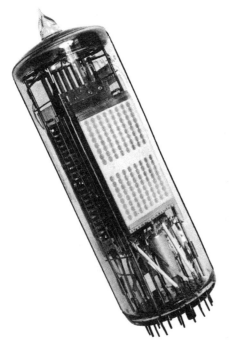

RCA electrostatic storage tube

J. Presper Eckert and John Mauchly form the Electronic Control Company, the first computer company. It was later renamed the Eckert-Mauchly Computer Corporation.

On June 16, the ENIAC patent is filed.

Frederic C. Williams at Manchester University in England develops a high-speed data storage method in which millions of charged spots are stored on the face of a cathode ray tube. This storage method is now called William's Tube Memory.

The Association for Computing Machinery (ACM), the largest computer related professional society, is founded on September 15. ACM is an international scientific and educational organization dedicated to advancing the art, science, engineering, and application of information technology, serving both professional and public interests by fostering the open interchange of information and by promoting the highest professional and ethical standards. The nine founding members of the ACM are Edward G. Andrews (Bell Laboratories), Edmund C. Berkeley (Prudential Insurance Company), Robert V.D. Campbell (Harvard Computation Laboratory), John H. Curtiss (National Bureau of Standards), J. Presper Eckert (Moore School of Electrical Engineering), John W. Mauchly (Moore School of Electrical Engineering), John B. Russell (Columbia University), Paul W. Taylor (Massachusetts Institute of Technology), and Samuel B. Williams (Bell Laboratories).

George B. Dantzig invents a method called the Simplex Algorithm to short-cut the process of examining all the combinations of variables. With it, complex problems with thousands of constraints and variables can be solved easily (with the help of computers).

Eckert-Mauchly Computer Corporation is awarded its first contract to build BINAC for Northrop Aircraft Company.

While Leonardo Torres y Quevedo had advocated the automatic control of industrial machines in 1913, the term "automation" is actually coined in 1947.

Richard Hamming of Bell Laboratories invents error-correcting codes.

Alan M. Turing publishes an article on "Intelligent Machinery" which launches artificial intelligence.

The Association for Systems Management (ASM) is founded.

The IBM Corporation decides not to invest in computers because the market is too small.

Only a year after the completion of ENIAC, the first large-scale electronic computer, Arthur Samuel proposes to build a computer to play checkers.

J. Lyons & Co., Ltd. in England, proposes to use an electronic computer in its office. As no commercial machine is available at this time, the company decides to build one. The computer, based on the Cambridge University EDSAC, is completed in 1953 and named LEO (Lyons' Electronic Office).

Large-scale calculating machines are for the most part thought of as expensive scientific specialty items. Yet, the Eckert Mauchly Computer Corporation starts to build the first computer designed for commercial use, the UNIVAC I.

The Harvard Mark II, under the direction of Howard Aiken, goes into operation. The Mark II is considerably faster than the Mark I.

1948

John Bardeen, Walter Brattain, and William Shockley announce the invention of the transistor and the world is generally unimpressed. The *New York Times* covers the news in four paragraphs on the next to last page. Scientists register much skepticism over the fragility, expense, and new production methods required. Such are the shaky beginnings of a technology which is destined to change the world. The transistor is a revolutionary replacement for the cumbersome vacuum tube.

Bardeen, Brattain and Shockley

The IBM Card Programmed Calculator (CPC) is released by the IBM Corporation.

Speech synthesis is based on the theory of visible speech, formulated by H.C. Green, G.A. Kopp and R.K. Potter, who show how phonemes correspond to graphic traces. Speech synthesis is used in many applications including computer games, educational software and automobiles.

Norbert Wiener

Norbert Wiener publishes *Cybernetics*, the science of control and communication in both animals and in machines. This widely read and influential book discusses some of the effects computers might have on society.

Alan Turing and David Champernowne write complete specifications for a one-move analyzing chess machine they name the "Turochamp." When the Manchester University's MADM computer is finished, Turing programs it to be the first machine capable of playing a complete game of chess.

Stimulated by Norbert Wiener and formalized this year by Claude E. Shannon, "information theory" treats communication as a problem in statistics. Like computers, the theory deals with "information" rather than meaning.

The computer industry's first "replaceable unit" is an assemblage of electronic parts in the IBM 604 multiplying punch. Service engineers can simply plug in a replacement.

M.E. Conway uses English abbreviations in computer programs, thus replacing all number programming requirements. This greatly advances programming.

Manchester Mark I computer goes operational. This "baby" version of a larger computer is being built at the University of Manchester in England. The baby machine is built by Frederic C. Williams and Tom Kilburn using a Williams Tube Memory.

The index register is invented by M.H.A. (Max) Newman and Tom Kilburn.

Jealous of ENIAC's success and miffed at Howard Aiken, who snubbed IBM at the Mark I dedication, Thomas J. Watson, Sr. orders the building of an ENIAC-like computer, the Selective Sequence Electronic Calculator (SSEC). With more than 12,000 vacuum tubes and 21,000 electromechanical relays, SSEC becomes the target of cartoonists and motion picture makers, who use its huge size and flashing lights to illustrate the outlandishness of computers of the period. The SSEC is a stored program computer.

Andrew Donald Booth creates a magnetic drum memory two inches long and two inches wide and capable of holding 10 bits per inch.

IBM Corporation produces the IBM 604 multiplying punch, based on vacuum tube technology.

Television is starting to become popular.

1949

The University of Illinois undertakes to build two copies of the John von Neumann machine: the ILLIAC I for use at the Urbana campus and the ORDVAC for use at the Aberdeen Proving Ground.

Maurice Wilkes of England's Cambridge University builds the Electronic Delay Storage Automatic Calculator (EDSAC). A student at Eckert's and Mauchly's Moore School lectures, Wilkes works with a copy of John von Neumann's draft on the Electronic Discrete Variable Automatic Computer (EDVAC) to beat out American designers. The EDSAC uses mercury delay lines, punched paper tape input, and teleprinter output. The EDSAC is a full-scale stored program computer.

Standards Eastern Automatic Computer (SEAC) and Standards Western Automatic Computer (SWAC) are built by the National Bureau of Standards as the first and second American electronic stored program computers using all-diode logic. These machines will be put into operation in the following year.

Short Code, the first computer language actually used on an electronic computing device, appears. It is, however, a "hand-compiled" language.

J. Presper Eckert and John Mauchly (Eckert-Mauchly Computer Corporation) complete the Binary Automatic Computer (BINAC) for Northrop Aircraft Company, making it one of the first operational stored program computers. The BINAC consists of two computers that simultaneously carry out the same calculations, whose results are then compared. It is never reliable enough to be put into routine service.

An Wang applies for a patent for magnetic core memories. Years later he sells the patent to the IBM Corporation for $400,000. He uses this money to start Wang Laboratories, Inc., a manufacturer of computer equipment.

Neurocomputer science is the science of computers whose architecture is modeled on that of the brain. The first machine to be built is the Perceptron, which is designed by Frank Rosenblatt. Later, engineers switch the focus of their research to artificial intelligence.

Edmund C. Berkeley publishes *Giant Brains: or Machines That Think*, a book well ahead of its time.

Plane of magnetic core

Jay Forrester

Jay Forrester, at Massachusetts Institute of Technology, conceives the idea of organizing magnetic core computer memories, a notion developed by An Wang, into a grid or matrix, providing a far greater practical application than serial connection.

In England, work begins on LEO (Lyons Electronic Office), a commercial version of EDSAC.

ENIAC is converted to a stored program computer by Richard Clippinger.

Thirty machine accountants meet at the Morrison Hotel in Chicago to form the National Machine Accounts Association. The organization, is founded in 1951 and later renamed Data Processing Management Association (DPMA).

The Harvard Mark III, under the direction of Howard Aiken, goes into operation. The Mark III uses an internally stored program and indirect addressing.

1950

Burroughs Corporation builds its first magnetic drum computer, a prototype of the UDEC and starts on the way to becoming a power in the computer field.

Hideo Yamashita leads a developing team that will create Japan's first large electronic computer, the Tokyo Automatic Calculator (TAC).

Claude E. Shannon, the founder of a branch of mathematics called "information theory," outlines a plan for coding a chess playing program that will make use of heuristic programming techniques. Shannon realizes the necessity of having a good scoring function (a chess master's most valuable asset is his ability to assess the merit of a position). Shannon, at Massachusetts Institute of Technology, builds a chess playing machine, called *Caissac*.

The ERA 1101 stored program computer is announced by Engineering Research Associates. The ERA 1101 is the beginning of the computer industry in the Twin Cities (St. Paul-Minneapolis, Minnesota).

Ferranti, Ltd. builds a special purpose computer called the Nimrod, to play the game of Nim.

SEAC (Standards Eastern Automatic Computer) completed at the National Bureau of Standards, Washington, D.C. is the first practical stored program computer to operate and be put into routine service in the United States.

A computer begins playing checkers.

ENIAC delivers the first computer weather forecast.

There are now a total of 60 computers in operation. Each one is individually designed and individually built.

Ferranti, Ltd. builds the Mark I, the first commercial computer in Great Britain. This follows an order for seven such machines from Britain's National Research and Development Corporation.

Kurt Vonnegut, Jr., writes about "EPICAC" in one of the first love stories involving a computer.

The word "automation" is first used to describe the increasing use of automatic machinery in making automobiles. Others begin using the word automation to mean the use of computers to control production equipment.

Using an 8 by 8 chessboard, Alan Turing writes the first computer program to simulate chess.

Edmund C. Berkeley designs and builds a simple automatic computer (called SIMON) containing 130 relays and a five-hole paper tape input.

K.H. Davies at Bell Laboratories builds the first machine to recognize ten numbers pronounced by a human voice as a series of sonic signals.

The Electronic Discrete Variable Automatic Calculator (EDVAC) is now complete. It is the first computer to use binary or digital mathematics.

Commercial color television begins in the United States.

Alan Turing proposes a test of machine intelligence. Suppose a person typing at a terminal exchanges messages with a hidden interlocutor who is occasionally a computer and occasionally a human being. If the person cannot tell whether the interlocutor is a person or a computer, then the computer has exhibited intelligent behavior.

The American military begins to use computers to simulate operations in its "war games."

The National Bureau of Standards Western Automatic Computer (SWAC) is put into operation at the University of California at Los Angeles (UCLA). SWAC is built by Harry Huskey. Two years later the SWAC completes in 13 minutes and 25 seconds a complicated problem that would probably take a human being 100 years to figure with the aid of a desk calculator.

W. Weaver and A.D. Booth first think of using a computer to help with language translation.

Yoshiro Nakamats at the Imperial University in Tokyo, Japan invents floppy disks. He grants the sales license for the disk to the IBM Corporation.

Remington Rand Corporation buys the financially troubled Eckert-Mauchly Computer Corporation. This marks the first time a large, established company enters the computer business.

There are 15 computer installations in the United States. The dollar value is $1 million.

Bell Laboratories Model VI relay computer is completed. This is the last of Bell Labs relay computers.

Maurice V. Wilkes at Cambridge University uses an assembler (symbolic assembly language) on the EDSAC.

The first universal digital calculator is constructed in Sweden, BARK (Binar Automatisk Relakalkylator), is a binary relay calculator. Three years later the BESK (Binar Elektronik Sekvens-Kalkylator) is completed.

Elliott Brothers, Ltd. in England develops Nicholas, a nickel delay line store machine.

The General Electric Company's first electronic digital computer (OMIBAC) is developed by the Aeronautics and Ordnance Systems Division in Schenectady, New York.

1951

Geophysical Service Inc. is renamed and called Texas Instruments Inc., a leading manufacturer of semiconductors, computers, terminals, and computer peripherals.

Alan M. Turing specified the design of a computer called the Automatic Computing Engine (ACE) for the National Physical Laboratory in 1945. Edward Newman and James Wilkinson produce a working model of ACE, which uses mercury delay lines for memory.

On December 26, the Data Processing Management Association (DPMA) is founded.

Wang Laboratories, Inc. is founded on June 30, selling core memories for $4 each. Dr. An Wang starts the company only six years after coming from China to study applied physics at Harvard University. The company will later become a major computer manufacturer.

The Whirlwind computer is completed at Massachusetts Institute of Technology by Jay Forrester, Kenneth Olsen, and others. It is the first real-time and control machine. The Forrester patent for magnetic core memory will come out of this project. The Whirlwind computer is the first machine to use magnetic cores for internal storage. Whirlwind performs calculations on data in parallel. It will influence the design of future computers.

Maurice V. Wilkes

Maurice V. Wilkes introduces the concept of microprogramming, which will have a profound effect on later mainframe, minicomputer and microcomputer design. By the early 1960s, microprogramming will be an established way of designing and building computer systems.

A Cybernetics Congress is held in Paris, France.

The Universal Automatic Computer, UNIVAC I, made by Remington Rand Corporation, is delivered to the U.S. Bureau of the Census as the first American commercially produced computer. The UNIVAC I gains general acceptance in the fields of science, the military, and very large corporations. The UNIVAC I is able to perform 2,000 computations a second.

On June 16, the first programming error is encountered at the Bureau of the Census.

First computer-animated movies are made at the Massachusetts Institute of Technology by taking pictures, frame by frame, of a computer display.

Lukasiewicz introduces parenthesis-free Polish notation.

The Computer Group of the Institute of Radio Engineers is founded on October 29 (it will be renamed the IEEE Computer Society in 1972).

In July, the first Joint Computer Conference is held.

Grace Hopper, working for Remington Rand Corporation, begins design work on the first widely known compiler, named A-0. When the language is released by Remington Rand, it is called MATH-MATIC.

John von Neumann

The IAS Computer, built by John von Neumann at the Institute for Advanced Studies at Princeton University, was started in 1946 and completed this year. A number of computers will be modeled after it, including ILLIAC I, JOHNNIAC, MANIAC and ORACLE. The IAS Computer is a stored program computer that uses a cathode ray tube memory. The initial test for the IAS Computer involves calculations integral to the design of the hydrogen bomb.

Compagnie Machines Bull in France announces its first electronic computer, the Gamma 3.

After Professor Frederic C. Williams and his colleagues at the University of Manchester in England had designed and completed two experimental computers with cathode ray tube storage, Ferranti, Ltd. replaces these in 1951 by an engineering version, the Ferranti Mark I computer. A copy of the Mark I will be installed at Toronto University (FERUT) and in 1953 a series of commercial versions are started, the Ferranti Mark I computers.

The First issue of *The Computing Machinery Field* is published. Two years later the publication is renamed *Computers and Automation*. For two decades this publication will keep readers abreast of the computer industry. This popular magazine contains information which is factual, useful and understandable. In 1980, the name of the publication becomes *Computers and People*. The publication will cease to exist in 1988 at the death of the editor and publisher, Edmund C. Berkeley.

William Shockley presents the world with the first reliable junction transistor, a kind of three layer germanium sandwich enclosed in a metal case that stands a half-inch higher.

Engineers at Northrop Aircraft develop a machine called Magnetic Drum Digital Differential Analyzer (MADDIDA) that uses a rotating drum on which successive approximations of the solution to a problem are computed and stored.

T. Raymond Thompson, John Simmons and their team at the Lyons Company introduce England's first business computer, the Lyons Electronic Office (LEO) computer.

Computer Research Corporation delivers the CADAC computer to the Massachusetts Institute of Technology. This computer has a 1024-word drum memory, 195 thermionic valves, and 2,500 germanium diodes, all packed into a small box with wheels. A production model of the CADAC is the CRC 102A. Computer Research Corporation later merges with National Cash Register Company, which markets the 102A and introduces an expanded decimal version, the 102D.

IBM Corporation announces its Defense Calculator and by 1953 the machine, renamed the IBM 701, will be in production.

Universal Automatic Computer (UNIVAC I)

1952

IBM Corporation announces the IBM 701 which can add a typewritten column of 10-digit numbers as tall as the Statue of Liberty in about one second. In one hour it can solve a problem in aircraft wing design that might take an engineer seven years with a desk calculator. The 701 is a portent of the larger, faster machines yet to come. Nineteen 701s will be shipped, mostly for government and research work. The IBM 701 is designed by Nathaniel Rochester. It performs 16,000 additions per second and uses a cathode ray tube for main memory.

In May, patent filed for Darlington amplifier.

Thomas J. Watson, Jr. becomes president of the IBM Corporation, which has forty thousand employees.

The EDVAC (Electronic Discrete Variable Automatic Calculator) is completed. The building of this machine was started in 1947.

Alick E. Glennie, in his spare time at the University of Manchester in England, devises a programming system called AUTOCODE, a rudimentary compiler.

The Nixdorf Computer Company is founded in Germany.

Grace Murray Hopper develops the first set of instructions or programs, to tell the computer how to translate mnemonic symbols into machine language. Hopper pioneers the writing of computer commands in English. She proposes use of the word "compiler" for her A-0 programming system. This is the beginning of the higher level language area.

Burroughs Corporation develops a memory system for ENIAC, the world's first large-scale electronic computer, which increases the computer's memory capacity sixfold.

Walter Cronkite touts UNIVAC I as that marvelous "electronic brain" during its CBS News television debut calculating presidential election returns. The machine predicts Eisenhower's victory just one hour after the polls close. The UNIVAC I used for this prediction is located at Lawrence Livermore National Laboratory.

John Diebold's *Automation: The Advent of the Factory* leads off the string of studies that will explore the computer's impact on employment and leisure time.

Using Teleregister's Reservisor System, agents for American Airlines can automatically request reservations by accessing information stored on a magnetic drum and updated by the computer.

Color television is introduced to the general public; forerunner for quality, economic computer display.

IBM Corporation introduces the Tape Drive Vacuum Column. Before tape can become a popular storage medium, it has to be kept from breaking when the drive suddenly starts or stops. IBM's solution: a chamber in which a loop of the tape is held down by a vacuum. This buffering technique will be widely adapted throughout the industry.

The IBM 701 is one of the first computers to use magnetic tape for reading, writing and storing information. Recording at 100 characters per inch, an 8-inch diameter reel is equivalent to 12,500 punched cards. It will be in production next year.

Automatic programming systems for the UNIVAC I computer are developed: "A-0," "B-0," etc. These are early attempts to make programming easier by moving away from numerical codes.

At the University of Toronto there are two relatives of ENIAC (Electronic Numerical Integrator and Calculator), the VTEC and the FERUT.

Svoboda's SAPO in Czechoslovakia is the first fault tolerant computer.

ILLIAC I (Illinois Automatic Computer) was developed at the University of Illinois.

The first computer simulated war game is conducted by the Rand Corporation.

Remington Rand Corporation buys Engineering Research Associates which was formed by William C. Norris. Five years later, Norris will leave to form Control Data Corporation, one of two major supercomputer makers in the world and a major force in computer services.

MANIAC is developed at Los Alamos under the direction of Nicholas Metropolis.

The IBM Corporation owns ninety percent of all punched card equipment in the United States.

The Digital Computer Association (DCA) computer user group is founded.

D.H. Wheeler computes the value of e to 60,000 decimals on the ILLIAC I, a computer located at the University of Illinois. It took the machine 40 hours to complete the job.

The first course on programming in the U.S.S.R. is taught by Lyapunov at Moscow University.

Raytheon Manufacturing Company builds the RAYDAC (RAYtheon Digital Automatic Computer). It is installed at the Naval Air Missile Test Center in California.

The Selective Sequence Electronic Calculator (SSEC) is dismantled after a modestly productive but short life.

In Germany, the Zuse Z5 relay computer is introduced.

Underwood purchases the Electronic Computer Corporation and introduces the ELCOM 100 computer. Underwood lingers for a while and in 1959 leaves the computer field.

Heinz Nixdorf, an engineer in Germany, develops a calculator and, in 1977 will form the Nixdorf Computer Company.

The Harvard Mark IV, the last of Howard Aiken's machines, becomes operational. The Mark IV uses a ferrite magnetic core memory.

The ORDVAC, a version of Princeton University's Insitute for Advanced Study (IAS) Computer, is now operational.

In the U.S.S.R., several universities start teaching a new specialty in "computing mathematics" in addition to the existing specialty in mathematics.

1953

The Telecommunications Research Establishment (TRE) in England develops the TREAC parallel computer which uses a Williams tube memory.

In the U.S.S.R., Y.Y. Vasilevsky of the Ministry of Automation builds STRELA, a computer with a Williams tube memory.

Andrew Donald Booth, the inventor of the magnetic drum memory, and his father sell magnetic drum memories for use in computerrs. This is the first time magnetic drum memories are marketed commercially.

The Burroughs Adding Machine Company changes its name to Burroughs Corporation.

The National Cash Register Company (NCR) purchases the tiny Computer Research Corporation (a spin-off of Northrop Aviation), which produces medium priced general-purpose computers, and in five years NCR will ship its first solid-state computer, the NCR 304.

Compagnie Machines Bull in France introduces the unsuccessful Gamma 3 computer.

IBM 701 data processing machine

After a slow start, IBM Corporation realizes the potential of computers in industry and launches its IBM 701, to be followed in two years by the IBM 702. Both computers compare well with Remington Rand's UNIVAC I, and IBM will increase its share of the world market to more than 70% within the next decade. A total of 19 IBM 701's are produced and sold.

Burroughs Corporation manufactures the Universal Digital Electronic Calculator (UDEC) at Wayne State University. UDEC weighs several tons, contains ten miles of cabling, uses three thousand vacuum tubes, and seven thousand transistors. Commenting on this machine when it is installed, Arvid Jacobsen, director of the computation lab, says "UDEC may never become obsolete."

The ERA 1103 is the first commercial computer to use interrupts.

By the end of this year, thirteen companies were manufacturing computers. The IBM Corporation and Remington Rand Corporation led the field with a combined total of nine installations.

Cybernetics, defined by American mathematician Norbert Wiener as "the study of control and communication in the animal and the machine" is born; its parents are electronic computers with feedback mechanisms. The new science explores the connection between the function of the human brain and nervous system and the equivalent programming and switching systems in computers.

The Postal and Telecommunications Services at The Hague, Netherlands, develops PTERA (Postal Telecommunications Electronic Automatic Calculator), a magnetic drum computer. PTERA will be dismantled in 1958 and replaced with more advanced computers.

The ORACLE (Oak Ridge Automatic Computer and Logical Engine) is installed at the Atomic Energy Installation at Oak Ridge, Tennessee. The ORACLE contains 3,500 vacuum tubes, about 20,000 resistors, and about seven miles of wire. It is built in 20 months at a cost of $350,000. The machine's memory operates successfully at 2,048 words and it can perform additions in 5 microseconds and multiplications in 500 microseconds.

National Cash Register Company introduces its CRC 1020 commercial computer.

Claude E. Shannon at Bell Laboratories develops several machines that play games: A rudimentary thinking machine that solves the ancient Tower of Hanoi puzzle; Nimwit, which plays expertly at Nim; and a mouse which solves a maze.

The IBM Corporation introduces the first magnetic tape device, the Model 726. It can pack 100 characters per inch and move at 75 inches per second.

The AVIDAC (Argonne's Version of the Institute's Digital Automatic Computer) is unveiled at the Atomic Energy Commission's Argonne Laboratory. The computer design is based on a machine being built by John von Neumann at the Institute for Advanced Studies at Princeton University. The machine contains 2,500 vacuum tubes, about 8,000 resistors and more then three and a half miles of wire. A bank of 355 storage battery cells, under constant charge from motor generators, provides the power for the computer which is constructed at a cost of $250,000. The first problem attempted on AVIDAC is one specified by Nobel laureate Enrico Fermi, then a University of Chicago physics professor and frequent Argonne visitor. The problem is to calculate trajectories of charged particles in a cyclotron's magnetic field. AVIDAC will serve Argonne until the latter part of 1957.

In May, the Johnson patent is filed for the phase shift oscillator.

Vacuum tube machines can multiply two 10-digit numbers in 1/2000 of a second.

In the 39 years between 1914 and 1953, the IBM Corporation has seen assets increase by a factor of 24, employees by 34 and data processing business by 316.

John von Neumann demonstrates the possibility of self-reproducing automation.

IBM Corporation initiates development of the IBM 702 for commercial applications.

Remington Rand Corporation develops a printer capable of printing 600 lines of 120 characters a minute.

1954

The first IBM 650 electronic data processing machine is delivered to a customer. The first mass-produced computer, it is cheaper than the IBM 701 and uses a magnetic drum memory. It is popular with businesses and universities. The IBM Corporation produces more than 1,500 of these machines in a 15-year span. The IBM 650 is the computer industry's Model T Ford.

IBM 650 data processing machine

In January, the Lyons Electronic Office (LEO) begins full-scale operation at the headquarters of the J. Lyons & Co. food and catering organization, Cadby Hall, London, England. LEO is used by Lyons for accounting and payroll preparation. It is the first electronic computer to be used in regular business use. Later in the year the first U.S. commercial computer is installed in a General Electric Company appliance plant in Louisville, Kentucky. It is a UNIVAC I computer. It amazes everyone by doing one thousand calculations a second.

IBM 704 computer system

A computer named JOHNNIAC (named for Johnny von Neumann) is built at the Rand Corporation in California.

Elliott Brothers Ltd., in England develops the Elliott 401 digital computer. The production model, the Elliott 402, is one of the first British machines in which an extensive use is made of plug-in units. Two other scientific computers, Elliott 403 and 404, will follow soon and a data processing machine, the Elliott 405, will be designed.

The Naval Ordnance Research Calculator (NORC) built by the IBM Corporation, is the most powerful computer of its time, with more than 9,000 vacuum tubes. NORC is built for the U.S. Naval Weapons Laboratory. The NORC was started in 1951 and was accepted by the Weapons Laboratory in June 1955. The NORC can perform 15,000 three-address operations per second.

IBM Corporation invents the computer "channel." Operating under its own program, the channel synchronized the flow of data into and out of the computer while computation is in process, relieving the central processor of that task. The channel is later widely adopted in the industry. The patent application for this invention is composed of 1,115 pages.

The first assembler is developed by Nathaniel Rochester for the IBM 701.

It is estimated that perhaps as many as 50 companies in the country could eventually use electronic computers.

S.E.A. (Societe d'Electronique et d'Automatisme) in France constructs its first general-purpose digital computer, called CUBA (Calculatrice Universelle Binaire de l'Armement). The first type of a commercial data processing system, the CAB 2000 series, will be built two years later.

Frederick Brown writes a science fiction story called *The Answer*, in which computers from different planets are linked together and asked if God exists. Their reply is "He does now."

IBM Corporation announces the IBM 704, the first commercial computer with hardware based indexing and floating point arithmetic. The 704 can do 40,000 additions a second.

The Association for Computing Machinery launches the *Journal of the ACM*.

Burroughs Corporation introduces the E-101, a desk-sized electronic digital computer for scientific, engineering and business applications.

English Electric starts building the DEUCE computer which is based on the Pilot ACE.

An operating system is a program that controls all operations within a computer system. This control program acts like the conductor of an orchestra, coordinating the functioning of the computer's different elements. The first operating system is designed by Gene Amdahl of the IBM Corporation for the IBM 704 computer. The first operating system for microcomputers will be CP/M (Control Program for Microcomputing) written by Gary Kildall in 1976.

J.H. Laning and Neil Zierler develop an algebraic compiler for the Whirlwind computer; the first high-level algebraic language for computers.

IBM Corporation announces the IBM 705 computer.

Metropolitan-Vickers in England commences work on designing a medium-speed digital computer and by the end of 1955 the first prototype is operating. A commercial version, the Metrovick 950 general-purpose digital computer, is later developed.

In England, R.A. Brooker introduces a new type of AUTOCODE for the Manchester University Mark I computer.

The Eastern Joint Computer Conference (EJCC) takes place in Philadelphia.

The General Electric Company develops the OARAC computer for the U.S. Air Force.

Physicist Gordon Teal at Texas Instruments Inc. perfects a way of making   transistors out of large, single crystals of inexpensive silicon instead of more costly germanium when the entire industry thought it was impossible.

An experimental programming language compiler (early Russian systems were called programming programs) for the STRELA computer is constructed by E.Z. Liubimskii and S.S. Kamynin.

1955

Radio Corporation of America (RCA) is the top vacuum tube maker in the world and the seventh largest transistor maker.

In the U.S.S.R. a computing center is established at Moscow University in which an M-2 computer is used for both research and instruction.

E.K. Blum at the U.S. Naval Ordnance Laboratory develops ADES (Automatic Digital Encoding System), a mathematical programming language.

Grace Hopper develops MATH-MATIC, the A-3 compiler, and follows this two years later with FLOWMATIC (B-0), the first English language data processing compiler.

The U.S. Navy uses NORC (Naval Ordinance Research Computer) and reflects the increasing use of electronic computers for weather forecasting. Working at the rate of 15,000 mathematical calculations a second, NORC can process the information needed for a 24-hour forecast and calculate a 30 day forecast over one hemisphere of the globe in a mere 5 seconds—a task that previously took a whole year for an unaided human.

At RCA Laboratories in Princeton, New Jersey, Harry Olson and Herbert Belar develop the RCA Music Synthesizer.

On July 20, IBM Corporation opens its new center for automatic electronic processing of data on the main floor of the company's headquarters in New York. There, a customer can bring his problem and make completely sure that his programming is correct in advance of the delivery of the machine he has ordered. Operating at the center are IBM 702, IBM 701 and IBM 650 machines.

The USE users group for UNIVAC computers is formed.

Sperry Gyroscope merges with the Remington Rand Corporation to become the Sperry Rand Corporation. To provide a more manageable structure, the Sperry Rand Corporation decentralizes its operations, and in 1962, UNIVAC becomes a separate division. The Sperry Rand Corporation is one of the IBM Corporation's chief competitors for a time.

Bell Laboratories introduces the TRADIC computer, the first transistorized electronic "brain" for automatic bombing and navigation. The machine can perform 62,500 computations per second. It takes only 1/20 the power needed by vacuum tube computers to operate. That is less power than a 100 watt bulb.

The beginning space program (NASA) and the military, recognizing the need for computers powerful enough to launch space vehicles to the moon and missiles through the stratosphere, fund major research projects.

IBM Corporation delivers the first IBM 704 mainframe computer. It is designed by Gene Amdahl and becomes one of IBM's most profitable computers.

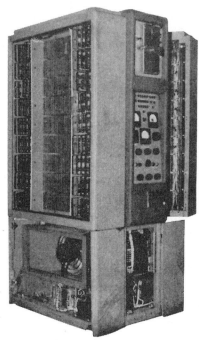

Bendix G-15 computer
The Bendix G-15 is announced—a popular small scale drum-based computer.

Computer Usage Company (CUC) is founded by John W. Sheldon and Elmer C. Kubie. It is the world's first computer software company. CUC's first project, completed in 1955 for California Research Corporation, is to develop an IBM 701 program that will simulate the radial flow of fluids to an oil well.

All the computers in the United States working together can do about 500,000 additions a second.

Minneapolis-Honeywell Regulator Company and the Raytheon Company create the Datamatic Corporation to develop and market large business computers. Most of the new company's 200 employees are engineers, mathematicians, and scientists who as early as 1943 had pioneered developments of electronic computation at Harvard University, the Massachusetts Institute of Technology and the Aberdeen Proving Grounds. Datamatics' first computer is a large, general-purpose, vacuum tube system called the Datamatic 1000. It is successor to the RAYDAC computer Raytheon had delivered to the Navy in 1953 and incorporates vacuum actuated magnetic tape drives.

ERMA (Electronic Recording Machine Accounting) is introduced on September 22 at a grand presentation that captures the imaginations of banking and engineering communities throughout the world. ERMA was built by the General Electric Company for the Bank of America.

The first artificial intelligence (AI) programming language, IPL (Information Processing Language), is invented by John Clifford Shaw, Allen Newell, and Herbert A. Simon. It is developed specifically to develop programs capable of resolving mathematical logic programs.

On October 2, ENIAC is retired. It is estimated to have done more arithmetic than the entire human race had done prior to 1945.

IBM Corporation introduces the IBM 608 calculator, the first all-transistor commercial calculator. Although only a few will be sold because of the high price of transistors, the 608 helps usher in a whole new generation of transistorized computers. The IBM 608 uses 2,200 transistors instead of the 1,200 vacuum tubes that would otherwise be required.

The Western Joint Computer Conference (WJCC) is held in Los Angeles.

SHARE users group meeting is held in the basement of Rand Corporation headquarters in Santa Monica, California. The members, including government, research, aviation and computer organizations, gather to exchange "homegrown" software in the absence of instructions for the newly available IBM 704 mainframe.

William Shockley, one of the inventors of the transistor, leaves Bell Laboratories to set up Shockley Semiconductor Laboratory in Mountain View, California. This company attracts a number of young, ambitious engineers and physicists. One of these is Robert Noyce, who (with seven others) leaves Shockley two years later to form Fairchild Camera and Instrument. The Silicon Valley syndrome of old companies spawning new ones is well under way. After a few years, Noyce will form the Intel Corporation, the world's largest manufacturer of computer chips.

The Sperry Rand Corporation introduces the UNIVAC II computer; it has a magnetic core memory.

Radio Corporation of America (RCA) enters the computer business. Its first computer, BIZMAC, is shipped to the U.S. Army. BIZMAC, installed at the Army Ordnance Tank and Automotive Command in Detroit in 1956, costs $6 million when it is first turned on but becomes obsolete within 3 or 4 years. In 1963, it will be retired and sold as scrap for $7,000. BIZMAC is a magnetic core computer.

General Electric Company's UNIVAC I computer is put to work on payroll—the first commercial application in the U.S.

IBM delivers the IBM 705—a large-scale computer that uses a magnetic core memory.

A magnetic drum store computer, ERMETH, is built by the Hasler AG in Switzerland.

In a speech before a congressional committee in Washington, D.C. on October 26, Ralph Cordiner, president of the General Electric Company, states, in part, "The computer derived technologies will create new industries and new products that will be a major source of new employment in the coming years."

NORC (Naval Ordnance Research Calculator) at Dahlgren, Virginia, is programmed to calculate π to 3,089 decimal places; the run takes 13 minutes.

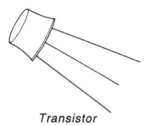

Transistor

1956

In 1951 there were only four companies making transistors. A year later there were eight, and in 1953, 15. In 1955, the top ten transistor making companies were Hughes, Transitron, Philco, Sylvania, Clevite, Motorola, Westinghouse, Texas Instruments, RCA, and General Electric. By 1956, the number of manufactures has risen to 26. However, by 1975 this number will be reduced to three survivors: Motorola, RCA, and Texas Instruments.

The ETL Mark 3, the first tranistor computer in Japan, is developed at the Electronics Division of the government's Electrotechnical Laboratory. The following year, the ETL Mark 4, an improved version of the Mark 3, is developed.

On February 28, Jay Forrester's patent is issued for magnetic core memory.

Sperry Rand Corporation starts work on its ill-fated LARC (Livermore Atomic Research Computer) computer, which is similar to the STRETCH (IBM 7030). The LARC will be the last major effort to create a machine based upon the decimal-only memory storage concept.

Joseph F. Engelberger, a young physicist, met George C. Devol, an inventor, and they created Unimation, Inc., a company that went on to develop thousands of computer controlled robots.

Allen Newell and Herbert Simon present a heuristic approach to prove both theorems in logic and the design of their list processing programming language, IPL II. They create The Logic Theorist, which uses recursive search techniques to solve mathematical problems. This is the first artificial intelligence (AI) program.

A chess program capable of playing on a 6 by 6 board is coded on the MANIAC I computer at Los Alamos Laboratory. The program is developed by Stanislaw Ulam.

Noam Chomsky invents context-free grammar, which is used three years later to describe Algol 60 and nearly all programming languages after this.

Doug T. Ross' APT (Automatic Programmed Tools) programming language for numerical control of machine tools becomes an early successful problem-oriented language. APT, created for the U.S. Air Force, provides the first use of digital control of machine tools and robots.

Automation in banking begins when the ERMA computer handles 32,000 accounts for the Bank of America.

William Shockley, Walter Brattain, and John Bardeen, at Bell Laboratories, are awarded the Nobel Prize in Physics for the development of the transistor. Shockley began working on the first transistor in 1947, but it wasn't perfected until 1952.

The first transatlantic telephone cable begins to operate.

Librascope introduces the LGP-30, a popular, small, inexpensive, general-purpose, drum-based computer.

The birth of the EDP supplies industry occurs on January 25, when the IBM Corporation agrees under an antitrust consent decree to make its punched card patents available to other manufacturers. With the end of IBM's monopoly, new card making organizations spring up with remarkable speed. A decade later there will be over 20 card manufacturers.

Burroughs Corporation acquires the ElectroData Corporation, a small company that had already installed 24 of its Datatron computers (about $120,000 each). It was not until 1964, however, that Burroughs undertook a concerted effort to develop its computer business.

Hideo Yamashita develops TAC (Tokyo Automatic Computer).

Ferranti's Pegasus is the first computer to use general-purpose registers.

The term "byte" is coined during the development of the STRETCH (IBM 7030) computer. The term will become a de facto standard in 1964 when the IBM Corporation introduces the System/360 family of computers.

The General Electric Company enters the commercial computer business.

First direct keyboard input is accomplished on the Whirlwind computer.

The birth of artificial intelligence. A number of researchers meet at Dartmouth College to discuss issues of mutual concern focused on the central question of how to program machines (digital computers) to exhibit intelligent behavior. Among the attendees are Marvin Minsky, John McCarthy (who suggests the term artificial intelligence), Allen Newell, and Herbert Simon. They give impetus to, and shape the direction of, research for years to come.

The Western Joint Computer Conference (WJCC) is held in San Francisco.

The first desk-sized computer, the Burroughs E-101 is made in Philadelphia and demonstrated in Paris and London. The computer is designed to fill the gap between mechanical adding machines and large electronic computers, and is intended for use by mathematicians and scientists, rather than by businessmen and accountants.

The IBM 704, UNIVAC II, and UNIVAC 1103 are the first commercial computers to use magnetic core storage.

National Cash Register Company introduces the first magnetic data storage on ledger cards. This technology will become the basis for the first electronic accounting machine, the Post-Tronic. The magnetic ledger principle is adopted by a number of other business equipment manufacturers.

Lejaren Hiller and Leonard Isaacson at the University of Illinois compose "Illiac Suite for String Quartet." Random numbers are generated, associated with notes and modified by computer. They are the first creative artists to produce computer music. Twenty years later, computers will be widely used in all fields of music, from pop music concerts to teaching.

The ATLAS computer project is started at Manchester University in Great Britain in conjunction with Ferranti, Ltd. The ATLAS computer is similar to IBM's STRETCH (IBM 7030) and Sperry Rand's LARC machines.

Edsger Dijkstra discovers the shortest path algorithm.

Bell Laboratories, the place where the transistor was invented in 1947, builds the Leprechaun, the first experimental transistorized computer. The on-off switching transistor fathers a new breed of more reliable, more economical machines. IBM, Philco, Sperry Rand, RCA, and General Electric quickly follow suit with second generation computers.

An estimated twenty million Americans watch a new electronic computer make its debut on Election Day, November 6, when Elecom 125, Underwood Corporation's new medium scale computer, successfully predicts the outcome of the U.S. presidential race over the combined TV and radio network of the American Broadcasting Company.

In the U.S.S.R., the M20 series computer is designed at the Institute for Precision Mechanics in Moscow.

The Swiss ERMETH computer was started in 1951 under the technical direction of Ambros Speiser and finished this year.

The first recorded computer application to medicine is an experiment on computer assisted diagnosis made in France.

The Symbotic Assembly Program (SAP) is developed for the IBM 704 computer.

In France, F.H. Raymond took out a patent relating to "associate memories." In 1960, Raymond will design an associative memory in the CAB 500 computer.

Remington Rand Corporation develops the 409-3 computer for the U.S. Air Force. In the next year a commercial version of this computer will be developed, the UNIVAC Solid State 80 Computer. This machine will be marketed in Europe and after the summer of 1959 in the United States.

A.I. Kitov publishes *Electronic Computers*, the first Russian textbook on computers for the mass audience.

1957

To demonstrate the automatic features of the Bendix G-15 computer at an automation exposition in New York, an electronic roulette game called "GAMBIT" is introduced to visitors at the Bendix Computer

Division exhibit. Players place "chips" on the board and when all chips are down the computer blinks lights, rings bells, figures the odds, and types out the winning numbers. "GAMBIT" derives its name from "Game for Automation-Minded Bigwigs Insensitive to Treachery."

Datamatic Corporation becomes the Electronic Data Processing Division of Minneapolis-Honeywell Regulator Company. The first product is the giant D-1000 computer system.

More than 7,000 IBM employees are assigned to the U.S. Air Force's SAGE air defense system. The IBM Corporation, installed and serviced the computers that comprised the SAGE system.

IBM Corporation hits $1 billion in sales.

Data processing takes a new direction when the IBM Corporation delivers the IBM 305 RAMAC (Random Access Memory Automatic Computer), the first computer disk storage system. Such machines become the industry's basic storage medium for on-line transaction processing. The system is capable of storing 5 million alphanumeric characters. In less than a second, the RAMAC's "random access" arm can retrieve data stored on any of 50 spinning disks.

Experiments at Bell Laboratories indicate that baud rates in excess of 750 bits per second are realistic. The data stored in a computer consist of bits and bytes. All transmission speed is measured in baud rate (the amount of time required to transmit one bit of data).

Two thousand people attend the Western Joint Computer Conference (WJCC).

Burroughs Corporation produces the first operational transistorized computer used in guiding the launch of the Atlas International Ballistic Missiles. A later version of this computer guides every launch in the Mercury and Gemini programs of NASA's manned

IBM 705 data processing system

space flights. The Atlas guidance computer is one of the first computers to use transistors.

Allen Newell, John Clifford Shaw and Herbert A. Simon write the pioneering "General Problem Solver." It is the first program that solves a problem that it hasn't been specially programmed to solve. The program uses means-ends analysis to solve problems. This ambitious program is made to potentially solve all problems.

The British Computer Society is formed. By 1970 they will have about 16,000 members.

When Edsger Dijkstra, a Dutch software expert, tries to get married in Amsterdam, he is asked his occupation when he applying for a marriage license. He says he is a programmer. The town authorities refuse to grant the license on the grounds there is no such occupation.

The IBM Corporation develops the first dot matrix printer.

Fortune magazine reports that there are now over 1,200 computers in use; more than 200 in the $1 million-plus class, more than 800 in the $100,000 to $500,000 class, and about 250 in the under $100,000 class.

Sperry Rand Corporation develops the UNIVAC ATHENA missile guidance computer.

The Eastern Joint Computer Conference (EJCC) took place in Washington D.C. in December.

Noam Chomsky writes *Syntactic Structures*, the first of many important works that will earn him the title "father of modern linguistics." This work seriously considers the computation required for natural language understanding.

Max V. Mathews at Bell Laboratories is one of the first researchers to take binary voltages and turn them into sound. Mathews is often referred to as the Father of Computer Music.

Datamation magazine begins publication as *Research and Engineering*.

The FORTRAN programming language is developed by John Backus and his team at the IBM Corporation. FORTRAN is one of the earliest and most widely used high-level programming languages. Designed mainly for scientists and engineers, it is still considered by many the single most importance advance in the field of programming. FORTRAN enables engineers and scientists using a computer to state a problem in familiar symbols, close to the

John Backus

anguage of mathematics. The first FORTRAN reference manual is also published.

Control Data Corporation (CDC), a major computer manufacturer, is founded by William C. Norris. CDC becomes one of the two top supercomputer makers in the world and a major force in computer services.

The first photograph is scanned, processed, and redisplayed by a computer.

The AVIDAC computer is retired from service at the Atomic Energy Commission's Argonne Laboratory.

The TX-0 computer is built at the Massachusetts Institute of Technology Lincoln Laboratory. It takes up nine thousand feet of floor space and is the first fully transistorized computer. The TX-0 is followed by the large-scale, 36-bit transistorized TX-2 computer. Digital Equipment Corporation's first computer, the PDP-1 will be patterned after these machines.

The Burroughs Corporation introduces the large-scale Datatron 220 computer system.

Kenneth Olsen leaves the Massachusetts Institute of Technology to form Digital Equipment Corporation (DEC) with $70,000 in venture capital. DEC opens in Maynard, Massachusetts, with three employees and 8680 square feet of production space in a converted woolen mill.

Cornell University begins the first computerized concor-dance, indexing the work of English poet and critic Matthew Arnold.

In England, the LEO II computer is introduced.

Computers are just beginning to be available in large numbers and the practical importance of higher level programming languages is first being demonstrated.

John McCarthy and Marvin Minsky establish the first artificial intelligence (AI) laboratory at the Massachusetts Institute of Technology.

General Electric Company develops the GE-312 Process Control Computer, a general-purpose computer that weighs three thousand pounds. The 312 was the forerunner of the GE-215, GE-225 and the GE-235 line of medium-sized business and scientific computers.

1958

Konrad Zuse publishes a description of the field computer, a parallel processor that solves differential equations. Zuse also designs and builds a computer controlled plotter, the Z64 or the Graphomat.

In May, a committee convenes to develop Algol 58. Peter Naur and committee design Algol over a period of years. The original name of the programming language was IAL (International Algebraic Language).

EDSAC 2 becomes operational at the University of Cambridge Computer Laboratory in England. It will close down on November 1, 1965.

Orren Evans at Hunt Foods develops the first decision table.

Southern California is considered the computer center of the world because it boasts a grand total of 32 digital computers in Los Angeles, California.

Business Week of June 21, publishes an eight page report entitled "Computers," saying among other things "Computers are no strangers in business today."

Leo Esaki, a Japanese scientist with the Sony Corporation in Japan, develops the tunnel diode.

The IBM Corporation introduces the IBM 709 electronic data processing machine.

Philco Corporation introduces the Transac S-2000 which features transistors, tape drives and data channels. The S-2000 forms the base for a family of upward compatible computers.

The Beijing Wire Factory in Beijing, China is developing and shipping vacuum tube computers copied after the Soviet BESM-2 and M3 machines.

John Diebold & Associates, Inc. reports that there are now 6,000 digital computers being used. Clearly, the digital computer has now arrived as a working tool of business and industry.

The UNIVAC Solid State 80/90 medium-scale drum computers are announced by Sperry Rand Corporation.

The Defense Advanced Research Projects Agency is established. This agency will fund much important computer science research in the future.

The Bendix G-15 Computer has faced, and bested, its first human adversaries in bridge. The program is written by Professor Robert F. Jackson of the University of Delaware.

NEC Corporation announces the NEC 1101 and 1102 computers. These are the first computers built in Japan.

Burroughs Corporation announces the B-220—the last major vacuum tube computer.

In China, for the next 14 years, factories and research organizations work independently of each other, and produce computers that are never compatible with each other.

The FORTRAN II programming language appears.

The U.S. Air Force's AN/FSQ-7 computer, developed by Jay Forrester and Robert Everett of Massachusetts Institute of Technology's Lincoln Laboratory, is the first computer to serve 100 simultaneous users. This 32-bit computer will be decommissioned in 1983.

The List Processor (LISP) programming language is developed by MIT's John McCarthy for artificial intelligence (AI) applications. LISP is a popular AI language and it generally requires fairly large computers to run it properly. LISP is developed on an IBM 704 computer.

Allen Newell, John Clifford Shaw and Herbert A. Simon design and use the first list processing program, IPL-V.

Sylvania develops the "Fieldata" family of computers. These computers, differing in size, are capable of running the same software.

Air Force's SAGE air defense system goes online at McGuire Air Force Base in New Jersey. The system allows online access, in graphical form, to data transmitted to and processed by its computers.

The East China Institute of Computer Technology starts developing computers for scientific applications. In 1960 they develop a vacuum tube computer similar to the Russian M3. In 1964 they develop the J501. In 1965 they develop the DJS 200 computer, and in 1973, the Model 655, China's first integrated circuit computer. In 1976, they develop the Model 1001, in 1979 the HDS 9, and the HDS 801, a computer with processing speeds of up to 500,000 instructions per second.

Computer firms spring up along Route 128, north of Boston, Massachusetts.

Allen Newell and Herbert Simon, artificial intelligence (AI) researchers, predict that within ten years a digital computer will be the world's chess champion.

The 8th Annual Eastern Joint Computer Conference (EJCC) took place in Philadelphia in December.

Sperry Rand Corporation introduces the UNIVAC II (Universal Automatic Computer) to the world. The UNIVAC II contains 5,200 vacuum tubes, 18,000 crystal diodes, 184,000 magnetic cores, hundreds of feet of plumbing, and countless miles of wires. It's a wonder that it works at all, but work it does—for the next 20 years. It is not only one of the most powerful computers of its time, it is also a veritable workhorse.

Elliott Brothers, Ltd. in England delivers the Elliott 802 computer.

El-Tronics purchases the computer business of Alwac Corporation, makes a stab at producing computers, and within two years will go out of business.

D. Starynkewitch in France develops PAF (Programmateur Automatique de Formules), a FORTRAN-like programming language for the SEA machine CAB 500.

The National Advisory Committee for Aeronautics is renamed the National Aeronautics and Space Administration (NASA).

This and the following year are very significant in the development of programming languages. Some of the events that occur are: the development of the (International Algebraic Language) report which became known as Algol 58; the development of NELIAC, MAD and CLIP (which eventually was the foundation of JOVIAL); John Backus' formalism for describing Algol (BNF); the formation of CODASYL (later renamed the COBOL committee); development of AIMACO, Commercial Translator, and FACT; start of work on LISP, development of COMIT; start of work on JOVIAL; the development of IPL V; the development of APT II for the IBM 704 computer; and the development of several other programming languages for specialized areas—DYANA, DYNAMO and AED.

1959

The first generation of computers ends as vacuum tubes, punched cards and machine codes give way to second generation transistors, magnetic tape, and procedural languages in computer design and operation.

Grace Hopper

An organization devoted to the development of computer business languages, Committee On DAta SYstems Languages (CODASYL) is founded. COBOL, for COmmon Business Oriented Language, is published within three months, whereupon the Department of Defense stipulates that all its suppliers must use the language. COBOL is based on Grace Hopper's FLOWMATIC language. Hopper invents a compiler that makes COBOL run on many types of computers.

The RCA 501 transistorized computer is introduced by the Radio Corporation of America and starts work in the offices of the New York Life Insurance Company. The programming language COBOL is later developed for the 501. RCA then begins work on the smaller RCA 301 computer which will become a hot

RCA 501 computer

IBM 7090 computer system

competitor with IBM Corporation and Sperry Rand Corporation computers, in the growing data processing race.

IBM Corporation engineers in Poughkeepsie complete the world's first fully automatic production line for transistors. By 1960, up to 1800 transistors will be produced and tested hourly.

Hitachi, Ltd., NEC Corporation, and Oki Electric Industry Co., Ltd. debut computers in Japan.

The STRETCH (IBM 7030) computer can make half a million decisions a second—100 times the speed of any other general-purpose computer. One section of the computer resembles a telephone exchange and allows simultaneous communication between input and output units and the computer memory.

The IBM Corporation introduces a transistorized version of the IBM 709 computer, the IBM 7090. It becomes the most popular large mainframe computer of the early 1960s. The IBM 7090 computer can, in one second, perform 229,000 additions or

IBM 1401 computer system

subtractions, or 39,500 multiplications, or 32,700 divisions.

The POGO programming system is developed for the Bendix G-15 computer.

IBM Corporation announes its popular IBM 1401 computer. More than 10,000 of these transistorized computers will be sold, making it by far the most popular computer up to this time.

The Eastern Joint Computer Conference (EJCC) is held in Boston, Massachusetts.

On May 27, the Whirlwind computer at the Massachusetts Institute of Technology is shut down.

Jack Kilby of Texas Instruments and Robert Noyce of Fairchild Semiconductor develop "the monolithic idea," creating the integrated circuit, a breakthrough that will allow the dream of smaller and more affordable computers to become a reality.

An IBM 704 computer is programmed to translate printed text into braille.

Sperry Rand Corporation announces specifications for the first real-time system, the UNIVAC 490, for commercial data processing which allows the simultaneous input and output of messages over many different lines. By this time, the UNIVAC FILE COMPUTER has already been used for communications for airline reservations systems and air traffic control for several years.

The first object produced using computer-aided design is an aluminum ashtray. It is produced at the Massachusetts Institute of Technology. Upon the ashtray's debut, the *San Francisco Chronicle* wrote: "The Air Force announced today that it has a machine that can receive instructions in English, figure out how to make whatever is wanted and teach other machines how to make it. An Air Force general said it will enable the United States to 'build a war machine that nobody would want to tackle.' Today it made an ashtray."

IBM Corporation introduces the 1620 data processing system—a popular, small-scale scientific machine.

Michael Rabin and Dana Scott introduce the notion of nondeterminism (the idea that a computer program can make guesses).

The IBM Corporation introduces the "chain printer" with the IBM 1401 computer. It can print 600 lines per minute. As computing speeds increase so does the printing speeds.

National Cash Register Company introduces the fully transistorized business computer, the NCR 304.

Inspired by a puzzle posed by John McCarthy, Michael Rabin defines the inherent computational difficulty of a problem.

The International Conference on Information Processing is held in Paris, France. Professor Howard H. Aiken, from Harvard University, gives the opening address.

An IBM 705 computer in North Carolina makes available long range climatological studies.

Frank Rosenblatt invents a pattern recognition machine called a "Perceptron."

John McCarthy suggests that designing programs with common sense is a worthwhile goal in artificial intelligence.

Lee Kaichen, a Chinese professor, beat computers with his abacus in contests in Seattle, New York, and Taipei.

The Burroughs Corporation introduces the B-251 visible record computer for banking applications.

Europe's smallest digital computer, the Ferranti Sirius, which is about the size of a refrigerator, makes full use of the latest transistorized techniques. Although not fast, its makers believe that its reasonable cost, easy method of programming and convenient size will attract many customers.

The Western Joint Computer Conference (WJCC) took place in San Francisco in March.

A computer called the URAL machine, has been produced in quantity in the U.S.S.R., and is used for university research and to solve engineering problems.

RCA's 501 computer handles the tallies during the Nixon-Kennedy presidential race. The 501 has high-speed magnetic core storage, with a transfer rate of 4 alphanumeric characters in 15 millionths of a second.

The ACE machine is constructed at the National Physical Laboratory in England.

Before his untimely death, Dudley A. Buck of the Massachusetts Institute of Technology was working on techniques which could ultimately put a powerful computer on the head of a pin.

In the movie *Desk Set*, Katherine Hepburn and her staff are worried they might be replaced by a computer Spencer Tracy is installing.

Bell Laboratories' Leprechaun, a computer with 5,500 transistors and 18,000 memory cores, allows programmers to add terms not included in the original programming language (macro instructions).

Francois Geyuys programmed an IBM 704 computer at the Commissariat a l'Energie Atomique in Paris, France, to generate π to 16,167 decimal places in 4.3 hours.

The second national meeting of the Association for Computing Machinery (ACM) is held at the Oak Ridge National Laboratory with a total attendance of about 150 people.

The Harvard Mark I (also called the Automatic Sequence Controlled Calculator-ASCC) is turned off for the last time.

The nontransistorized KIEV computer is built at the Computing Center of the Ukranian Academy of Sciences in Kiev.

The FORTRAN language becomes popular in the scientific community. Most of the manufacturers of scientific computers have adopted the use of this programming language rather than trying to develop a new scientific language of their own.

By now the computer industry, which had developed from work done in the universities, is firmly established. The day of the one-of-a-kind computer has gone.

1960

Fujitsu, Ltd. in Japan manufactures the PC-2 Computer for the University of Tokyo.

Cyborg, a contraction of "cybernetic organism," is first used by Manfred Clynes. It describes the hybrid of human and machine, simultaneously biological and technological, which results from procedures in biomedical engineering.

In January, a committee convenes to develop the Algol 60 programming languare.

The January issue of *Computers and Automation* magazine publishes a list of 310 types of computer applications. Within a few years this list will grow to over 2,000 applications.

Benjamin Gurley at Digital Equipment Corporation (DEC) develops the world's first small, interactive minicomputer, the PDP-1. The first system is sold to Bolt, Berenak, and Newman. On advice from the venture capital firm that financed the company, DEC does not call it a "computer" but a "Programmed Data Processor" instead.

The Western Joint Computer Conference is (WJCC) held in San Francisco, California.

The COBOL programming language now runs on UNIVAC II and RCA 501 computers. Programming no longer must be done separately for each brand of computer.

Ted Nelson conceives his futuristic vision for hypertext—Xanadu. His idea inspires countless products.

The annual Eastern Joint Computer Conference (EJCC) is held in New York.

CDC 1604 computer system

Control Data Corporation delivers the CDC 1604 Computer System to the Naval Post Graduate School in Monterey, California. The CDC 1604 proves to be one of the fastest and most versatile electronic computers on the market, yet it is priced at about half that of comparable systems offered by major competitors. The CDC 1604 is built by Seymour Cray. CDC president William Norris adds the firm's address, 501 Park Avenue, to the nomenclature of the last machine he worked on, the UNIVAC 1103, to give the machine its 1604 designation.

The International Federation of Information Processing (IFIP) is founded.

The Datamatic Division of Minneapolis-Honeywell Regulator Company introduces the H-400 computer.

The NCR Company develops a new magnetic Rod memory. The Rod assembly consists of glass rods of 0.010-inch diameter which are electro-plated with a magnetic alloy and wound with many small coils.

Keyboards are first used to enter data into a computer.

Bull (Compagnie des Machines BULL) in France is the largest manufacturer of data processing equipment in Europe and the third largest in the world.

The first robot able to imitate the grasping motion of the human hand is employed in a nuclear plant. Handyman's 9 foot (2.7 meters) arms, which are operated by remote control, can perform 10 basic movements.

There are about five thousand computer-like "things" in the world. In twenty-five years there will be several million.

The total number of digital machines (electronic calculating punches included) of pure European construction is estimated to be about 2,000.

The Bendix Corporation announces the G-20 computer. Its speed is 45,000 floating point operations per second. A G-20 for scientific problems rents for about $10,000 per month. It contains 5,000 transistors, 30,000 diodes, and has an expandable magnetic core memory.

The first electronic switching central office becomes operational in Chicago, Illinois.

Bell Laboratories releases SNOBOL, a programming language for manipulating strings of characters.

Robert S. Bell, president of Packard Bell Electronics Corporation, says that the day is coming when diseases will be diagnosed electronically by advanced computers. They will determine the disease and recommend appropriate drugs and treatments according to the patient's age, height, weight, and other data and symptoms.

Sylvania Electric Products, Inc. announces the Sylvania 9400, a multiple-computer system capable of performing four separate tasks on a continuing basis at the same time that its primary function is being carried out.

Maurice Halstead develops the NELIAC programming language, an Algol derivative defined for Naval Electronics Laboratory (NEL) use. The language is defined so as to make it easy to build a compiler for it. The compiler is also coded in its own language, an idea so daring for its time that it boggles the software mind. NELIAC is a language for systems and scientific programming.

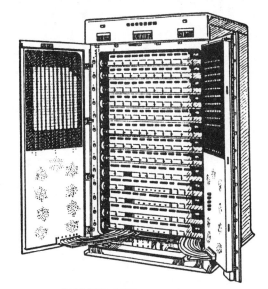

AN/USQ-20V computer

Transistors in early integrated circuits have features approximately one-third the diameter of a human hair. By 1990, advanced commercial transistors will be 100 times smaller than a hair. Nanotechnology involves features 3,000 times smaller than a hair—a little more than a hundred atoms across.

Manual office typewriters are still outselling electric typewriters.

The U.S. Navy develops the Naval Tactical Data System (NTDS). This system consists of computers which send information to a series of consoles that display schematic pictures showing targets, their types and movements, and the defensive and offensive postures of friendly ships and aircraft. The UNIVAC Advanced Navy Computer, a real-time machine designated AN/USQ-20V, collects, processes and evaluates naval tactical data in a combat situation and recommend courses of action. NTDS is the first floating computer command and control system.

IBM Corporation delivers the IBM 7070—a popular, large-scale business-oriented machine.

Theodore H. Maiman at Hughes Research Laboratories in Malibu, California announces the operation of a laser (Light Amplification by the Stimulated Emission of Radiation) based on a crystal of synthetic ruby.

The U.S. banking industry adopts MICR (Magnetic Ink Character Recognition) which allows machines to read the data printed on checks.

There are about 400 digital computers installed in the U.S.S.R. More than 300 of them are URAL's, a small-sized magnetic drum computer.

Royal Precision Corporation announces the RPC-4000 digital electronic computing system. The computing system is capable of operating on 9-digit numbers at rates up to 4,000 operations per second.

A beginning computer programmer's starting salary is between $5,000 and $7,500.

The term "automatic programming" is an advanced concept. Visions of a computer performing the programmer's work captures the imagination.

Packard Bell Computer Corporation introduces the PB-250 computer which costs $30,000 and can perform up to 40,000 operations each second.

The term "software" is widely accepted throughout the computer industry.

About 6,000 computers are in operation in the United States.

IBM 7070 business-oriented computer system

Bethlehem Steel becomes the first company to use its computer, a UNIVAC, to handle orders, inventories, and production control on a real time basis.

The Monroe Calculating Machine Company, Division of Litton Industries, announces the Monrobot Mark XI general-purpose computer.

The Association of Data Processing Service Organization (ADAPSO) is founded.

On August 12, Echo I, the first U.S. communications satellite is launched.

Control Data Corporation introduces the CDC 160 desk-sized, all-transistorized computer.

Association for Computing Machinery publishes the first volume of the *ACM Computing Reviews*.

The first computer-written TV scripts are aired on CBS on October 26 on a show about computers called "The Thinking Machine."

Sperry Rand Corporation introduces the UNIVAC LARC, a solid-state supercomputer.

The first checker program to improve its own performance—by using "heuristics," or rules of thumb to make guessing more intelligent—is written by Arthur L. Samuel of the IBM Corporation. The program analyzes games between human checkers experts to ferret out winning strategies for its own use. This computer program performs as well as some of the best checker players of the time.

The National Cash Register Company announces the NCR 315 computer.

The U.S. Department of Defense issues a requirement that all computers supplied to it must be capable of compiling the COBOL programming language.

Minneapolis-Honeywell Regulator Company delivers the first H-800, a large solid-state computer system. It has several features far beyond the existing state of the art. Parallel processing, for example, enables the H-800 to run eight independent programs at the same time.

High-level programming languages of the day are FORTRAN, Algol, XTRAN, MAD, NELIAC, CORREGATE, AP2, CLIP, COBOL, APT, COMIT, SNOBOL, ALTAC, COMMERCIAL TRANSLATOR, FACT, SURGE, CL/1, IPL, LISP, MIMIC, JOVIAL, SIMCOM, TABLEMAKER, MORTRAN, FORTRANSIT, SIMSCRIPT and COLINGO.

Bull (Compagnie des machines BULL) in France starts marketing the Gamma 60 computer. A dozen machines will be built.

JOVIAL (Jule's Own Version of International Algebraic Language) is developed.

The Institute for Advanced Study (IAS) computer is retired and put on display at the Smithsonian Institution in Washington, D.C.

SEA in France develops the CAB 500, a microprogrammed and microprogrammable computer. About 50 of these computers will be built.

The NCR Corporation coproduces with the Control Data Corporation the NCR 310 computer. NCR follows the 310 with the NCR 315 and NCR 360, both successful general purpose mainframe computers.

The MAD (Michigan Algorithm Decoder) higher level programming language is developed at the University of Michigan.

1961

Hitachi, Ltd. makes a technical aid agreement with RCA in an effort to bring advanced computer technology to Japan. The Hitachi-RCA agreement is the first of several similar Japanese-American agreements to be formed.

Max Palevsky, son of a house painter, starts Scientific Data Systems (SDS) with an investment of $100,000 and $900,000 venture capital. SDS is a manufacturer of minicomputers and will be sold to Xerox Corporation in 1969 for $1 billion.

The 16th National Conference of the Association for Computing Machinery (ACM), in September at Los Angeles, is attended by more than 2,000 computer technologists and industry leaders. It is the first ACM conference to include equipment exhibits and the first to be held in a major hotel (instead of on a university campus).

The IBM Corporation announces two modular electronic computers, for scientific data processing. The IBM 7040 and 7044 are compatible with each other and with the IBM 1401. In one second the IBM 7044 can perform 400,000 logical decisions, 200,000 additions or 33,333 multiplications.

More than 100 computers are installed in American universities. In 1955 the number was less than 25.

IBM programmers are early leaders in providing users with prewritten computer programs. Such systems software includes instructions for sorting and merging data, controlling input and output, and generating reports. Users of the IBM 7090 computer, for example, can take advantage of more than 1 million such prewritten machine instructions.

Burroughs develops the NORAD combat operations computer complex and data display system for the U.S. Air Force. The computer is used to make split-second evaluations of threats to the North American continent using input from satellites and radar throughout the world.

Fred Brooks assembles a team that includes Gene Amdahl, John Cocke, and Elaine Bone, to design the instructions for the future IBM System/360 family of computers.

The first mobile computer center, using a UNIVAC SS 90, goes to work.

On April 25, Robert Noyce's patent, is issued for the semiconductor.

Machine Translation, Ltd. develops a system to translate one language into another by means of a digital computer. At a demonstration they translate an article from a Russian newspaper into English at the rate of 60,000 words per hour or 17 words per second.

A patent is filed for the electronic clock.

A fully-automated television station, with both broadcast programming and station business procedures under complete control of a computer system, has been developed for the broadcasting industry by Radio Corporation of America.

On April 27, the patent is issued for multilayer circuit boards.

James Slagale writes a Symbolic Automatic INTegrator (SAINT) to solve elementary symbolic integration problems at the level of a good college freshman.

The Elliott Computing Division of the Elliott Automation Group is the largest British computer manufacturer. This year they produced 62 percent of the computers manufactured in the United Kingdom. They have over 150 machines installed throughout the world.

The invention by G. Gordon of GPSS (General Purpose Systems Simulation), the first language designed to provide a simple way to simulate natural systems, is announced by the IBM Corporation. GPSS made simulation a practical tool for people to use.

The first patient monitoring system is implemented at the National Health Institute Clinic in Maryland.

Daniel D. McCracken's book:*Fortran II Programming* is published by John Wiley & Sons. This book becomes one of the most popular FORTRAN books of the early 1960s.

A UNIVAC I computer is programmed to play bridge.

Robert Lindsay at the Carnegie Institute of Technology programs the SAD-SAM (Syntactic Analyzing Machine). The program accepts English sentences about kinship relations, builds a database and answers questions about the facts it has stored.

The NCR Company develops CRAM (Card Random Access Memory), a new memory configuration which exhibits characteristics heretofore seen only independently in magnetic tape systems or random access systems.

On May 10, the American Federation of Information Processing Societies (AFIPS) is founded.

The first computer to be designed by another computer is completed. Destined for the Army's Nike-Zeus anti-missile system, the computer is the brainchild of the Bell Laboratories.

The Burroughs Corporation introduces the B-200 series of small to medium-scale solid-state computers.

ATLAS, Europe's fastest computer, is installed at Great Britain's Atomic Research Establishment at Harwell, Oxfordshire, to aid atomic research and weather forecasting. ATLAS is developed by Ferranti, Ltd. in Great Britain.

Computer Control Company announces the DDP-19, a compact, modular medium-sized computer. The DDP-19 is a 19-bit machine with a 5-microsecond core storage to 4,090 and 8,192 words. An average multiply operation is performed in 36 microseconds, and a divide operation in 57 microseconds.

Robots are dumb. The second company to buy a computer-controlled robot, Doehler-Jarvis, nicknames it "Knucklehead."

The first time-sharing computer system is placed in operation at the Massachusetts Institute of Technology by Fernando Jose Corbato.

The STRETCH (IBM 7030), built by IBM Corporation and delivered to Los Alamos, is the most powerful computer of its day. Its 150,000 transistors can execute 100 billion instructions per day. It can cope with more than one instruction at a time and prepare itself for future work. STRETCH is a pioneer in various advanced systems concepts: look-ahead, overlapping/pipelining of instructions, error-check-ing and correction, control program operating systems and the 8-bit byte. STRETCH is 75 times faster than its vacuum tube predecessor. Many of its innovations will become part of the IBM System/360 (which will be introduced three years later.)

There are over 14,000 computer installations in the United States.

The Eastern Joint Computer Conference (EJCC) is held in Washington, D.C. Over 5,900 people attend this conference.

The Burroughs Corporation introduces the B-5000 solid-state modular data processing system. The B-5000 is regarded as the most advanced business and scientific computer offered by any manufacturer. It departs from traditional concepts of computer design, and features such pioneering concepts as automatic multiprogramming, exclusive use of compiler languages, Burroughs Master Control Program, and "virtual memory."

The June issue of *Computers and Automation* magazine lists 500 application areas where computers are used.

Iannis Xenakis applies mathematical formulas (Markov chains, Poisson distributions, etc.) to the creation of music.

Sylvania Electronic Systems develops the mobile general-purpose digital computer MOBIDIC 7A. This computer is ruggedized for use in the field; it occupies 3 standard 30-foot U.S. Army trailer vans.

Thomas J. Watson, Jr.

Thomas J. Watson, Jr. becomes chairman of the IBM Corporation.

A fast digital computer is in operation at the Massachusetts Institute of Technology's Lincoln Laboratory. Known as the FX-1, this computer is a working model for a future generation of computers.

A byte is a group of eight bits (binary digits). The byte appears as a basic unit of information on the STRETCH (IBM 7030), a high-powered, transistorized computer built by the IBM Corporation. The byte will become very popular in 1964 when IBM introduces the System/360 family of computers, and in the future the byte will be universally used to represent a character (letter, figure or special symbol) and as a basic unit of computer storage.

President John F. Kennedy, addressing a joint session of Congress, says, "I believe we should go to the moon," thereby launching Project Apollo, which will provide the impetus for important research in computer science.

Burroughs Corporation announces MADDAM (MAcro-module and Digital Differential Analyzer Machine), a miniaturized computer—the size of a loaf of bread yet capable of performing calculations at the speeds of a room-sized computer. MADDAM weighs 12 pounds and can perform 33,000 calculations per second.

The IBM Corporation introduces the Selectric typewriter with a removable, ball-shaped, single element.

The Data Processing Management Association (DPMA) announces the computer industry's first program for professional certification—Certificate of Data Processing (CDP). Later the program will be officially turned over to the Institute for Certification of Computer Professionals (ICCP).

The RCA 301, a popular small business computer, is announced by the Radio Corporation of America.

In England, a group of people propose a method for overlaying portions of stored programs in computer memory without the programmer being aware it is happening. Within ten years, virtual memory will become available on most computers.

Hewlett-Packard Company stock is first offered on the New York Stock Exchange for trading. Hewlett-Packard becomes a major computer manufacturer and in the 1980s, a major producer of laser printers for personal computers.

Steven Hofstein devises the field-effect transistor used in MOS integrated circuits.

Control Data Corporation introduces the CDC 160A desk-sized computer.

The GE-225 computer, introduced by the General Electric Company, can handle both scientific and business data processing. Years later it will be followed by the higher speed GE-235 and the smaller GE-205 and GE-215. Many installations of this GE-200 family will be in service a decade later.

1962

The National Cash Register Company begins shipping the NCR 315 computer, an improved version of the NCR 304. Approximately 700 will be sold. The 315's ability to process information punched into paper tape by NCR's cash registers is one of many customer driven features that contributes to its success.

The sale of a used computer is an event occurring with increasing frequency in the computer field. The advances in computer technology during the past several years have encouraged many users to exchange "first generation" computers for more modern solid state units. The result has been the appearance of a brisk market for used computers. Some 1962 prices for used computers are: IBM 650 with Magnetic Tape Unit ($244,000), LGP-30 ($18,000), Burroughs E-101 ($40,000), Clary Corp. DE-60 ($12,000), and Alwac IIIE ($27,000).

Scientific Data Systems,Inc. (SDS) introduces a pair of second generation, solid-state, general-purpose computers: SDS 910 and SDS 920. SDS is a California company founded by Max Palevsky.

Japanese engineers build an analog computer to help control water levels at hydro-electric power plants.

The first wide hot-strip steel mill to have an integrated computer system is the one at the Richard Thomas and Baldwin Company in Great Britain.

Burroughs Corporation demonstrates the B-260 punched card computer.

Canada is the largest single foreign supplier of computers to the United States (44 percent of total computer imports).

Cheaper and smaller electronic gadgets can be made now that the MOS (metal oxide semiconductor) integrated circuit has been perfected. Developed by scientists at RCA, it allows more circuits to be crammed into one chip.

A computer smaller than a person's head and capable of making many million basic decisions a second, is destined to be used in rail, road and air traffic control, in language translation and in weather forecasting.

Minneapolis-Honeywell Regulator Company develops Pico, an 18-pound computer, approximately the size of a table radio, for missile and space guidance applications.

The market for integrated circuits widens as the government places a contract for 300,000 circuits for the Minuteman Missile program.

Computer industry revenues reach the $1 billion mark for the first time.

Minneapolis-Honeywell Regulator Company introduces a larger version of the H-800, called the H-1800 computer system.

The General Electric Company develops WIZ, a compiler, for the GE-225 computer that automatically translates algebraic expressions into computer language for solving engineering problems.

The Spring Joint Computer Conference (SJCC) is held in San Francisco, California. This conference is the direct successor to the Western Joint Computer Conference (WJCC) of previous years.

Sperry Rand Corporation develops the UNIVAC 490 online real-time computer system.

IBM Corporation introduces the removable disk pack, the industry's first removable disk storage units. Each pack can hold well over two million characters, and packs can be exchanged to run different applications.

The CTSS Time-Sharing System is developed at the Massachusetts Institute of Technology.

Tractor, an automatic computer tape storage system developed by IBM Corporation for the U.S. National Security Agency, is designed to attach to an enhanced STRETCH computer. Tractor can store the equivalent of 88 billion characters in 160 cartridges. Its read/write speed of 1.1 million characters per second is to be the fastest achieved for magnetic tape during the 1960s.

Sperry Rand Corporation introduces the large-scale UNIVAC 1107, the first computer to employ magnetic thin film memory.

Richard Greenblatt and D. Murphy develop the TECO text editor, one of the first word processing systems, for use on the PDP-1 computer at the Massachusetts Institute of Technology.

Kenneth Iverson of the IBM Corporation develops APL (A Programming Language), a concise language in which a problem can be solved with relatively few instructions.

UNIVAC 1107 computer

QUOTRON, a computerized stock quotation system, is introduced. This popular stockbroker program which runs on a Control Data Corporation computer, signals the end of the stock market "ticker tape."

Sperry Rand Corporation develops the UNIVAC III commercial computer system.

Thompson Ramo Wooldridge, Inc. develops the TRW-530 industrial control computer.

Brian Josephson, a physicist at Oxford University in England, develops the fastest electronic circuit in the world, dubbed the Josephson Junction.

Alan Kotok, an MIT undergraduate, writes a chess program that almost goes unnoticed, but five years later it will be used as the basis of the Stanford University program that plays a four-game match with a program from Moscow. This is the first time that Russian efforts in the field of computer chess are widely publicized, but work had been going on in Russia since the mid-1950s.

The IBM Corporation demonstrates an experimental machine that can recognize handwritten numbers in a variety of styles and convert them automatically into computer code.

Burroughs Corporation installs the first of their B-5000 computers, large scientific machines featuring hardware to accommodate the Algol programming language and employing some of the advanced features pioneered by the British Ferranti ATLAS computer.

Edward Thorp writes the book *Beat the Dealer* on using a computer to win at blackjack. Thorp used a computer to work out the odds on blackjack. Thorp's system is so successful that several casinos bar him from playing the game.

A General Electric Company GE-312 process control computer is installed at the Big Rock Point Nuclear Power Plant in Michigan. This is the first installation of a process computer at a large nuclear plant.

On October 1, the first computer science department is formed at Purdue University. Twenty years later Computer Science will become one of the most popular undergraduate majors in universities and colleges.

Joseph Engelberger founds Unimation, Inc., the first industrial robot company.

H. Ross Perot founds Electronic Data Systems (EDS) Corporation in Dallas, Texas.

Ivan Sutherland designs Sketchpad, a line-drawing system for draftsmen. Using a cathode ray tube display, the system features an electronic stylus, or light pen, to display calculations at any stage of design. Sketchpad is the forerunner of future graphic design systems. This is the first use of a light pen in conjunction with a computer graphic system.

IBM Corporation introduces IBSYS, an operating system developed for the IBM 7090/7094 computers. This operating system supervises the loading and execution of jobs. It also provides language processors, a program linkage editor and subroutine libraries to help in program preparation.

James Slagle at the Massachusetts Institute of Technology designs a program that does freshman calculus about as well as a freshman.

Today, the question for a business is not whether to get a computer, but what kind to get.

Westinghouse Electric Corporation introduces the Prodac 510 and Prodac 580 process control computer systems.

Wang Laboratories, Inc. builds Linasec, a text justification machine, for Compugraphic, a typesetting manufacturing company.

IBM Corporation announces the IBM 7094, one of the IBM Corporation's most powerful computing systems.

The second congress of the International Federation for Information Processing (IFIP) is held in

Munich, Germany.

On election night, November 6, three teams of computer companies and broadcasting companies report and make predictions: NBC and Radio Corporation of America using the RCA 501 computer; CBS and IBM Corporation, using IBM computers; and ABC and Minneapolis-Honeywell Regulator Company, using a Honeywell H-400 and a Honeywell H-800.

IBM Corporation, with American Airlines, begins linking up high speed computers and data communications to handle seat inventory and passenger name records from terminals in more than 50 cities. The system, called SABRE, is the first system of its kind to operate over telephone lines in real time. SABRE, which uses an IBM mainframe, is the first computerized airline reservation system. By 1968 it will handle over 100,000 calls per day from passengers, travel agents, and other airlines. By 1995 there will be 45 million fares in the database, with up to 40 million changes entered every month. SABRE will become so popular that American Airlines will market the software to other airlines. SABRE is an acronym for Semi-Automated Business Research Environment.

It is estimated that more than 16,000 computers are installed in the United States.

William C. Norris

William C. Norris, CEO of Control Data Corporation, believes that computers can contribute to solving social problems. For the next two decades, his company will market the computerized education program called PLATO and make it available to over a hundred cities across the nation.

The estimated $500 million spent this year in computer programming in the United States indicates the importance of effective programming languages and programming aids called "software."

General Electric Company develops the GE-304 (an in-house version of the NCR 304), a large general-purpose computer.

General Electric Company develops the M236, a large-scale solid-state computer designed for use in the U.S. Air Force's Atlas missile tracking system. Years later, GE will use this machine as a model for the GE-600 line of commercial computers (GE-615, GE-625, GE-635 and GE-645).

Control Data Corporation develops the CDC 160G computer for use in the NASA Apollo space program. The 160G is a 13-bit word version of the CDC 160 computer and is used in Apollo spacecraft checkout stations.

In England, the LEO III computer is introduced.

For the first time, IBM Corporation's annual computer revenue (at $1 billion) surpasses its other revenue.

Manchester University in Great Britain installs the first Ferranti ATLAS computer.

The General Motors Corporation starts using computer-controlled industrial robots in the manufacturing of automobiles. GM puts a 4,000 pound Unimation robot to work in a New Jersey factory.

The *New York Times* sends pages to its edition in Paris, France via photo facsimile.

Fairchild Semiconductor and Texas Instruments, Inc. began mass-producing the integrated circuit.

The SAPIENT assembly program is developed for the RCA 301 computer.

English Electric in England introduces the transistorized KDN2 computer.

1963

In October, UNIVAC I, developed by Mauchly and Eckert, is retired after more than 73,000 hours of continuous operation. It is given to the Smithsonian Institute.

A new digital computer is introduced in the United States by SAAB (Svenska Aeroplan Aktiebologet). This Swedish system, called the D21, is a general-purpose, binary computer. An autocode system called DAC is used in programming the D21 computer.

General Electric Company announces the GE-215 computer, designed to allow smaller businesses and industries to convert to electronic data processing at minimum start-up costs.

Pacific Data Systems, Inc. develops two small-scale computers, the PDS 1020 and the PDS 1068.

The *Daily Oklahoman-Oklahoma City Times* becomes the first newspaper to set all editorial and classified copy by computer.

MIT professor Joseph Weizenbaum develops ELIZA, a computer program that simulates a conversation between a therapist and a patient.

Sperry Rand Corporation announces the UNIVAC 1050 off-line computing system. It is designed to be a subsystem to UNIVAC large-scale computers .

There are currently over 825 computers being used in Department of Defense installations.

Charles Tandy of Tandy Corporation acquires the assets of Radio Shack (9 stores). He pays nothing for the company as it is virtually bankrupt, and he agrees to pay the bills. In the late 1970s, Radio Shack microcomputers will become popular in schools and homes throughout America. Radio Shack goes on to be a major developer and supplier of microcomputer systems and equipment.

Conversational graphics consoles (DAC-1) are developed at the General Motors Corporation. One of the first uses of computer-aided design (CAD). DAC stands for Design Augmented by Computer.

Sperry Rand Corporation demonstrates the UNIVAC 1824 Microtronic Aerospace Computer. Designed for aerospace applications, the computer is six inches square, seven inches high and weighs less than 17 pounds. The computer can perform 125,000 additions per second. The 1824 costs about $100,000.

The Spring Joint Computer Conference (SJCC) is held in Detroit, Michigan.

There are over 280,000 people currently employed in the computer and electronic data processing industry.

Today's price for execution of a computer operation is roughly 1,000,000 additions per dollar.

The IBM Corporation delivers the IBM 7040 computer.

Making and servicing electronic computing machines is now a $3.4 billion industry.

The IBM Corporation installs the first tunnel diode memory unit in an operating computer system, the STRETCH. Its purpose is to modify instructions to the computer at extremely high speeds.

Minneapolis-Honeywell Regulator Company introduces a larger version of the H-400, called the H-1400.

Autonetics develops Monica, a family of miniaturized computers for use in inertial guidance, flight control and automatic checkout as required for missiles, space vehicles, advanced aircraft and navigation systems for submarines.

The National Aeronautics and Space Agency (NASA) uses Control Data CDC 924 computer systems in the Nimbus weather research project. The computer systems are used in gridding of picture data, real-time assessment of the Nimbus Satellite, and in long-term engineering evaluation of the satellite.

A computer eases the frustration of Toronto traffic jams. The device controls the timing of traffic signals according to the number of passing vehicles, which it detects magnetically.

The General Electric Company adds a new computer to its medium-priced line of electronic data processing systems. The GE-235 computer is designed for use by financial institutions, manufacturing industries and scientific/engineering users.

Magnetic Ink Character Recognition (MICR) is now well established in banking in the United States.

Mauchly Associates, Inc., the company started by John W. Mauchly, co-inventor of ENIAC, introduces the NTC-18 SkeduFlo, a computer small enough to be carry-on luggage when taken on an airplane.

Seat reservations in transatlantic flights of BOAC (British Overseas Airways Corporation) are now being made by a computer, which can answer booking queries in as little as four seconds.

The computer industry is now growing twice as fast as the electronic industry as a whole.

The Librascope Division of General Precision, Inc. introduces the L-2010, a small, high-capacity, general-purpose digital computer. The L-2010 weighs 60 pounds and measures only 2 cubic feet in volume.

The IBM Corporation announces the IBM 1440, a low-cost computer for small- to medium-sized business firms. The price range is approximately $90,000 to $315,000 depending on accessory systems.

Thompson Ramo Wooldridge, Inc. develops the TRW-230 digital computer for scientific and engineering use.

The Bell Punch Company of England produces the first fully transistorized four-function calculator.

IBM Corporation introduces the "train" printer with printing speeds to 1,100 lines per minute.

John McCarthy leaves the Massachusetts Institute of Technology and founds the Artificial Intelligence Laboratory at Stanford University.

John Clifford Shaw introduces the JOSS interactive system at the Rand Corporation.

Philco Corporation announces the Philco 4000 family of solid-state, stored program computer systems.

Sperry Rand Corporation announces the Standard Communications System with a capacity of 32 communications lines.

Approximately 3,600 new computer systems are installed this year.

Packard Bell Computer Corporation develops the PB-440 computer.

Project MAC is established at the Massachusetts Institute of Technology for computer science research.

The Hughes Aircraft Company develops the H-330, a large-scale, real-time computing system.

From practically no installations or sales in 1951, the computer industry has grown to a point where there are now 10-12,000 computers in use. An estimated cumulative total of 116,187 computers have been installed to date.

President John F. Kennedy says, "It would be difficult to imagine how the government or industry could work effectively today without the help of electronic computers."

Overflow crowds fill the Bendix Corporation booth at the Fall Joint Computer Conference in Philadelphia as Bendix presents the earliest known type of computer—the human brain. Wallis Dysart, the famous mental arithmetician, astonishes conferees with 23 performances of mathematical wizardry in square and cube root problems.

The Digital Equipment Corporation announces the PDP-5, an early minicomputer and Digital's first 12-bit minicomputer.

Over 5,400 people attend the Spring Joint Computer Conference (SJCC) in Detroit, Michigan.

Sperry Rand Corporation announces the UNIVAC 1218 Military Computer. It is a stored-program, medium-scale, general-purpose digital computer.

Digital Equipment Corporation launches the PDP-1 timesharing system.

There are approximately 2,800 computer systems installed and on order in Western Europe, plus 389 installations in Great Britain. West Germany leads in overseas computing installations with 472 systems, Great Britain is second with 389, and France is third with 342 systems.

"The industrial revolution effectively releases man from being a beast of burden; the computer revolution will similarly release man from a dull, repetitive routine..." Richard Hamming makes this comparison and this prediction of a bright tomorrow during a National Educational Television series entitled *The Computer and the Mind of Man*.

General Electric Company announces the DATANET 30 data communications system.

Commercial computing power in the United States (more than 10,000 general-purpose computers) can be measured as the ability to perform 110,000,000 operations per second—95 percent of the world's computing power.

Control Data Corporation introduces the CDC 6600. This brainchild of Seymour Cray runs three times faster than IBM's STRETCH. IBM President Thomas J. Watson Jr.'s comments about the computer's announcement: "I understand that in the laboratory developing the 6600 there are only 34 people, including the janitor. I fail to understand why we have lost our industry leadership position by letting someone else offer the world's most powerful computer." Seymour Cray will go on to form Cray Research, Inc. and Cray Computer Corporation, and to develop many advanced supercomputers.

Computers range in price from $18,000 to more than $2,000,000.

Friden, Inc. develops the Friden 6010 Electronic Computer System. The 6010 can be plugged into any standard wall outlet and requires no air conditioning.

CDC 3600 computer system

There are more than 20 companies manufacturing electronic computers; more than 200 companies are making peripheral and accessory equipment.

The computer industry is now making equipment deliveries of approximately $1.5 billion a year.

Control Data Corporation acquires the Bendix Corporation computer division, developers of the Bendix G-15 and G-20 computers.

The computer industry now employs more than 1,000,000 people. It has created wholly new skills, professions, and technologies.

The term *word processing* is introduced by the IBM Corporation to sell dictation equipment. In 1967, IBM will also use it as part of an advertising campaign for its magnetic tape Selectric typewriters.

Current large computers cost about 10 cents per second.

Scientific Data Systems introduce the SDS 9300 computer, intended for general-purpose computation. The SDS 9300 can execute typical floating point programs at rates in excess of 100,000 instructions per second. It adds in 1.75 microseconds and multiples in 7 microseconds.

Data Systems, Inc. develops a real-time general-purpose digital computer, called the DSI 1000. It is priced to sell starting less than $10,000.

Douglas Engelbart invents the mouse at the Stanford Research Institute. Xerox Corporation further develops the mouse concept in the early 1970s at its Palo Alto Research Center (PARC), under the direction of Jack S. Hawley. Unlike Engelbart's mouse, which used variable resistors and had an analog-to-digital conversion circuit, Hawley's is the first digital mouse. Much of Hawley's basic design will be carried into the modern mouse used with personal computers.

Electronic Associates, Inc. acquires control of Pacific Data Systems, Inc., a firm specializing in low-cost digital computers (PDS 1020 and PDS 1068 computers).

For the first time in the history of the computer industry, a complete line of computers will be marketed by franchised sales representatives—a method similar to that used to sell automobiles, appliances, and other more familiar products. General Precision, Inc. announces the establishment of a nationwide network of franchised representatives to market its three low-cost computers (LGP-21, LGP-30, RPC-4000) to business, scientific, industrial, and educational concerns.

General Electric Company releases IDS, the first commercial database management system (DBMS).

Over 2,000 people attend the Association for Computing Machinery (ACM) Annual Meeting in Denver, Colorado.

IBM Corporation develops AUTOCHART, a programming system that enables a computer to automatically "draw" a flowchart in about 15 seconds.

A Japanese color computer is shown for the first time in the United States. The Toshiba CC-1 color computer combines a recording spectrophotometer and a digital computer. The CC-1 is designed to be used for color control or to select new shades for lipsticks, fabrics, etc.

The first computer movie film is made by Bell Laboratories. The product is the forerunner of computers in the film industry.

Advanced Scientific Instruments announces the ASI 2000 digital computer.

Approximately 2,600 computer executives, engineers, and programmers attend the Fall Joint Computer Conference (FJCC) in Las Vegas, Nevada.

The Los Angeles Times uses a RCA 301 computer to perform newspaper editing functions. The computer outputs an edited paper tape for direct input into typesetting machines.

The trend toward large-capacity disk files for random access memories continues. In spite of the trend to disks, magnetic tape is still the predominant low-cost-per-bit storage medium.

RCA Laboratories develop a new solid state element, combining some desirable properties of transistors and vacuum tubes. This metal oxide semiconductor transistor is designed to be used in portable, battery-operated, high-speed computers and other equipment.

Stanford University and Rancho Los Amigos Hospital develop a computer controlled orthotic arm designed to aid a paralyzed person.

Radio Corporation of America introduces the RCA 3301, an advanced all-purpose business computer.

General Motors Research Labs produces the first computer-designed auto part: the trunk lid for Cadillacs. The computer system is DAC-1 (Design Augmented by Computer), whose screen displays an image that can be modified with a light pen.

The computer field may well remember this year as the big year of "drop-outs" in the race to capture a sustaining sector of the computer market. By June of this year, we see several firms waving the white handkerchief and going back to the pits. General Mills has now stopped marketing its AD/ECS-37 computer, Advanced Scientific Instruments no longer sells its ASI 210 and ASI 420 computers, the Autonetics Division of North America Aviation waves the white handkerchief on its RECOMP line of computers, and after almost nine years of competition, the Bendix Corporation sells their G-15 and G-20 computers to Control Data Corporation. Now the CDC-15 and CDC-20 computers are new banners in the computer field.

The U.S. Air Force uses approximately 175 NCR 390 data processing systems to process electronically the payroll for over 800,000 military personnel.

General Electric Company develops the GEPAC 4000 process control computer for on-line process functions in chemical, petroleum, steel, paper, cement and electric utilities.

In England, the main computer interests of Ferranti, Ltd. are sold to International Computers and Tabulators (ICT).

Control Data Corporation starts to deliver the CDC 3600 computer which is a much faster, much improved version of the CDC 1604, its first computer.

4.5 million chips are manufactured in the United States. Eight years later over 600 million will be made. The cost of a chip will also drop from $50 to $1.

Engineers on the Minuteman II intercontinental ballistic missile and Apollo space capsule decide to adopt chips for these vehicles. The result is that nearly all the chips made in the United States go to either the Minuteman or Apollo programs.

Wesley Clark of M.I.T.'s Lincoln Laboratory develops the LINC computer.

SEA in France develops the CAB 1500, the first French computer with virtual memory.

Radio Corporation of America (RCA) makes the first CMOS transistor and will introduce the first chips using CMOS five years in the future. Later on, CMOS will be re-engineered by Hitachi of Japan to give comparable performance to other technologies without losing any of its low-power characteristics.

English Electric in England delivers the high-speed transistorized KDF9 computer.

Philco Corporation first delivers the Philco 212 computer. This computer can compete with the CDC 3600 and the IBM 7094 computers. Philco Corporation lacks financial resources and will later be sold to the Ford Motor Company. After a short while, Ford will close down the computer branch.

Integrated circuits make their appearance in a commercial product— the hearing aid.

The American Standard Code for Information Interchange (ASCII) is developed to standardize data exchange among computers.

About 500,000 integrated circuits are sold this year; sales quadruple the next year, quadruple again the year after that, and quadruple again the year after that.

This year marks the end of a crucial period in the history of the computer. Machine architecture, the main means for input and output, the main types of other resources and the means for exploiting them, and the main programming languages have all been defined.

The range of computer applications have become so wide that computer science is no longer the private territory of mathematicians and engineers but has become a new science in its own right.

1964

More than 70 percent of all computers in the world are manufactured by the IBM Corporation.

The Spring Joint Computer Conference (SJCC) is held in Washington, D.C.

Ken Iverson and Adin Falkoff are trying to design a character set for Iverson's new APL programming language. There is no easy way to transfer the APL language symbols to a standard typewriter so they configure them around a ball. IBM Corporation likes the idea so much it will employ the ball for all its typewriters in 1971.

Minneapolis-Honeywell Regulator Company, a large computer manufacturer, shortens its name to Honeywell, Inc.

The General Electric Company announces the GE-205, a small computer for business data processing and the scientific and engineering markets. The GE-205 is the fourth and lowest priced member of the Compatibles-200 family of computers, and is GE's first entry into the low cost computer market.

The final day of SEAC operation occurs on October 20.

Operator using the console of an
IBM System/360 computer

IBM Corporation introduces the IBM System/360 family of modular, compatible general-purpose mainframes. IBM System/360 machines are designed with micro-miniature circuits (Solid Logic Technology). This is the first major compatible family of computers introduced by IBM. Software and peripherals work virtually interchangeable on processors of different sizes. Results: boosts in customer productivity and easier conversion to greater computing

IBM System/360 computer system

power. The new technology, which paves the way for portable and desktop computers, will spread like wildfire.

Computers with multiprocessing capabilities are first sold.

Robert Moog designs the first commercial synthesizer. By 1995, many personal computers and relatively inexpensive circuit boards will provide high-quality music output.

Sperry Rand Corporation announces the low-cost UNIVAC 1004 computer system and the UNIVAC 1050 family of small- and medium-scale systems.

A computer controls biscuit-making in the Netherland's Royal Verkade Factory.

IBM Corporation introduces RPG (Report Program Generator), a program generator designed for business reports.

Robert Noyce forms Intel Corporation with Gordon Moore to create complex integrated circuits.

The IBM Corporation has installed more IBM 1401 computers than all other computer systems in the world combined.

Burroughs Corporation announces the B-5500 data processing system—a third generation version of the B-5000. The B-5500 is the first of Burroughs "500" Systems family of computers. This very successful line, which ranges from the small-scale B-500 through the medium-scale B-2500, B-3500 and B-4500 to the large-scale B-5500 and B-6500, offers significant advances in computer technology and performance.

Robert Noyce

Sara Lee, maker of frozen pastries, becomes the first fully automated factory. The plant uses a

Honeywell H-610 computer to change equipment speeds and oven temperatures and to determine what products are needed in filling orders.

Digital Equipment Corporation introduces the PDP-6, a large computer system that will be widely used for research on artificial intelligence (AI) and time-sharing.

IBM Corporation develops the Extended Binary Coded Decimal Interchange Code (EBCDIC) for use on IBM System/360 family of computers.

Digital Equipment Corporation introduces the LINC (Laboratory Instrument Computer). This machine is a scientific workstation that includes a personal filing system, keyboard and interactive display, and it is transportable. It costs about $40,000.

IBM Corporation introduces Hypertape, a cartridge loading tape system that can read or write 340,000 characters per second. This innovation is the fastest commercially available tape through the mid-1970s.

Honeywell, Inc. introduces the H-200 Series—a series of popular business machines designed to attack IBM's installed base of IBM 1401 systems. These small computers are faster than the IBM 1401 machines and they have the unique ability to automatically convert IBM 1401 programs into H-200 programs. The H-200 is a successful competitor to the IBM 1401 machine.

The University of North Carolina is one of the first universities to form a computer science department.

The term "byte," coined during the development of the STRETCH (IBM 7030) computer, is now a de facto standard with the introduction of the IBM System/360 family of computers.

General Electric Company announces a family of four business data processing systems, known as the Compatibles-400. The computers are the GE-425, GE-435, GE-455 and GE-465.

David Bobrow develops Student, a natural language program that can solve high school level word problems in algebra.

On February 4, the ENIAC patent is issued. The patent will be invalidated in 1973.

Sperry Rand Corporation develops the UNIVAC CP-667 military computer, which while compact, is comparable in speed and memory capacity to the largest commercial machines presently available.

The East China Computer Research Institute designs the 501, a large-scale computer.

The third generation of computers starts as integrated circuits become prominent in computer construction and usage.

Honeywell, Inc. announces the H-2200, a moderate cost, high-performance computer.

The graphic tablet is developed by M.R. Davis and T.D. Ellis at the Rand Corporation.

General Electric Company acquires Compagnie Machines Bull and Olivetti's computer operation.

Peter Foldes uses computer graphics in his film *The Hunger*. However, it is Steven Lisberger, twenty-two years later, that is the first to use all of the computer's possibilities in the Walt Disney movie *Tron*.

In *Texas vs. Hancock* a programmer who stole his employer's computer software, worth about $5 million, is convicted and sentenced to five years. This constitutes the first computer crime leading to criminal prosecution.

Two general-purpose digital computers, the SDS 925 and the SDS 92, are announced by Scientific Data Systems, Inc. With the two new machines, SDS is now marketing six compatible general-purpose computers.

The IBM Corporation introduces the first word processor, the MT/ST (Magnetic Tape/Selectric Typewriter). Second thoughts about a phrase no longer means retyping a page. IBM Corporation's word processor stores typed material in coded form on magnetic tape. To correct, the operator types new words over the old, the tape incorporates the amendments and the typewriter automatically retypes the entire folio.

Harris Intertype Corporation introduces three models of a computer designed specifically for typesetting.

Control Data Corporation introduces the CDC 3400 computer. This versatile, large-scale computer system uses a 48-bit word and has a machine cycle time of 1.5 microseconds.

IBM Corporation introduces PL/I (Programming Language One), a high-level programming language for use with System/360 computers.

Gordon Moore, one of the founders of Fairchild Semiconductor Corporation and later one of the founders of Intel Corporation, makes a statement that the number of individual circuits on a chip will double every year. This theory known as Moore's law, will prove true for decades to come.

Control Data Corporation delivers the CDC 6600 supercomputer, which uses 60-bit words and parallel processing. The CDC 6600 is the first modern supercomputer and will be the world's most powerful computer for several years.

The largest single customer of the electronic computer industry continues to be the Federal Government. Its use of computers has soared from ENIAC (installed at the Ballistic Research Laboratory) in 1949 to an estimated 1,248 computers in 1963, and an additional 317 are planned for installation during fiscal year 1964 for a total of 1,565.

Mainframe computer

There are an estimated 18,000 computers in use in the United States. The number of computers in Western Europe is approximately 5,400 machines.

Thompson Ramo Wooldridge, Inc. announces a medium-sized tactical military computer, the TRW-133, an advanced version of the TRW-130 (AN/UYK-1) model.

American technology and marketing skill have captured the major share of the European computer market. This is clearly evidenced by the fact that 25 percent of the computers now installed in Western Europe are manufactured in the United States and another 54 percent are manufactured in Western Europe by American firms or American licensees. Only 21 percent of Western Europe's computing power in 1964 is manufactured by independent European concerns.

A total of 45 new computer systems are announced this year, only eight of which are IBM systems.

The theatrical side of computers is shown at the World's Fair in New York. In the egg-shaped IBM Pavilion, 500 spectators at a time are hauled by a sloping "people wall" inside the ovoid to see a nine-screen movie on computers.

The Olympic Games in Tokyo, Japan utilize a large IBM Olympic data center to provide up-to-the-minute results of the games for worldwide distribution. The center is the largest computer installation in Asia to date and contains more than 100 units, including eight computers.

Advanced Scientific Instruments announces the ADVANCE 6020, a small scale system, and the ADVANCE 6040, a larger high-performance machine.

A general programming language called BEFLIX (Bell Flicks) is introduced by Bell Laboratories, for making simple animated films quickly and inexpensively with a computer. BEFLIX is developed by Kenneth C. Knowlton.

The February 29th issue of *Business Week* magazine contains a report titled "New Tool, New World." This report contains much interesting information and some important ideas concerning computers.

Computer Control Company, Inc. introduces the DDP-116 computer which performs up to 294,000 computations per second. The DDP 116 sells for around $30,000.

General Electric Company develops the large-scale GE-625 and GE-635 computer systems. The GE-635 is the largest computer in the GE line with a price tag of $2 million and up. The GE-625 is priced at approximately 25 percent less.

Trenton Junior College, Trenton, New Jersey becomes the first college in the Northeastern United States to offer an Associate in Science Degree in Computer Technology.

A new 35-pound airborne computer, the NDC-1000, is announced by Northrop Corporation, and is said to be capable of feats of computation and data handling worthy of many large ground-based computers.

A computing record to date of 18,000 hours is set in designing the XB-70 airplane to meet the demands of trisonic flights. The staggering amount of computer time is logged on several IBM 7094s by North American Aviation to help engineers create the revolutionary design. By comparison, 1,235 computer hours were used to help translate engineering plans into the hypersonic X-15 research rocket plane.

NCR Company announces the NCR 395 electronic accounting system which combines the performance of a small computer with the economy of a conventional accounting machine.

The FORMAC (Formula Manipulation Compiler) programming language is developed.

In the U.S.S.R., the MINSK22 computer series is built in Byelorussia to the order of the Ministry of Radio. MINSK2 and MINSK22 are the most used general purpose computers in Russia. 2,000 of them and their derivatives will be built by 1976.

The Systems Development Corporation develops the first computerized encyclopedia.

The JOSS (JOHNNIAC Open Shop System) is a development of the Rand Corporation in Santa Monica, California. It will be implemented on a PDP-6 computer two years later.

In England, English Electric Leo Computers Ltd. acquires the Marconi Company's commercial and scientific computer interests. Three years later, the company will merge with Elliott Automation and its name will change to English Electric Computers.

1965

The Simula programming language is developed by Kristen Nygaard and Ole-Johan Dahl in Norway.

Ted Nelson coins the term "hypertext."

The Conversational Programming System (CPS) is developed by the Allen-Babcock Corporation in co-operation with the IBM Corporation. The language contains a PL/I-like kernel.

Harvard University and the Massachusetts Institute of Technology start computer dating services.

The TRAC higher level programming language is developed.

The Numerical Analysis Problem Solving System (NAPSS) is a programming language designed both for interactive and for non-interactive use. It is developed at Purdue University in Indiana.

There are now around 50 major software businesses in the United States.

Donald Davies invents "packet switching," which involves breaking down a message into small pieces and sending them to a new location over communications lines. The technology will play an integral part in the premise of the Internet.

Hitachi, Ltd. in Japan introduces the HITAC 8000 line of computers which are patterned after the RCA Spectra 70 computers.

There are now over 80 major computer manufacturers in the United States.

Computer Control Company, Inc. announces the DDP-124, a 24-bit word computer constructed with monolithic integrated circuits.

Bell Laboratories releases L[6], a programming language that allows programmers to manipulate complexly linked data, write fast-running programs, and use computer storage more efficiently.

Control Data Corporation establishes a computer training school known as Control Data Institute. The purpose of the training facility is to train high school graduates to qualify for positions as electronic technicians in the computer industry.

Sperry Rand Corporation announces the UNIVAC 1108—a popular, large-scale, scientific machine.

Edward Feigenbaum, Bruce Buchanan and Nobel laureate Joshua Lederberg conceptualize expert systems and start the Dendral project, the first true expert system. Its purpose is to experiment on knowledge as the primary means of producing problem solving behavior.

Computers are beginning to be widely used in the criminal justice system.

Bunker Ramo Corporation announces the BR 335, a small, fast, low-cost, control computer system for industrial applications.

IBM Corporation's share of the total U.S. computer market is 73.7 percent. Sperry Rand Corporation place second place in the U.S. computer market with a 6.6 percent share, Control Data Corporation holds third place with 4.5 percent, followed by Burroughs Corporation with 3.14 percent and Honeywell, Inc. with 3.07 percent. RCA, General Electric Company and NCR Company follow in that order.

During the five years that follow, the growth of the computer industry will be reflected in the announcements of some two hundred new machines by over eighty major manufacturers.

Control Data Corporation introduces the CDC 6400 and CDC 6800 computers with execution speeds of one million and twelve million instructions per second, respectively.

Several Wall Street financial firms turn to computers for security analysis and accounting.

Computer time-sharing speeds up theater and airline bookings, improves warehouse stock control and brings computer technology within the reach of many more businesses. A central computer can present answers to several users simultaneously.

Honeywell, Inc. develops two low-cost general-purpose digital computer control systems for industrial applications, the Honeywell H-21 and the Honeywell H-22.

More than 250 electronic computers across the nation now can exchange work and information as part of a communications network placed in operation by the IBM Corporation. The network links computing centers at 16 IBM plant, laboratory, and headquarter locations from Boston, Massachusetts to Los Angeles, California.

Scientific and professional knowledge is beginning to be codified in a machine-readable form.

Control Data Corporation begins development of the STAR 100 supercomputer system which will eventually realize a capability of running one hundred million operations per second.

There are now more than 30,000 computers in operation throughout the world.

Sperry Rand Corporation announces the UNIVAC 490 modular real-time computer system.

Donald Knuth describes how to perform bottom-up left to right parsing, the basis of all modern language translators.

Beginner's All-purpose Symbolic Instruction Code (BASIC) programming language is developed by John Kemeny and Thomas Kurtz of Dartmouth College. Nine years later BASIC will be adapted for use on microcomputers by William Gates and Paul Allen, the founders of Microsoft Corporation. In the future

John Kemeny

BASIC will be the standard language of all home, school and office microcomputing. It is the easiest to use of all programming language

Thomas Kurtz

The first IBM computer to rent for less than $1000 a month is announced by IBM Corporation. The desk-sized IBM 1130 is designed for individual use by engineers, scientists and mathematicians.

Lofti Zadeh, a researcher at the University of California, invents Fuzzy Logic.

China develops its first solid state computer.

General Electric Company announces its entry into the small computer market with the introduction of the GE-115. The computer is developed by the Olivetti organization in Italy. The GE-115 general-purpose computer is designed for small data processing applications.

Raj Reddy founds the Robotics Institute at Carnegie Mellon University. The institute becomes a leading research center for artificial intelligence (AI).

The Department of Agriculture reports to the President that its computers are saving the Government $7 million each year. One example it gives concerns preparation of the Agriculture payroll by one computer at an estimated savings of $500,000 a year. This task used to be done by 87 separate payroll offices in Agriculture.

A 59-pound on-board IBM guidance computer is used on all Gemini space flights, including the first spaceship rendezvous.

Wang Laboratories, Inc. releases its first Wang-only product, a $65,000 logarithmic calculating machine called Loci (LOWsigh). This machine performs calculations previously reserved for mainframe computers.

The computer installed by the New York Stock Exchange gives spoken answers to telephone inquiries.

Burroughs Corporation expands its commercial data processing lines with the introduction of the B-300 computer.

Ivan Sutherland at the Massachusetts Institute of Technology develops the Eyephone, a head mounted display that gives the operator an astonishing sense of immersion in an image. The image reacts to the movement of the head.

Westinghouse Electric Corporation introduces the Prodac 50 and Prodac 550 digital process control computer systems which are designed to solve a full range of electric utility problems.

The Internal Revenue Service begins using a person's Social Security Number as a tax identification number.

There are now an estimated 225,000 people working in the computer industry. Approximately 140,000 are analysts or programmers, or a combination of the two.

The third congress of the International Federation for Information Processing (IFIP) is held in New York City.

PDP-8 minicomputer
Digital Equipment Corporation (DEC) introduces the PDP-8, the first mass-produced minicomputer. Before long 50,000 systems—at one-sixth the price of

a PDP-1, one-fiftieth the cost of a mainframe will be put to work in business, production, and research. The PDP-8 realizes the dream of putting computers directly in the hands of the people who can use them. In the years to come the PDP-8 will help popularize computing, radically condensing the circuitry so that computers will be ever faster, cheaper, more reliable, and more accessible to more people than ever before. The PDP-8 is designed by Edson deCastro (who later forms Data General Corporation) and engineered by Gordon Bell. The PDP-8 is fast, small enough to fit in a cabinet, and sells for under $20,000. DEC will sell thousands of them and build its fortune and reputation in the process.

A miniaturized computer weighing less than 200 pounds and occupying only four cubic feet of space has been introduced by Sylvania Electric Products, Inc. The MSP-24 is designed to perform the high-speed computations of conventional computers. The MSP-24 uses 3,500 integrated circuits which contain the equivalent of 24 components.

The total number of computers in Israel is 26 and an additional 30 are on order from various manufacturers. Of the 26 installed computers, 25 are American machines, the other is manufactured in Great Britain. In addition, the country has two native computers, the GOLEM at the Weizman Institute and the SABRAC at the Scientific Department of the Ministry of Defense.

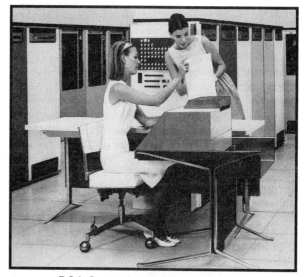

RCA Spectra 70 computer system
RCA Corporation introduces the Spectra 70 series of computers, which can run the same software as the IBM Corporation's System/360 machines. The Spectra computers are the first commercial machines to use integrated circuits.

On December 5, Richard L. Wexelblat is awarded the first Ph.D. in computer science, at the University of Pennsylvania.

The phrase "IBM (Snow White) and the Seven Dwarfs" is coined to describe the relationship between dominant IBM and the seven companies struggling to catch up. The seven companies who attempt to compete with IBM during the formative days of the computer industry are General Electric Company, RCA, Sperry Rand Corporation, Honeywell, Inc., Burroughs Corporation, NCR Corporation and Control Data Corporation.

1966

Honeywell, Inc. purchases Computer Control Company (CCC), a maker of digital logic modules and minicomputers.

The Australian Computer Society is formed on January 1. The total membership of the Society is approximately 1,500.

United States manufacturers introduce hand-held electronic calculators to the retail market.

Scientific Data Systems, Inc. announces the Sigma 2, a small, low-cost, real-time computer for scientific, engineering and process control applications.

In Great Britain, computers make major inroads into industry. BOAC announces a massive scheme for computerizing design, administration, planning and control, while Shell UK installs in a tanker a sophisticated remote control system which will eventually monitor the ship's machinery. Also, a computer is running an industrial alcohol plant.

In the first federal case involving criminal use of computers, *U.S. vs. Bennett*, a bank programmer is convicted of adjusting a computer to ignore all his overdraft checks.

The Spring Joint Computer Conference (SJCC) is held in Boston, Massachusetts.

Burroughs Corporation announces two new processors, the B-2500 and B-3500, which incorporate the key features of third generation equipment; i.e. (1) modularity, (2) compatibility, and (3) modularity.

The first ACM Turing Award is awarded to Alan Perlis.

The FORTRAN 66 programming language appears.

NLS pioneers hypertext, outline processing, and video conferencing.

Computers are widely used to analyze the results of Great Britain's General Election. Programmed with data from previous elections, and then fed fresh results, the computers are able to forecast the final result.

Charles W. Adams Associates, Inc. starts publishing the *Computer Display Review*, a single source publication that contains up-to-date information on available computers and peripheral devices. This handy aid helps computer professionals and businesses keep up with the rapidly changing computer business.

Honeywell, Inc. develops the small-scale DDP-416 minicomputer. Nine months later, the DDP-516 will be announced.

Texas Instruments, Inc. invents thermal printing. In the future, when microcomputers become popular, thermal printers will be used as output devices for several of these machines.

Digital Equipment Corporation, manufacturer of the PDP series of minicomputers, makes its first public stock offering.

Almost all medium to large computers run under an operating system. Jobs are typically submitted by users as decks of punched cards, either to the computer room or by remote job entry terminals, i.e., card reader and printer equipment connected by telephone lines to the computer. A large computer can run several hundred or even thousands of jobs per 24-hour day with only one or two professional operators in the machine room.

General Electric Company announces its largest to date computer system, the GE-645, designed specifically for large-scale time-sharing operations.

Operation Match computer dating service opens in Cambridge, Massachusetts.

The artificial intelligence program ELIZA, written by Joseph Weizenbaum at the Massachusetts Institute of Technology, tries to assume the role of a non-directive therapist. It turns sentences into questions and responds to key words about feelings and family.

Collins Radio Company introduces the C-8500, an integrated communication/computation/control system designed to implement the multiprocessing approach for diversified and geographically separate operations.

Western Union went into the business of supplying computer services over Teletype lines.

Texas Instruments unveils the first solid-state hand-held calculator. It has no electronic display, but prints out answers on a strip of heat sensitive paper.

Sperry Rand Corporation announces the first members of their 9000 computer series: UNIVAC 9200 and UNIVAC 9300.

Railroads in the United States and Canada are currently using 192 computer systems. These computers are located at 97 installation sites in 59 separate railroad firms.

IBM Corporation introduces the System/4 Pi computer, for use aboard aircraft and missiles.

The nation's first computerized medical school course is taught at the University of Oklahoma Medical Center.

There are 28,500 computers being used in the United States. West Germany has a total of 2,750 computer installations. Japan, Great Britain, and France have 2,100, 1,700 and 1,550 computers respectively. Italy has 1,150 installations and both Canada and the U.S.S.R. have 1,000 computer installations.

Burroughs Corporation announces the B-6500 computer system, however, it will be twenty months before the first machine will be delivered. This announcement-to-delivery delay is longer than that of any other system in its price class in the history of the computer industry!

George A. Zimmerman, Vice-President of Scientific Control Corporation says in an article "Someday primary schools will have children using small computers, and parents will have one at home for mom, dad, and the kids." Two decades later, Zimmerman's statement will be a reality.

Lear Siegler, Inc. announces the LSI 8000, a third-generation, general-purpose digital processor.

All over the world, it seems, there is a thirst for knowledge about computers: what they really are; how to apply them, how to make them; what their implications are. Throughout the world, more computer societies are being formed, computer books are being written, computer magazines are being published, computer conferences and seminars are being held, and universities and colleges are offering more computer courses and degree programs.

Since 1951, the average annual cost of computer hardware has declined from approximately $750,000 to $125,000, both through improved technology and the advent of smaller, faster hardware. However, the annual costs of operating and development personnel costs has increased from about $120,000 to $190,000.

The Kiewit Computation Center at Dartmouth College is built. This high-speed computer facility will keep the college in the forefront of one of the most significant recent developments in computer technology—time sharing. The center uses a large-scale GE-625 computer system. The BASIC programming language is also developed at this facility.

Scientific Data Systems, Inc. introduces the Sigma 7 computer, the first unit in a series of real-time computer systems designed for "multi-usage" environments. The medium-sized system is priced at $200,000 to $1 million.

The August issue of *Computers and Automation* magazine contains the winners of their first annual "Computer Art Contest." All of the computer art displays are produced using computers and digital plotters.

Northrop Corporation introduces the NDC-1051, a 28-pound airborne computer.

France's president, General Charles DeGaulle, is stepping up his government's efforts to eliminate the dependence of his country on American computer technology. He plans to "beef-up" the computer industry within France. The background reason behind this decision is that French-owned industry accounts for only 15 percent of the computers used in France.

Westinghouse Electric Corporation introduces the Prodac 250 process control computer system.

"HELP WANTED" advertisements for programmers and analysts are to be found every day in the nation's major metropolitan newspapers. Because the field is growing, because there is a shortage of qualified people to operate data processing installations, and because employers want those they want *now*, there is a real scramble for available talent. Salaries for programmers and analyst are at premium levels.

The New York Stock Exchange completes automation of its basic trading functions.

Interstate Electronics Corporation announces the IEC 1010, a 16-bit word length general-purpose digital computer.

What the computing industry has predicted will be the way of the future—computer power distributed through wall outlets similar to ordinary electric outlets—is now a reality at the Rand Corporation in California. The installation is believed to be the first of its kind in the world. In years to come, this type of system will be called a local area network (LAN).

The Federal Government now uses over 2,600 computers at 1,141 different locations. The value of this equipment is $1.5 billion.

The Ferranti company in England, which many regard as leaders of British electronic technology, announces the Argus 400 and Argus 500 computer systems.

Fifteen thousand people attend the Fall Joint Computer Conference (FJCC) in San Francisco, California.

There are over 44,000 electronic computers in operation throughout the world. In contrast, ten years ago less than 800 computers were installed and they had a total calculating power of under 5 million operations per second.

The Illinois Institute of Technology in Chicago, Illinois develops the DIALOG language system.

Stephen B. Gray forms the first personal computer club, the Amateur Computer Society.

The AMTRAN (Automatic Mathematical Translation) system is developed by NASA for the IBM 1620 computer.

1967

Fujitsu, Ltd. in Japan announces the FACOM 230/60 large scale computer system.

Scientific Data Systems, Inc. announces the Sigma 5 computer designed specifically for scientific and business applications.

Pat McGovern launches *Computerworld*, a weekly newspaper geared to the computer industry. First issue is published on June 12.

Control Data Corporation introduces the CDC 449 computer, measuring a mere four by four by nine inches. It is the world's smallest operational data processing system. This tiny computer contains the computing power of a standard-sized, general-purpose computer system. The CDC 449 performs limited tasks on board Grumman aircraft.

A fairly sophisticated chess playing program Mac Hack IV becomes the first program to compete successfully against human chess players. The program is written at M.I.T. by Richard Greenblatt. The development of game playing programs will have much influence on the emerging field of artificial intelligence.

Electronic Associates, Inc. introduces the EAI 690 hybrid computing system, which includes both digital and analog computers.

A light-sensitive pen, a display screen and a computer are the components used by the IBM

Corporation to create new computer-assisted circuit designs. Instead of re-drawing the whole circuit, any design changes can be made simply by manipulating the computer-generated images with the light pen.

S.G. Tucker coins the term *emulation* to mean hardware assisted simulation.

Burroughs Corporation announces the B-340 electronic data processing system.

children using LOGO

Seymour Papert and his associates at the Massachusetts Institute of Technology begin working on LOGO, an education-oriented programming language that will be widely used by children.

Data Machines, Inc. announces the DATA 620 and DATA 620-I minicomputers. The DATA 620-I comes complete with software and ASR 33 Teletype and is priced at $13,900. Data Machines will later become a subsidiary of Varian Associates and their name will become Varian Data Machines. The DATA 620-I computer's name will become Varian's DATA 620i.

Arthur L. Samuel develops the first checkers playing program. It uses "heuristics" by analyzing losing games and isolating the factors that led to the losing move. It reigns as the champion of checker playing programs until it is defeated in 1977 by a program named Paaslow developed by Eric C. Jensen and Tom R. Truscott at Duke University.

IBM Corporation invents the dynamic memory cell—using only one transistor per bit of information—permitting major increases in computer memory density. This technology will later be adapted throughout the industry.

Systems Engineering Laboratories, Inc. develops the SEL 810 general-purpose 16-bit digital computer.

The world's smallest ferrite cup core has been developed for the U.S. Army by Indiana General Corporation. Its outside diameter is 0.125 inches, ground to a 0.035-inch thickness.

The United States has a shortage of computer programmers. Fifty thousand programmers are needed right now to help write programs for the computers already in operation.

Burroughs Corporation introduces the B-3200 computer system.

The August issue of *Computers and Automation* magazine contains several entries in their annual "Computer Art Contest." The winner this year is "Sine Curve Man" by Charles Csuri and James Shaffer.

Chevrolet's Camaro, perhaps more than any other 1967 car, is a product of the computer age. Computers are used extensively in all phases of its design and manufacturing.

The IBM System 360/85 is the first commercial computer to use a cache memory.

A federal grant through the Defense Department Research Project Agency creates ARPANET. Over a million scientists and engineers begin to share expensive computers over a network that can withstand a nuclear attack. ARPANET helps 'spark' the Internet. And the High Performance Computing and Communications Initiative, a federal research and development program, helps 'spark' the World Wide Web.

General Electric Company announces the medium-scale GE-420 time-sharing system which can handle 30 communications lines concurrently.

The world's largest manufacturing corporation, General Motors Corporation, heads the list as the world's largest computer user among manufacturers. General Electric Company, Boeing Aircraft Company, Lockheed Aircraft, and Ford Motor Company follow, respectively.

Twenty-two of the high schools in New York City offer their students a course in computer mathematics.

Digital Equipment Corporation introduces the PDP-10, a large computer system that will be popular for research on artificial intelligence (AI) and time-sharing.

Via private telephone lines, seven state colleges in Maryland share a single Honeywell H-1200 computer system.

The General Electric Company offers time-sharing as a commercial service on the GE-635 computer system.

Shipments of semiconductor memory, as a replacement for magnetic core memory, begins.

Friden, a division of The Singer Company, develops the 5610 Computyper Data Processor for use in business application.

Gene Amdahl proposes the idea of parallel processing (using several computers together to work as one).

Fifteenth century, Leonardo da Vinci, who dabbled in almost everything, also dabbled with calculators. He designed one that could register up to 13 digits; but this was not known until it is rediscovered in the *Madrid Codices* in 1967.

Standard Computer Corporation demonstrates the IC-6000, a third-generation computer designed to use second generation software.

The Internal Revenue Service completes computerization of income tax processing, with a central facility in Martinsburg, West Virginia and satellite locations around the United States.

Control Data Corporation announces the CDC 3500 large-scale, general-purpose, multiprogramming computer system.

The first computer association in Taiwan is formed, and has the name "The Chinese Society for Automation and Electronic Data Processing." The use of computers in Taiwan is in its infancy.

There are about 14,000 banks in the United States. About 943 of these banks have computers and another 2,055 banks use off-premise computer services.

IBM Corporation delivers the IBM System/360 Model 91 computer. The Model 91 is IBM's most powerful computer with speeds ranging up to 16 million additions a second.

A.H. Bobeck at Bell Laboratories develops magnetic bubble memory. Magnetic bubble memory, which stores information on tiny "bubbles" of magnetism and allows any detail to be retrieved within 100 microseconds, improves the memory power of computers. Each chip contains hundreds of thousands of bubbles which retain data even if the power supply is cut off.

Interdata, Inc. announces the Interdata Model 3 minicomputer. The machine has been designed for the control field.

Fred Brooks sets up a virtual reality laboratory at the University of North Carolina.

General Electric Company develops Audrey, a talking computer.

Control Data Corporation introduces the CDC 6500 dual processor computer system which utilizes two CDC 6400 processors.

First United States picture processing via electronic scanning and transposing of photographs took place at Bell Laboratories. It will eventually allow for the replacement of chemical photography as the dominant form of photography.

The Fall Joint Computer Conference (FJCC) is held in Anaheim, California.

Gamco Industries, Inc. announces the Math-Master ECP-18A Computer specifically for use in business, science and mathematics classes.

The number of computers used in typesetting applications has increased over four times in the last two years. All major American digital computer manufacturers are by now active in the typesetting market.

Logic Corporation announces the LC 1000, a low-cost, general-purpose computer for the businessman, educator, and scientist.

The First Annual Computer Conference of the Institute of Electrical and Electronics Engineers (IEEE) is held in Chicago, Illinois.

A Control Data Corporation CDC 6600 computer was programmed by French mathematicians Jean Gilloud and Michele Dechamph to compute π to 500,000 decimal places in 28 hours and 10 minutes.

CSSL (Continuous Systems Simulation Language) is developed.

A group under Alan Perlis at Carnegie Mellon University developed the IT programming language for the IBM 650 computer. The language simplifys the process of communicating algorithms to the computer. IT translates the source program into the assembly language SOAP, which then translates into machine language.

English Electric Computers in England releases the System 4 computer. The System 4 is based on the RCA Spectra 70 Series and compatible with IBM System/360 Series computers.

1968

The Spring Joint Computer Conference (SJCC) is held in Atlantic City, New Jersey.

Varian Data Machines introduce the DATA 520i minicomputer which sells for less than $10,000.

The Association for Computing Machinery (ACM) National Conference is held in Las Vegas, Nevada. A special feature of this conference is a Computer Music and Art Festival.

Hewlett-Packard Company announces a compact computer priced at only $9,950. The HP 2114A computer uses software already developed for other H-P computers.

General Automation, Inc. announces the SPC-8 digital computer which is designed particularly for use in custom data processing and control systems, in R & D laboratories, and in universities.

Over 4,000 people attend the International Federation for Information Processing (IFIP) Congress in Edinburgh, Scotland. In the opening address, Dr. A.P. Speiser of Switzerland, president of IFIP, comments that the cost of one million arithmetical operations is about 25 cents, and that the computing power for a given amount of money has increased 60 times in 10 years.

Dynamics Research Corporation introduces the DRC-44 general-purpose computer. The 24-bit machine has a one microsecond memory cycle.

A complete, stand alone computer graphics system, with comprehensive user language programs, and full graphics input and output facilities can be purchased in 1968 for about $20,000.

Computer Automation, Inc. introduces the PDC 816 digital controller.

The August issue of *Computers and Automation* magazine contains the results of its Sixth Annual "Computer Art Contest." The winning entry is "Hummingbird" by Kerry Strand. The drawing is done on a GE-425 computer and output on a CalComp digital plotter.

Datacraft Corporation develops the DC-6024 digital computer which is designed for use in simulator, process control and scientific applications.

There are 3,700 computers installed in Japan.

Data General Corporation, a manufacturer of minicomputers, is founded on April 15 by Edson De Castro, former Digital Equipment Corporation PDP-8 chief engineer.

The Sixth National Conference of the Computer Society of Canada is held in Kingston, Ontario.

La Compagnie Internationale pour l'Informatique in France announces the IRIS 50 medium-scale computer.

The exhibition, "Cybernetic Serendipity" is shown world-wide, creating interest in the potential of the computer in the arts.

Lockheed Electronics Company announces the MAC 16 computer for the OEM systems market.

The Association of Independent Software Companies is formed.

Scientific Control Corporation enters the 16-bit computer market with their SCC 4700 digital computer.

Three years ago there were probably no more than ten people in top management who could write a computer program; in 1968 there are at least 1,000 companies where the presidents can write programs faster than trainees.

Decade Computer Corporation announces the Decade 70 digital computer.

There are 533 computer installations in Australia.

K & M Electronics Company, Inc. introduces the KM-220 general-purpose computer.

The American Society for Information Science is created. Information science deals with diverse fields that comprise communication: recording, microfilming, indexing, abstracting, translating, filing, storing, retrieving, publishing, and disseminating the ever-growing output of research data in all fields of knowledge.

General Electric Company broadens its line of small-scale business computers with the announcement of the GE-130 computer.

Hewlett-Packard Company develops the HP 2116A minicomputer. This computer will be followed by a family of minicomputers, peripherals, and desktop calculators/workstations.

On September 28, Raymond Schoolfield stood naked in front of the IBM Building in Atlanta, Georgia, carrying a sign that said, "Computers are Obscene."

Leeds & Northrup Company introduce the LN5000 Digital Computer System, designed for process control applications.

Edsger Dijkstra starts the structured programming movement in a March article in *Communications of the ACM*, declaring that "GO TO" statements should no longer be used in computer programs. Since then, virtually all programming textbooks have adopted the structured techniques.

Data Technology Corporation introduces the DT-1600 general-purpose minicomputer.

The FCC decision permitting other vendors' attachments to telephone lines is protested by AT&T.

General Automation, Inc. introduces the SPC-2 Control Computer with a price tag of $6,400.

Hewlett-Packard Company introduces the HP 2000A, a 16-terminal Time-Sharing System. User terminals are standard ASR-33 or ASR-35 teleprinters.

Joshua Lederberg and associates at Stanford University create Dendral, the first medical diagnostic computer program.

Intel Corporation is incorporated on July 18 by Robert Noyce, Gordon Moore, and Andrew Grove. Intel is formed to pursue the potential of integrating large numbers of transistors onto silicon chips. The firm promptly acquires an international reputation and revolutionizes the way computers are designed and applied. Formed with only twelve employees, Intel will become the world's largest manufacturer of chips.

Scientific Data Systems,Inc. announces the SDS 945 time-sharing computer system which can accommodate up to 24 simultaneous users.

The salary of a computer programmer is about $6,900 a year; a data processing manager, $12,800. By 1982, a junior programmer will draw a salary of $28,000, while managers will make $52,000.

Decade Computer Corporation designs the Decade 70 general-purpose computer.

The first software patent (for a sort) is issued to Martin Goetz.

Honeywell, Inc. announces a new family of integrated circuit computers for scientific and control use. The H-632 computer is the first of the Honeywell Series 32 line of computing systems.

Douglas Engelbart at the Stanford Research Institute invents the computer mouse.

Sperry Rand Corporation introduces the UNIVAC 418 Real-Time Computer System. The 418 is designed for communications oriented applications, such as message switching and data collection and distribution.

The first computer to diagnose and cure its own faults is completed at the Jet Propulsion Laboratory in Pasadena, California for space programs of the future. When, using its built-in error detecting code, it notices a fault, it automatically switches power to a spare module while it tests the faulty one. It then requests a replacement module if necessary.

Computer Automation, Inc. introduces the PDC 808 digital controller which is designed to serve where control, monitoring, and data logging systems require a versatile interface.

A computer wins the transatlantic yacht race—the *Sir Thomas Lipton* follows a course plotted daily by computer.

Honeywell, Inc. announces the H-100 central processor, ninth and smallest in the Series 200 family of computers.

Engineer Gilbert Hyatt invents the first microprocessor chip. However the U.S. Patent Office did not issue a patent until July 17, 1990.

Potter Instrument Company, Inc. introduces the PC-9600 general-purpose digital computer designed for use with Numerical Control machine tools.

Burroughs Corporation announces the B-500 electronic data processing system.

The New York Stock Exchange lists its first computer software company: Computer Science Corporation.

Honeywell, Inc. introduces the DDP-324, a general-purpose dual processor computer which will process more than 500,000 operations per second.

Stanley Kubrick's movie "2001: A Space Odyssey" is released. In this movie, the sentient HAL 9000 computer runs amok and kills four humans in deep space. In the movie, HAL becomes operational on January 12, 1992. This day came and went in 1992 without the world having a machine that can tie shoelaces or find its way home, or basically learn very much from experience. HAL is simply a creature of science fiction.

NCR Corporation introduces the Century 100 computer.

Integrated circuits are used in the Apollo Guidance Computer.

Burroughs Corporation introduces the B-8500 supercomputer which costs $10 million and upward.

Joseph Engelberger flies to Japan and grants Kawasaki the right to build Unimation robots in exchange for royalties. These are the first robots built in Japan.

Wang Laboratories, Inc. announces the Wang 380 desktop computer.

The Algol 68 language, a monster compared to Algol 60, appears. Some members of the specifications committee protest its approval. Algol 68 proves difficult to implement.

Scientific Control Corporation adds the SCC 2700 digital computer to its product line.

Robert Mallary at the University of Massachusetts is the first person to design sculptures with a computer.

Standard Computer Corporation announces a dual-memory, multi-lingual data processing system—the IC-4000 general-purpose computer.

The term "Software Engineering" is coined at a NATO Conference, in response to the perception that computer programming has not kept up with advances in computer hardware.

Elbit Computers, Ltd. from Israel introduces the ELBIT 100, a low-cost digital computer designed specifically for integration into a system or control loop.

Sperry Rand Corporation develops the UNIVAC 9400, the third system to be introduced in the 9000 Series of compatible computers.

Complementary MOS (CMOS) first goes public at the 1968 International Electron Device Meeting in Washington, D.C. CMOS is a premier semiconductor memory technology. However, many obstacles have to be overcome before the process can become commercial. Frank Wanlass invented complementary MOS in the mid-1960s and patented his invention on December 5, 1967. The first demonstration circuit, a two-transistor inverter, consumed just a few nanowatts of standby power, six orders of magnitude below the consumption of equivalent bipolar PMOS gates.

Hewlett-Packard Company introduces the HP 9100 which has a CRT, keyboard, magnetic storage for programs and data, and a printer. The HP-9100 has a small memory and sells for $6,000.

IBM Corporation introduces cache memory. A cache, or buffer memory is a small, extremely fast memory that relieves demands on the main memory by supplying data or instructions most often needed in processing.

Viatron, a spin-off company from the Mitre Corporation, announces a small computer designed to work remotely from larger systems but connect to them by wires. Viatron obtained thousands of orders for their forward-looking machine, however, they were unable to manufacture them and the company was finally liquidated in 1974. Viatron was trying to produce a machine seven years ahead of its time.

The Fall Joint Computer Conference (FJCC) is held in San Francisco, California.

Data General Corporation announces the NOVA, a small-scale, general-purpose minicomputer. The NOVA is one of the most compact minicomputers in its class.

Harvey Matusow forms the International Society for the Abolition of Data Processing Machines.

CSMP (Continuous System Modeling Program) is developed.

English Electric Computers and International Computers and Tabulators (ICT) merge to form International Computers Ltd. (ICL) thus bringing all the major British computer manufacturers under one roof.

Seiko markets a miniature printer for use with calculators.

Burroughs Corporation produces the B-2500 and the B-3500 integrated circuit computers.

The ATLAS (Abbreviated Test Language for "All" Systems) higher level programming language is developed.

Fairchild Semiconductor, founded in 1957, was the eighth largest transistor company in the world by 1960. Five years later it was number 3, and by 1968 it is the world's largest transistor manufacturer.

In England, over 1,000 ICT 1900 series computers have been installed.

The Speakeasy higher level programming language is developed.

1969

Bell Laboratories develops CARDIAC, a hand-operated, cardboard model teaching computer for high school students.

Honeywell, Inc. becomes the first major large-system manufacturer to explore the area of minicomputers. The H-316 model weighs 115 pounds, costs $9,700 and has more than 500 software packages. By 1969 there are at least a dozen other minicomputer companies.

On June 23, IBM Corporation "unbundles" its software, allowing customers to purchase hardware and software separately. Overnight, the multi-billion dollar software business is born.

Systems Engineering Laboratories introduces the SYSTEM 86 and SYSTEM 88 real-time, medium-scale, computer systems.

The American Federation of Information Processing Services (AFIPS) surveys thirty thousand computer people and determines that 34 is the average age.

General Electric Company introduces the GE-105, a small-scale information processing system.

IBM Corporation introduces the IBM System/3, a low-cost system designed especially for small business. The System/3 uses a new punched card that is about 1/3 the size of a traditional 80-column card, yet holds 20 percent more information. Cartridge disk drives are supplied with the System/3.

Computers begin to be used to control industrial processes as the Molins Machine Company in Great Britain shows that computers can manufacture a variety of components in a relatively short time.

Digital Equipment Corporation introduces the PDP-12 minicomputer for laboratory applications.

The Bunker Ramo Corporation applies for a patent for the use of a central time-sharing computer, which can simultaneously control many industrial machines.

Motorola Inc. introduces the MDP-1000, a small-scale digital computer that sells for about $8,000.

Centronics Data Computer Corporation introduces the first commercially successful dot matrix printer.

Siemens of Germany announces the Siemens System 4004 family of digital computers.

Edgar F. Codd proposes a relational database model to the IBM Corporation.

Martin Allen forms the Computervision Corporation. It will become a leading producer of CAD/CAM systems in the U.S.

General Electric Company announces the GE-120 computer, fourth in the GE-100 series.

Forty-one thousand people attend the Spring Joint Computer Conference, causing the largest traffic jam in Boston's history.

DataMate Computer Systems announces the DataMate 16 digital computer.

The Advanced Research Project Agency (ARPA) Net is established. It eventually links computers across the country and lays the foundation for computer networking and the Internet.

Control Data Corporation introduces the CDC 6700 supercomputer.

Micro Systems, Inc. introduces the MICRO 800 digital computer, designed for direct integration into control and processing system applications.

The U.S. Department of Justice files a case against the IBM Corporation that will become one of the longest and costliest antitrust cases in history. It produces hundreds of thousands of pages of documents. The Justice Department will drop the case in 1982.

Sperry Rand Corporation adds a new addition to its family of 1100 series computers—the UNIVAC 1106 computer.

Automatic Teller Machine (ATM)
The first Automated Teller Machine (ATM) appears. The use of ATMs for depositing and withdrawing money, transfers between accounts, and other banking services will become a way of life for many people. By 1988, there will be 72,500 ATMs installed across the country.

General Automation, Inc. announces the GA 18/30 industrial computer system.

It is generally recognized in the electronics industry that it is theoretically possible to use metal-on-silicon (MOS) semiconductor manufacturing technology to put all of the function of a calculator on a single chip. Three years later, the Intel Corporation will ship the first Intel 4004 chips and the microprocessor revolution will begin.

Burroughs Corporation introduces the L2000 desk-sized electronic billing computer.

Honeywell, Inc. expands its operations into the computer education field by establishing the Honeywell Institute of Information Sciences.

General Electric Company introduces the GE-410 Time-Sharing System which will serve up to 10 keyboard terminals simultaneously.

Shakey, the first integrated robot system equipped with a TV camera and other sensors, is developed at the Stanford Research Institute. Shakey is guided by the remote radio control of an SDS 940 computer. Shakey is the first mobile robot with vision.

Westinghouse Electric Corporation introduces the P-2000 computer.

Neil Armstrong and Edwin Aldrin become the first humans to walk on the moon. Their landing is almost canceled in the final seconds because of a problem with the Apollo Guidance Computer's memory, but on advice from the Earth control center they ignore the warnings and land safely.

Digital Equipment Corporation introduces the PDP-15 computer.

Digital Scientific Corporation introduces the META 4 logical processor controlled by a random access read-only memory (ROM). This computer has been designed to emulate instruction sets from other computers at several times their speed.

Kenneth Thompson and Dennis Ritchie at Bell Laboratories develop the UNIX Operating System.

Control Data Corporation introduces the CDC 7600 computer system that can perform a staggering 36 million operations per second.

Data General Corporation introduces the NOVA, a 16-bit minicomputer. The NOVA is one of the first commercial machines to use medium-scale integrated (MSI) circuits and is the first 16-bit minicomputer. Earlier minicomputers were 8-bit and 12-bit machines. It costs $8,000 and is one of the least expensive and most successful of the early minicomputers.

Control Data 7600 CDC computer system

Interdata, Inc. introduces the Model 15 minicomputer designed for "front-end" teleprocessing needs of a large computer.

General Electric Company announces a new member of the GE-600 computer family, the GE-615.

The Association for Computing Machinery (ACM) National Conference is held in San Francisco, California.

Siemens in Germany announces a sixth model to the System 300 family of computers—the Model 306.

Victor Scheinmam at Stanford Research Institute constructs the first successful electrically-powered computer-controlled robot arm.

The IBM Corporation introduces the MC/ST (Magnetic Card/Selectric Typewriter).

Niklaus Wirth

Niklaus Wirth develops the Pascal programming language. He names the language after the French mathematician and philosopher Blaise Pascal. The language is developed to aid college students in writing structured programs. The language is more powerful than the BASIC programming language and will be widely used in high school and college computer science classes. The language is originally installed on the CDC 6400 computer.

Computer Automation, Inc. introduces the CAI 208, an 8-bit, parallel computer designed as a communications controller. CAI also introduces the CAI 216 minicomputer for control applications.

Xerox Corporation purchases Scientific Data Systems, Inc. for $1 billion and forms a Xerox Data Systems subsidiary. The XDS Sigma 3 is the first computer to start life as a Xerox data system.

EMR Computer announces the EMR 6135 computer which is designed for real-time data acquisition and data reduction applications.

Computer Automation, Inc. announces the CAI 808 process control computer.

The Department of Defense adopts the USA Standard COBOL, and all future COBOL compilers delivered to the department must either provide for the full standard or one of the standard subsets.

Lockheed Electronics develops the MAC 16 computer.

Winners are announced for an international computer/plotter art competition sponsored by California Computer Products (CalComp). First prize goes to Gordon Hines, a doctoral student from Canada. His winning entry is titled "Cross."

Standard Computer Corporation introduces the IC-7000 time-sharing computer system.

The first International Joint Conference on Artificial Intelligence is held in Washington, D.C.

The Honeywell, Inc. Kitchen Computer System is advertised in the Neiman Marcus holiday catalog (the system includes a H-316 minicomputer and a modern looking keyboard console). It is priced at $10,000 (in 1969, $6,585 buys a new Cadillac Coupe DeVille automobile).

The August issue of *Computers and Automation* magazine contains the results of the "7th Annual Computer Art Contest." The first prize in this contest is entitled "Circus" by Tom Childs.

Honeywell, Inc. announces the H-3200 communications-oriented computer system.

The Fall Joint Computer Conference (FJCC) is held in Las Vegas, Nevada. Associated with this conference is a computer art exhibit.

MUMPS (Massachusetts General Hospital Utility Multi-Programming System) is developed.

Four Stanford University electrical engineers—Gene Richardson, Kenneth Oshman, Walter Loewenstein, and Robert Maxfield—establish Rolm Corporation. The company name is an acronym of their names. They had hoped to turn out a line of rugged military computers but later switched to producing sophisticated telephonic equipment.

Gary Starkweather at the Xerox Corporation invents the laser printer.

The charge-coupled device (CCD) memory device is invented by Willard S. Boyle and George Elwood Smith of Bell Laboratories.

1970

The first book composed entirely by machines—from manuscript to print-ready page-sized negatives—is issued by New York publisher William Morrow & Company. The book by V.C. Clinton-Baddeley, titled *Death's Bright Dart*, was previously published in England.

IBM Corporation employs almost 50,000 programmers.

IBM Corporation introduces the System/7, a system developed for process, manufacturing, and laboratory applications.

The Information Processing Association of Israel (IPA) holds its 6th National Data Processing Conference in Tel Aviv, Israel.

The Fall Joint Computer Conference (FJCC) is held in Houston, Texas.

Digital Equipment Corporation (DEC) announces the PDP-11 minicomputer family. The PDP-11/20 is the first of many models using the PDP architecture, which by 1980 will be the most widely used minicomputer architecture in the world. The PDP-11 family of computers are 16-bit minicomputers. From 1970 to 1990, DEC will build four generations of PDP-11 systems, ranging from a small 4-user system to a large 64-user machine. In 1975, a new generation of hardware technology, Large Scale Integration (LSI), will further streamline the PDP-11 design.

There are 2,700 computer installations in Canada. Almost half of these installations are IBM machines.

The IFIP World Conference on Computer Education is held in Amsterdam, Netherlands.

Xerox Data Systems XDS Sigma 9 computer system

Burroughs Corporation introduces the B-5700, B-6700 and B-7700 computers as the first members of the "700" System family of large-scale computers.

The August issue of *Computers and Automation* magazine contains the results of the "Eighth Annual Computer Art Contest." First prize is awarded to Lillian Schwartz and Ken Knowlton of Bell Laboratories. The title of their winning entry is "Tapestry I."

Donald Knuth and Peter Bendix publish an algorithm that explores the consequences of mathematical axioms.

General Electric Company introduces the small-scale GE-58 computer aimed at first time business users.

The first Parke-Bernet auction of computers is a flop. The prestigious New York auctioneer is unable to sell used mainframes: an IBM 7070 (a million dollar machine) sells for $2,250; a UNIVAC Solid State 80 computer (a $300,000 machine) sells for $485. No one will pay $15,000 for an IBM 7094 computer which in its heyday was a $3 million machine.

Xerox Data Systems introduces the XDS Sigma 6 computer, designed for business applications.

Intel Corporation creates the Intel 1103, the first generally available RAM chip. This memory chip can contain more than 1,000 bits of information.

Hewlett-Packard Company announces the HP 2114B minicomputer, designed for data communication, instrumentation and education systems.

Charles Moore writes the first significant programs in his new programming language, FORTH.

Bell Laboratories develops the first semiconductor laser. Until now, lasers were bulky glass-filled tubes, usually confined to research laboratories or large-scale instrumentation.

The Nanking Telecommunications Factory introduces the CTJ-I, a Chinese version of a Tektronix desktop calculator. The factory also manufactures a DJF-11-8 control system for the Peking subway, and a Model 702 computer which is used in a weather radar application.

Researcher Edgar F. Codd of the IBM Corporation develops the relational database concept. This process makes computers much more amenable to the lay user by automatically arranging data into easy-to-interpret tables. By filling in blanks on a display screen, users can specify what they want the computer to do—without telling it how to do it. The term "relational database" will become a popular buzzword in the mid-1980s.

The "Software" art show at the Jewish Museum in New York is the first art exhibit that contains computers and automata in it.

General Electric Company announces its largest and fastest processing system to data, the GE-655 system.

Amdahl Corporation, a computer manufacturer, is founded by Gene Amdahl, the chief architect of the IBM System/360. Amdahl, in 1981 will leave his own company to form Trilogy Systems, a company whose plan is to build a monumental computer—an IBM compatible supercomputer made with very large-scale integration (VLSI) circuits. However, Trilogy Systems will never produce the supercomputer.

Computer-controlled composing systems have broken into the printing trade worldwide. Used by a total of 1,200 companies, they consist of a single computer serving many keyboard inputs.

Major airlines now use computers to trace lost luggage.

Mediator, a computer-assisted system, helps air traffic controllers monitor the crowded skies.

EMR Computer introduces the EMR 6120 computer system.

The recently developed "floppy disk" recorder provides three times more storage space and much faster access than any other computer memory device on the market. Now integrated into IBM's 3740 system, it kills competition almost overnight and establishes an industry wide standard.

The United States Census Bureau uses the Fosdic "sensoread" system to eliminate manual keypunching of the data on census questionnaires.

Honeywell, Inc. introduces the H-1530 computer for scientific and commercial use, and the H-1540 for communications processing. This is Honeywell's first entries into the fast growing small scientific/commercial market.

Computer-controlled industrial robots begin to be put to work in factories and manufacturing facilities around the world.

IBM Corporation introduces monolithic main memory. In monolithic technology, circuits are fabricated on thin wafers of silicon, and later diced into chips.

Xerox Data Systems introduces the XDS Sigma 9 computer system.

P. Thomas develops SYSTRAN, a universal language translation system.

The Icon programming language, a descendant of SNOBOL 4, appears.

Burroughs Corporation introduces the first model of their B-4500 Series of data processing systems, the B-4504.

China has a total of approximately 1,000 installed large- and medium-scale computers for a saturation ratio of about one machine per one million people.

Cincinnati Milling Machine Company introduces two real-time digital computers, the CIP/2000 and CIP/2100.

Jack Myers and Harry Pople of the University of Pittsburgh create Internist (later renamed Caduceus), a comprehensive medical diagnostic computer program, capable of identifying more than 500 diseases and 3,000 manifestations.

Interdata, Inc. introduces the Model 5 and Model 1 general-purpose computers.

Artificial Intelligence (AI) is recognized as a computer science discipline.

Monitor Data Corporation introduces the MD 708, an 8-bit general-purpose computer.

The General Electric Company develops the first flight simulation programs for NASA, In the future, many of the larger airline company's will use computer-controlled flight simulators to train their pilots.

Arthur D. Little, Inc., in an unprecedented review of the computer industry, predicts that the computer field will ultimately become polarized—with only very large and very small computers remaining. The small computers will also be terminals of the large computers, forming an octopus-like network of inter-related equipment. Thus every computer can ultimately be attached to every other computer, forming a worldwide information system available at any terminal.

Raytheon Company introduces the 704 minicomputer.

Fiber optic technology is developed to conduct light through fine, flexible clear glass wires. By carrying sound waves as light pulses, the fibers prove capable of transmitting enormous amounts of information. Optical circuits have a speed and capacity advantage over conventional metal wire or cable. Corning Glass Works, Inc. produces the first fiber optic cable.

General Automation, Inc. introduces the compact SPC-16 computer, designed for manufacturing and production applications.

W.S. Boyle and G.E. Smith of Bell Laboratories develop the charged-coupled device (CCD).

Signal Processors, Inc. introduces the 16-bit, general-purpose digital computer, CSP-30.

Athena Systems, based in the Boston area, intended to mount computerized card readers near gas station pumps to record transactions. However, the company is dissolved before the systems could be built.

Data General Corporation ships the SuperNova mini-computer.

Walt Disney Studios produces the movie *The Computer Wore Tennis Shoes* starring Kurt Russell.

Datacraft Corporation introduces the DC 6024/3 high speed computer.

Computer Space is the first computer video game to become a commercial video arcade game.

The Singer Company introduces the System Ten, a low-priced computer system.

Ralph Baer at Sanders Associates originates the home video game when he develops an electronic unit with hand controls that sends broadcast signals to a TV set.

Varian Data Machines introduces the DATA 620f minicomputer.

In August, the Association for Computing Machinery (ACM) holds its first computer chess tournament in New York. Six computer programs take part and the tournament, a three round event, is won by CHESS 3.0 which was written at Northwestern University.

Philips' Data Systems introduces the P9200 Time Sharing System which can accommodate up to 245 users. Philips also announces the P1075 computer, a new addition to the P1000 computer series.

On April 7, The Netherlands issues a set of five postage stamps containing designs made with a computer coupled to a plotter. The computer is a CORA 1, at the Technological University in Einghoven. All five stamps are 25 x 36 mm, and are printed in two colors by Enschede en Zonen in Haarlem, who are also the printers of Dutch banknotes. The designs of the stamps are originated by R.D.E. Oxenaar, one of the graphic artists of the Post Office Department.

Ferranti's Automation Systems in England introduces the ARGUS 600 digital computer.

The first meeting of the International Joint Conference on Artificial Intelligence (IJCAI) is attended by 200 people.

The first computerized supermarket, Telemart, opens in San Diego. Shoppers use their touch-tone phones to select groceries for delivery. It later closed when so many shoppers called that the computer overloaded.

On September 30, John Burlingame, general manager of the General Electric Computer Department, invited his staff to a luncheon at which he presented each man with a beautiful ice bucket, engraved with a tombstone inscribed "I.S.E.D., 1.1.68-9.30.70, RIP." The next day the Information Systems Equipment Division (more commonly called the GE Computer Department), became a part of Honeywell Information Systems, Inc. The King of the Seven Dwarfs (GE) throws in the towel on the computer business.

computer chip

Today the chip industry can sell you a computer chip with 1,000 components on it. In 1994, it will be able to sell you a chip with 16 million components on it for a comparable price.

BLISS (Basic Language for Implementation of System Software) is developed.

Xerox Corporation establishes the Palo Alto Research Center (PARC) to perform basic computing and electronic research. In the future, many innovative computer products will be developed at PARC, including the graphical user interface (GUI) and the popular mouse.

1971

The Japanese government starts providing the Japanese computer industry with subsidies in order to encourage research and development by the industry and to make Japanese computer manufacturers competitive in the international market place.

There are six Japanese computer manufacturers; Fujitsu, Hitachi, Mitsubishi, NEC, Oki, and Toshiba.

IBM Corporation introduces the IBM System/370 Model 145, the first computer with an entire main memory of monolithic technology, very dense, large-scale integration of both memory and logic technology brought major gains in speed, capacity and reliability. The System/370 family of computers is faster than the System/360, yet operates on the same instructions. Larger models handle up to 15 program tasks at once.

It is estimated that there are 100,000 computers in use worldwide.

The IBM Corporation introduces the first flexible magnetic disk, or diskette, to feed instructions to the IBM System/370 mainframes. Such "floppy disks" greatly increases the convenience of data handling.

Control Data Corporation delivers the CDC 7600—a supercomputer with a central processor cycle time of 28 nanoseconds.

The Spring Joint Computer Conference (SJCC) is held in Atlantic City, New Jersey.

There are around 100 companies making small computers (minicomputers).

Xerox Data Systems introduces the XDS Sigma 8 computer for scientific and engineering applications.

Hitachi, Ltd. of Japan announces the development of an ultra high-speed, large-scale integrated (LSI) circuit.

The Data Processing Management Association (DPMA) observes its 20th anniversary. Membership is now around 30,000 members belonging to over 200 chapters.

IBM System/370 computer system

Burroughs Corporation installs the one-of-a-kind ILLIAC IV computer at NASA's Ames Research Center. This $40 million computer is financed by the U.S. Army and is designed at the University of Illinois. The ILLIAC IV consists of a battery of 64 "slave computers." It can handle 200 million instructions a second. ILLIAC IV will operate for the next few years and will be dismantled in 1981.

The Computer Group of the Institute of Electrical and Electronic Engineers (IEEE) becomes the IEEE Computer Society. In 1971 the Computer Society has over 17,000 members.

The IFIP Congress 71 is held in Ljubljana, Yugoslavia.

The August issue of *Computers and Automation* magazine contains the winners of its "Ninth Annual Computer Art Contest." "Sea Horses," winner of the first prize is produced by a FORTRAN program on a GE-425 computer and plotted on a CalComp plotter. The artist is Derby Scanlon.

On June 21, the STRETCH (IBM 7030 computer) retirement ceremony is held.

Wang Laboratories, Inc. introduces the Wang 1200, a typewriter with a brain—basically a Wang 700 calculator (which was introduced in 1969) hooked up to an IBM Selectric typewriter. The Wang 1200 is the first word processing machine.

Mass produced pocket calculators are introduced in the United States.

Terry Winograd of M.I.T. develops AHRDLU, a program that combines parsing (analyzing) English statements, putting events into context, problem solving, and natural language response.

The second computer chess tournament is held at the ACM Annual Conference in Chicago. Eight programs participate in the tournament and the winner is CHESS 3.5 from Northwestern University.

NCR Corporation introduces the Century 50 computer.

The IBM Corporation has grown to a worldwide total of 269,000 employees.

The Italian computer company, Olivetti, enters the word processing market.

London's Heathrow airport becomes the first airport in the world to computerize the control of incoming cargo.

Digital Equipment Corporation introduces the DECsystem-10 computer system.

The first home video game console is marketed using a patent originally granted to Sanders Associates. The name of the game is Odyssey. The company that sells the game is Magnavox Corporation.

Computer Automation Inc. introduces the Alpha-16 minicomputer.

Harlan Mills advocates the use of the chief programmer team.

France installs its first industrial robot, a Unimate, at Renault's plant to build LeCar.

The 719 computer is built at Fudan University in Shanghai, China.

Direct telephone dialing on a regular basis begins between Europe and parts of the United States.

John V. Blankenbaker forms the Kenbak Corporation and announces the Kenbak-1 personal computer. The machine is billed more as an educational tool rather than as a full-blown machine for executing application programs. The Kenbak-1 will never become popular. Only 40 machines will be sold to schools and a dozen to individuals over the next two years. In 1973, the Kenbak Corporation will close its doors. However, the Kenbak-1 has the distinction of being the first personal computer.

Journalist Don Hoefler refers to a 100-square-mile valley southeast of San Francisco as Silicon Valley because of the number of high-tech firms prospering there. The area's identity, once based on crops of plums, pears and prunes, is changed forever.

The Institute of Computer Technology in Beijing, China develops the DJS 111 computer to facilitate Kanji input. Three thousand Kanji characters are stored in the machine's memory.

Poketronic—the first pocket calculator is introduced.

Stephen Cook publishes a paper on non-deterministic polynomial complete (NP-complete), defining a new family of problems that is not computable in a practical sense.

Honeywell, Inc. announces a large-scale data processing system consisting of six models—the H-6030, H-6040, H-6050, H-6060, H-6070 and H-6080.

A computer-on-a-chip microprocessor is developed with a simple core of logic for general-purpose use.

The chip is the size of a child's fingernail. The microprocessor is the Intel 4004 and it is developed by a team headed by Marcian E. Hoff of Intel Corporation. This chip holds most of the elements of an entire computer. The 4-bit 4004 has 2250 transistors on a chip one-sixth of an inch long and one-eighth of an inch wide. The 4004 paves the way for the microcomputer revolution.

Alan Kay develops the first object oriented programming language, Smalltalk, at Xerox PARC.

Dendral, which was started in the mid-1960s, mimics the behavior of an expert chemist who is determining the structure of molecular compounds.

IBM computers help guide Apollo 14 and Apollo 15 moon landings and enhance photos taken by Mariner 9, the first spacecraft to orbit Mars.

Datacraft Corporation introduces the Model 6204 and Model 6205 minicomputers.

Sperry Corporation establishes a Grace Murray Hopper award, in honor of computer language pioneer, Grace Hopper.

Time magazine and the American Federation of Information Processing Societies (AFIPS) conducts a major survey to determine the public's attitudes towards computers. The survey results are extensive and lengthy, however one observation is that almost half of the working public has some contact with computers.

Control Data Corporation introduces the CYBER 70 family of computers.

In September, Radio Corporation of America (RCA) announces its intentions to withdraw from the computer industry and sell its Computer Division. The Sperry Corporation will take over the RCA computer product line.

The ILLIAC IV is the first computer to have 64 parallel processors. It had a parallel processing design that sought to break away from the model proposed in 1945 by John von Neumann in his EDVAC report.

ISPL (Instruction Set Processor Language) is developed.

1972

The video game business begins. Though it had roots as far back as 1948 with the invention of a computer checkers game by IBM scientist Arthur Samuel, the modern video game really begins with a maverick 28-year old engineer named Nolan

Bushnell. Bushnell and his company Atari, Inc. first develop Computer Space (which is overly complicated) and Pong, a simple, electronic form of Ping-Pong. Pong and its descendents sweep the consumer market. Atari, Inc., soon purchased by entertainment conglomerate Warner Communications, becomes one of the youngest billion dollar companies ever. Competitors, such as Coleco, Magnovox, Mattel, and Bally quickly spring up to participate in the video game business. Pong makes Atari a household word. It is followed by Space Race and Pong Doubles, the first sequel game in video history. Atari, Inc. will go on to develop the Atari 400 and Atari 800 personal computers.

video game

Hewlett-Packard Company announces the HP 35 calculator for $395. This is the first scientific hand-held calculator. Bill Hewlett, one of the founders of Hewlett-Packard, is about the only one sure that engineers and scientists will buy a $395 calculator over a $20 slide rule. As it turns out, the HP 35 is the hottest product ever advertised in the computer trade press, and by 1980, scientific calculators will drive the slide rule manufacturers out of business.

Ken Thompson of Bell Laboratories invents a language called B; Dennis Ritchie extends it to form programming language C.

The Association for Computing Machinery now has a membership of 28,838. Fifteen years in the future the membership will be almost 73,000.

The Summer Olympic Games in Munich, Germany, are the first games to use computers as judges of times and finishes.

A group of Californians dedicated to demystifying computers form the People's Computer Company which publishes a popular computer newspaper and several entry level computer books.

The third annual computer chess tournament is held at the ACM Annual Convention in Boston, Massachusetts. There are eight entries, and for the third consecutive year, Northwestern University claims the first prize with its CHESS 3.6 program.

IBM Corporation announces the System/32, a desk-sized computer system.

The first pacemakers with chips appear.

IBM System/370 main memory uses tiny silicon chips mounted on 1/2-inch modules, each pair of modules containing more than 4,000 bits of data—the same as 4,000 magnetic cores. This monolithic memory is more reliable and four times faster than the core memory it replaced.

There are 111,867 computers in use in the United States (42,000 of these computers are IBM mainframes).

Gary Kildall, a professor at the Naval Postgraduate School, writes PL/M, the first programming language for the Intel 4004 microprocessor.

England's Clive Sinclair creates and markets a hand-held calculator. He later belted out the low-cost Sinclair ZX-80 and ZX-81 microcomputers.

Jack S. Kilby, Jerry D. Merryman and Jim H. van Tassel of Texas Instruments, Inc. develop the first electronic pocket calculator.

Using electron scan technology, developed by IBM Corporation, 100,000 transistors will soon be squeezed onto a single silicon chip only a few millimeters square. As a direct result of this dramatic reduction in the size of integrated circuits, cheaper, more efficient electronic gadgets will be available by the middle of the decade.

Intel Corporation introduces the 8-bit 8008 microprocessor. This is the first integrated circuit capable of supporting a true microcomputer. In the future, Intel will replace this microprocessor with the 8080.

The August issue of *Computers and Automation* magazine contains the winners of the "Tenth Annual Computer Art Contest." The first prize is awarded to Bharat K. Shaw whose entry is "Peacock Courtships," produced using an IBM System/360 Model 44 computer and a CalComp plotter.

Xerox Corporation develops the Alto microcomputer at the Pala Alto Research Center (PARC). This machine introduces the Graphical User Interface (GUI). Both the Macintosh and Windows user interfaces will be based on concepts developed at PARC and implemented in the Alto.

Inexpensive calculators start to flood the market.

In a move to reduce clutter in the newsroom, newspaper publishers start using CRT's and keyboards for writing and editing stories.

LUNAR, a natural-language information retrieval system is completed by Kaplan, Nash-Webber and Woods at Bolt, Beranek and Newman, Inc. LUNAR helps geologists access, compare and evaluate chemical analysis data on moon rock and soil composition from the Apollo 11 mission.

Cray Research, Inc., the producer of the most powerful supercomputers in the world, is founded by Seymour Cray, a leading designer of large-scale computers at Control Data Corporation. The company's first supercomputer will be the CRAY 1, which will be, for a short time, the fastest computer on earth.

Microprocessor chips are first sold in large quantities.

The first articles about microprocessors begin to appear in such publications as *Electronics, Electronic News*, and *Datamation*.

Jerry Schneider penetrates Pacific Telephone Company's computers to defraud them of over $1 million. He is subsequently caught, and sentenced to a ninety day jail sentence.

IBM Corporation introduces N-channel FET technology. FET which stands for field effect transistor becomes the basic technology for Large Scale Integration (LSI) semiconductor memory.

Computers turn to the problem of job finding. Computer job banks are being used to update printouts of vacancies.

Digital Equipment Corporation designs the VAX minicomputer.

Beijing University builds the DJS 18 computer which uses assembly language and the BD-200, a high-level FORTRAN-like language which uses Chinese symbols.

Intel Corporation develops the Intel 1702, the first erasable programmable read-only memory (EPROM).

Prime Computer, Inc. is founded by seven engineers from Honeywell, Inc. to manufacture minicomputers.

Roy Tomlinson, an employee of ARPANET contractor Bolt, Beranek & Newman, was first to use the @ symbol in Internet E-mail addresses.

Computers are now becoming common in high schools, and have become frequent even in elementary schools.

Five million pocket calculators are sold in the United States.

There are over 170 programming languages in use in the United States. Many of these languages, however, are designed for specialized applications.

Radio Shack introduces its first calculator.

Intel Corporation finds that they can put a primitive computer—consisting of a little over 3,000 transistors—on a single chip. However, the achievement went almost unnoticed in the computer industry. In retrospect, this may seem surprising, since the event may be said to mark the beginning of very large-scale integration, something which had been long heralded, but had been seemingly slow to come.

There have been over 200 higher level programming languages developed during the past 20 years. However, only 13 are deemed of major significance.

Hitachi, Ltd. in Japan introduces the HITAC 8700, a large business computer. The machine is compatible with the smaller HITAC 8500 and 8300 systems.

Pioneering work at Xerox Palo Alto Research Center (PARC) on the use of personal computers and servers connected to an Ethernet has a profound effect on the development of computing.

T.A. Standish and several co-workers at Harvard University design the Polymorphic Programming Language (PPL) and implement it on a Digital Equipment Corporation DEC-System-10 computer.

1973

Interactive laser disks make their debut.

French scientist Alain Colmerauer and logician Philippe Roussel at the University of Marseilles in France invent PROLOG (PROgramming in LOGic), a logic-based artificial intelligence (AI) programming language.

Scelbi Computer Consulting creates the Intel 8008-based Scelbi 8H microcomputer.

The first National Computer Conference (NCC) is held in New York in June. IBM makes its first appearance at a national data processing show since 1970 and shows its System/3 and System/370 Model 145 computer systems. Senator Philip Hart, in his keynote address, warns that the computer industry must restructure itself or face government regulation. NCC replaces the Fall and Spring joint conferences.

First year that the NCR Corporation turns a profit in computers.

Don Lancaster introduces the TV Typewriter which makes it possible, for the first time, to display personally generated alphanumeric information on an ordinary unmodified television set. The design is published in the September issue of *Radio Electronics* magazine as a home assembly project that uses only $120 worth of components. Lancaster's design attracts considerable attention as its extreme low cost proves that home video terminals and video displays for personal computers are practical. High resolution bit mapped displays will follow within a few years, enormously enhancing the utility of personal computers.

In China, factories and educational institutions start developing computers in series.

Alan Kay's Smalltalk language inaugurates object oriented programming systems (OOPS), but the idea doesn't catch on for thirteen more years.

Frenchman Thi T. Truong creates the Micral microcomputer as a replacement for minicomputers in applications where high performance is not required. The Micral is the earliest commercial non-kit computer based on an Intel 8008-based microprocessor. The first Micrals are sold to industry for process control and to the French government to help collect demographic information in France's African colonies. The Micral's low cost of $1,950 and bus architecture attracts great interest. By 1974, 500 machines will be sold; 2,000 will be sold over the next two years. However, following an unsuccessful attempt to penetrate the U.S. market, Truong can no longer finance the growth of his business, R2E (Realisations Etudes Electroniques). In 1979 he will sell Micral to the major French computer maker Bull.

The used computer market is $75 million a year, divided among 40 to 50 companies.

Computer chess tournaments are now becoming something of a major competitive sport. The tournament at the ACM Annual Convention in Atlanta, Georgia draws twelve participants and is won by Northwestern University's CHESS 4.0 program.

IBM Corporation introduces Winchester disks, the project name for IBM's 3340 disk storage unit. This technology, the industry's standard for the next decade, doubles the information density of disks to nearly 1.7 million bits per square inch.

On August 13, the Institute for Certification of Computer Professionals (ICCP) is founded.

The Dataspeed 40 terminal takes the AT&T Corporation onto computer turf.

Wang Laboratories, Inc. introduces the Wang 2200 minicomputer. With this product Wang shifts its focus from electronic calculators to minicomputers.

William Millard founds IMS International, predecessor to ComputerLand. In two years IMS will develop the IMSAI 8080 microcomputer. The following year IMS becomes IMSAI and ComputerLand is incorporated. In 1979, IMSAI goes bankrupt. In 1984, there are more than 783 ComputerLand franchise computer retail stores in 24 nations and sales go over $1.4 billion. In 1987, Millard will sell ComputerLand.

Computer arts are still in the highly experimental stage of emergence.

The transistor—the invention that started the computer revolution and the space age, and created a multi-billion dollar industry—is twenty-five years old. Originally developed as a solid-state replacement for vacuum tubes in telephone applications, the Nobel Prize-winning invention has become virtually ubiquitous in American life. Most people are never more than a few feet away from a transistor. Man would probably not have landed on the moon without the transistor; it makes possible visual and aural communication between Earth and the astronauts, is used in the complicated and vital guidance equipment and in all manner of data-logging equipment.

The basic mission of a computer is to solve problems. This year's issue of the *Computer Directory and Buyer's Guide* lists 2,400 applications of computers.

The August issue of *Computers and Automation* magazine contains the winners of the "Eleventh

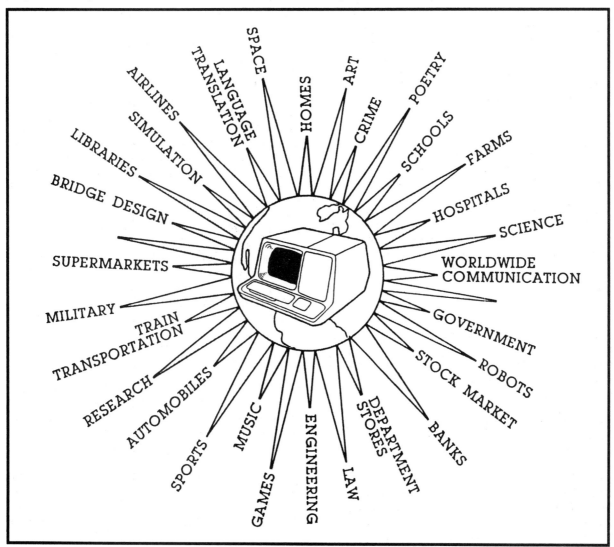

computer applications

Annual Computer Art Exposition." There is a name change this year from "Art Contest" to "Art Exposition."

The East China Computer Research Institute develops China's first magnetic disk drive.

John Atanasoff

John Atanasoff wins a U.S. District Court decision recognizing him as the official inventor of the computer after a lengthy patent trial involving Honeywell, Inc. and Sperry Rand Corporation.

Integrated circuit computers become commonplace.

The East China Institute of Computer Technology in Shanghai, China develops the Model 655 computer. This is the first Chinese computer that uses integrated circuit technology. The 655 is a large computer similar to the IBM 7030 (STRETCH). The production model of the 655 is the TQ-6.

Robert Metcalfe at Xerox PARC invents Ethernet.

The U.S.S.R. aims to monitor its complete economy by computer. Emphasizing improved efficiency rather than greater productivity, the Soviet Government plans to introduce 930 computerized management systems into business, and install new equipment in 2,000 computer centers.

Forensic scientists may now catch crooks by using a computer that matches slivers of glass.

Computer-coded labels are introduced into supermarkets to speed the changeover to electronic cash registers. The cashier simply passes a scanner over the label on each product and the price is extracted from a computer memory.

On October 19, the ENIAC patent is invalidated.

Charles H. Moore forms FORTH, Inc. a firm created to provide application programming services and package FORTH programming language systems. FORTH combines the benefits of an interpreted language with those of a compiled language. FORTH has a small, but very loyal, following.

Richard Schroeppel, a mathematician and computer programmer, uses a Digital Equipment Corporation PDP/11 minicomputer, to determine that there are 275,305,244 magic squares of order 5 (excluding rotations and reflections).

1974

In January, the first issue of *Computers and People* magazine is published. The previous name for this publication was *Computers and Automation* which began publishing information for computer enthusiasts in 1953.

The First World Computer Chess Championship contest is held at the IFIP Congress in Stockholm, Sweden. The Russian computer program, KAISSA, designed by V.L. Arlazaroff and Donskoy wins. The computer used is an ICL System 4/70 located in Moscow. There are twelve other participants, CHESS 4.0 (USA), TECHII (USA), CHAOS (USA), OSTRICH (USA), MASTER (England), FREEDOM PROGRAM (Norway), TELL (Switzerland), RIBBIT (Canada), FRANTZ (Austria), A16CHS (England) and SCHACH MVS.1 (Germany). The main interest in the contest is in the clash between Soviet entry KAISSA and the leading American program CHESS 4.0. The end result is that KAISSA played much better than its rivals.

Control Data Corporation develops the STAR 100 supercomputer.

Pocket calculators have now become household items.

In March, Digital Equipment Corporation ships its 30,000th computer system.

Texas Instruments, Inc. develops the ASC supercomputer.

Ted Nelson writes the first book about personal computers—*Computer Lib and Dream Machines*.

The first UPC-reading scanner is installed at Marsh's Supermarket in Troy, Ohio. The first item scanned is a 10-pack of Wrigley's gum marked "69 cents." Marsh's price is actually 67 cents, a fact the scanner notes correctly.

Banks begin to experiment with automatic teller machines (ATM).

David Ahl starts *Creative Computing*, the first magazine devoted to recreational and educational uses of computers. In 1981, Ahl will sell the publication to the Ziff Davis publishing empire and, a few years later, the publication will be terminated.

Musicians now have a formidable array of computer tools to help them create and perform music.

IBM Corporation delivers the first digital submarine sonar system to the U.S. Navy. It provides a coherent picture of sound sources picked up by the submarine's hydrophones.

In New York City, a programming error causes $7.5 million in welfare checks to be issued to people whose cases have been closed. An embarrassed official says, "We save a lot of money when it works right."

Gordon Moore, one of the founders of Fairchild Semiconductor and later one of the founders of Intel Corporation makes this prediction: There will be twenty million computers in operation by the year 1984. This is an utterly astounding pronouncement at a time when only two hundred thousand computers exist. Moore is a year off, hitting his prediction in 1985.

64K of computer memory costs about $7,000.

National Semiconductor introduces PACE (Processing And Control Element), the first 16-bit microprocessor.

The "Twelfth Annual Computer Art Exposition" is published in the August issue of *Computers and People* magazine.

The fifth ACM (Association for Computing Machinery) computer chess competition takes place in San Diego, California and is won by the Canadian program TREEFROG. TREEFROG (formerly called RIBBIT) had won the first Canadian computer chess championship and it placed third at the International Computer Chess Tournament in Stockholm Sweden.

Computer Law and Tax Reporter, a magazine which documents legal battles in data processing, is published.

Intel Corporation introduces the 8-bit 8080 microprocessor, which is designed by Masatoshi Shima. It is ten times faster than the 8008, and has four times the memory capacity. This chip really founds the personal computer industry and is used in nu-merous personal computers. The 8080 is first widely used as a traffic light controller, however, it finds its way a year later into the MITS Altair personal computer.

The second National Computer Conference (NCC) is held in Chicago, Illinois. Vice-President Gerald Ford, the keynote speaker, warns users that computers have raised issues concerning privacy that will not be easily solved.

The first computer-controlled industrial robot is developed.

The SUMEX-AIM computer communications network is established to promote the development of applications of artificial intelligence to medicine.

The first advertisement for a personal computer appears in an amateur radio magazine. The computer is the Scelbi 8H.

John Cooke at the IBM Corporation designs the first RISC (Reduced Instruction Set Computer) machine.

If you invest $10,000 in the following computer firms, your stock will be worth the indicated amount in 1980—six years in the future.
  Commodore International (personal computers) $1,715,520
  Prime Computer (minicomputers) $557,430
  Computervision Corporation (computer graphics systems) $335,780
  Tandy Corporation (personal computers) $478,000
  Wang Laboratories, Inc. (word processing systems) $328,000

Privacy Act, which protects against the misuse of computer data, zips through Congress.

Zilog, Inc. is founded by two leading designers from Intel Corporation to create the Z-80 chip, which competes directly with Intel's new 8080 microprocessor. The Z-80 will become the heart of the first major generation of non-Apple personal computers, the CP/M machines. The Z-80 chip will become available in 1976.

RGS Electronics announces the RGS-008 microcomputer kit that sells for $375 and is based on the Intel 8008 microprocessor. The printed circuit board version of the RGS-008 is described in September 1975 in the first issue of *BYTE* magazine.

The first ACM SIGGRAPH conference is held.

Edward Shortliffe develops MYCIN, an expert system designed to help medical practitioners prescribe an appropriate antibiotic by determining the precise identity of a blood infection.

Tandem Computers, Inc., a manufacturer of fault tolerant computers, is founded.

Digital Equipment Corporation introduces MPS, their first microprocessor.

The first programmable pocket calculator is introduced by the Hewlett-Packard Company. No larger than a person's hand, the HP 65 can be programmed to solve scientific, engineering and statistical problems.

Radio Corporation of America produces the world's first 164,000 element chip.

Texas Instruments, Inc. patents its first hand-held calculator in June. The Datamath, sells for over $100 and provides only addition, subtraction, multiplication, and division.

Digital Equipment Corporation enters the Fortune 500, ranking 475th in sales among U.S. industrial corporations.

The Intel 8080 microprocessor chip sells for $360. In 1983 the price of this chip will be reduced to $3.70.

The first Toshiba floppy disk drive is introduced.

In England, International Computers Ltd. (ICL) announces the ICT 2900 series of computers.

Scelbi (for SCientific ELectronic and BIological) announces a personal computer in the March issue of QST, a ham radio magazine. Four months later, the Scelbi 8H microcomputer has its first competition—*Radio Electronics,* a magazine for experimenters, runs an article about the building of a machine called the Mark-8. Both the Scelbi 8H and the Mark-8 are based on the Intel 8008 microprocessor chip.

1975

The United States air traffic control is fully computerized.

Microsoft Corporation is founded by William Gates and Paul Allen. Gates and Allen write the first BASIC interpreter for the MITS Altair 8800 microcomputer. Microsoft will go on to become the largest software company in the world.

MITS Inc., a firm in Albuquerque, New Mexico introduces the Altair 8800 microcomputer kits, which are based on the Intel 8080 microprocessor. The Altair 8800 is featured on the cover of *Popular Electronics* as the "World's First Minicomputer Kit to Rival Commercial Models." The Altair sells for $395 (or $498 fully assembled), but up to $2,000 worth of peripherals are needed to make it go. MITS will ship about 2,000 of the machines the first year. This is the start of the personal computer age.

William Gates

Paul Allen

Altair 8800 microcomputer kit

B.W. Kerninghan introduces RATFOR (RATional FORtran), a preprocessor that allows C-like control structures in FORTRAN.

In February, Digital Equipment Corporation adds the LSI-11, Digital's first 16-bit microcomputer, and the powerful PDP-11/70 to the PDP-11 family.

Medicine is becoming an important area of applications for artificial intelligence (AI) research. By now, four major medical expert systems have been developed: CASNET, Internist, MYCIN, and PIP.

The 753 computer is built at Fudan University in Shanghai, China.

Over nineteen different microprocessors are available.

IBM Corporation introduces the IBM 3800, the first laser printer in the industry. This high-speed nonimpact printer bounces a laser beam off a many-sided mirror rotating at high speed to print high-quality documents at over 20,000 lines per minute. It is an extremely expensive and bulky machine, designed for high-speed printing. Laser printers do not become popular until 1984 when the Hewlett-Packard Company introduces the LaserJet for use with personal computers.

On July 15, Dick Heiser opens the world's first microcomputer retail store in West Los Angeles. It is called *The Computer Store*.

Burroughs Corporation begins introducing the "800" family of computer systems with the announcement of a series of computers designed for medium- to large-scale applications.

Liquid crystal displays for pocket calculators and digital clocks and watches are sold for the first time.

Radio Corporation of America delivers the first full-scale all-optical memory to NASA.

The Sphere I microcomputer is introduced. It uses a Motorola 6800 microprocessor and offers 4K bytes of RAM, a keyboard, video interface, and ROM-based monitoring, all for $650.

The pocket calculator boom peaks with world production hitting 50 million.

A computer helps prove that the left-field wall at Boston's Fenway Park is actually 9 feet shorter than the posted 315 feet from home plate at the foul line. It took an aerial photograph, a computer, some basic trigonometry, and World War II mapping lenses to solve the mystery.

MOS Technology announces the 6501 and 6502 microprocessors, which cost only $20 and $25, respectively, versus $150 for an Intel 8080. The 6502 will later become the heart of the Apple II personal computer line.

Michael Shrayer, a previous member of the executive staff of the TV program *Candid Camera*, develops the Electric Pencil, the first word processing program for microcomputers.

Thirty-two thousand computer professionals travel to Anaheim, California to attend the National Computer Conference (NCC).

Paul Terrell and Boyd Wilson open the first Byte Shop (computer store) in Mountain View, California. A couple of years in the future, Paul Terrell will sell a chain of 74 Byte Shops for $4 million.

Ed Roberts, founder and president of MITS (Micro Instrumentation and Telemetry Systems) and developer of the Altair 8800, coins the term "personal computer (PC)." Distinguishing PCs from hobby machines, demonstration machines, industrial machines and development systems, his view is that PCs have to be used for applications typically run on a minicomputer or larger computer. The PC also has to be affordable, easily interfaced with other devices and feature a conventional console with a keyboard, CRT or something similar. It should have an operating system and mass storage.

IBM Corporation introduces the IBM 5100 portable computer that weighs 50 pounds.

The role of knowledge in intelligent behavior is now a major focus of artificial intelligence (AI). Bruce Buchanan and Edward Feigenbaum of Stanford University pioneer knowledge engineering.

Bob Albrecht and Dennis Allison introduce the Tiny BASIC programming language which runs on a microcomputer in 2 kilobytes of RAM.

SouthWest Technical Products Corporation (SWTPC) introduces the SWTPC 6800 microcomputer, one of the first computers to be based on the Motorola 6800 microprocessor. The computer is sold as a kit, costing $395 for the basic system which includes 2 kilobytes of RAM and a serial Teletype interface. With its complete set of peripherals, the SWTPC 6800 is one of the first low-cost systems on which software can be developed and run in a reasonably convenient fashion.

The Homebrew Computer Club is founded by Fred Moore in Gordon French's Menlo Park, California garage. This is the first microcomputer club.

MOS Technology announces the KIM 1, an assembled single-board computer based on the 6502 microprocessor, with 1 kilobyte of RAM, LED read-out and a monitor.

G.L. Steele and G.J. Sussman introduce the Scheme programming language, a LISP dialect.

The retail price of the Intel 8080 microprocessor chip is $150.

Benoit Mandelbrot writes *Les objet fractals: Forme, hasard, et dimension*, his first long essay on fractal geometry, a branch of mathematics that he develops. Fractal forms are widely used to model chaotic phenomena in nature and to generate realistic computer images of naturally occurring objects.

The first German computer chess tournament is held in Dortmund. The winner of the tournament is TELL, a program written in Zurich and the only non-German entry.

The Defense Advanced Research Programs Agency launches a program to stimulate research in the area of machine vision.

EPA Associates introduces the Micro-68, a microcomputer trainer based on the Motorola 6800 microprocessor. Victor Wintriss develops the Micro-68 as a low-cost tool for training engineers in the use of microprocessors. EPA will go out of business in 1978.

The "Thirteenth Annual Computer Art Exposition" is published in the August issue of *Computers and People* magazine.

On July 21, the Xerox Corporation announces to the world it is throwing in the towel in the computer business—Xerox Data Systems closes its doors and withdraws from the mainframe computer industry.

Scelbi Computer Consulting announces the Scelbi 8B microcomputer, a successor to the 8H. Both are based on the Intel 8008 microprocessor.

There are three specialists for every computer. In another decade there will be one hundred computers per specialist. By 1996 there will be several thousand microcomputers per specialist.

The Institute of Computing Technology starts development of the 757, China's first large-scale computer.

Transistors are now so small and the circuits on them so compactly etched they are referred to as microchips.

IBM Corporation introduces the IBM 3850 Mass Storage System—a beehive of electronic activity. It can store up to 472 billion characters of information.

In September, the first issue of *BYTE* magazine is published by Wayne Green and Carl Helmers.

Congress drafts Consumer Communications Reform Act, much to the consternation of the AT&T Corporation.

Object Design of Tallahassee, Florida, offers Encounter, the first commercial personal computer game, in assembly language on paper tape.

Fudan University in Shanghai boasts the first computer science department in China. The university has built several computers, including the 719 (built in 1971), the 753, and a DJS 130 mainframe which is similar in architecture to the Data General Corporation's NOVA 1200.

In September, Digital Equipment Corporation delivers its 50,000th computer system, 15 years after Digital's first computer was introduced.

The sixth ACM (Association for Computing Machinery) computer chess competition takes place in Minneapolis, Minnesota and is won by the program CHESS 4.4 of Northwestern University. Earlier versions of this program had won the first four ACM matches, but in the fifth competition, played in San Diego, California in 1974, first place was taken by the Canadian program TREEFROG.

1976

Stephen Wozniak proposes to the Hewlett-Packard Company that it create a personal computer. Steven Jobs proposes the same to Atari Corporation. Both are rejected. Both Steve's go on to form Apple Computer, Inc.

Design System Language, considered to be a forerunner of PostScript, appears.

Chuck Peddle of MOS Technology develops the 8-bit 6502 microprocessor. It will be used in several microcomputers including the popular Apple II computer.

Dr. Dobb's Journal of Computer Calisthenics and Orthodontia: Running Lights Without Overbyte is first published by the nonprofit People's Computer Company.

Steven Jobs

Stephen Wozniak

CRAY 1, the first commercial supercomputer, is developed by Cray Research, Inc. This supercomputer is one of the most powerful in the world. It can make 167 million calculations per second. The U.S. Government will use the CRAY 1 to make top-secret weapons research calculations, and the U.S. National Weather Bureau will use the computer to make weather forecasts. The CRAY 1 is introduced as the fastest computer on earth. The first CRAY 1 is shipped to Los Alamos National Laboratory. It contains 200,000 integrated circuits.

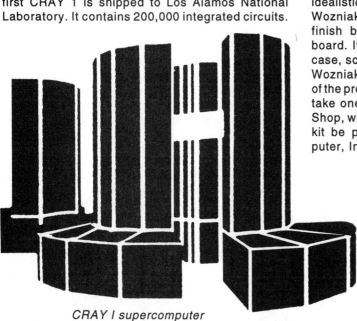

CRAY I supercomputer

The *New York Times* starts to convert to electronic editing and typesetting on a Harris 2550 system.

The National Bureau of Standards approves an IBM data encryption technique. Without the correct key, it is estimated that it would take hundreds of years to decode information stored this way.

Zilog, Inc. releases the Z-80 microprocessor chip, a faster and cheaper version of Intel's 8080 microprocessor. The operating system CP/M and leading software will be written for the Z-80.

Apple Computer, Inc. is founded on April Fool's Day by an idealistic pair of visionaries: Steven Jobs and Stephen Wozniak. Working out of a garage, Wozniak and Jobs finish building a pre-assembled computer circuit board. It is called the Apple I and has no keyboard, case, sound, or graphics. Jobs sold his VW bus, and Wozniak sold his HP calculator, and they used $1,350 of the profits to launch the company. Jobs and Wozniak take one of the Apple I microcomputers to the Byte Shop, who order a few dozen on the condition that the kit be preassembled. Thus was born Apple Computer, Inc.

Apple Computer's first logo

Lee Felsenstein introduces the first implementation of a memory-mapped alphanumeric video display for personal computers. This makes it possible, for the first time, to use personal computers for highly interactive uses such as real time games. The Visual Display Module (VDM) prototype is demonstrated at the World Altair Computer Convention in Albuquerque, New Mexico. Variants of the VDM board were immediately incorporated into many personal computers; the design had a great influence on the development of personal computer video displays. Felsenstein himself will use the design in the Processor Technology Sol microcomputer and the Osborne-1 portable microcomputer.

China starts to import advanced computer technologies from other countries. Prior to this time they used only Chinese technology.

Data General Corporation displays a computer chip in the navel of a belly dancer at the National Computer Conference. (And everyone thought computer people were just stuffy technology nerds).

Tandem Computer, Inc. introduces the first fault-tolerant computer, the T/16.

Worldwide revenue of Burroughs Corporation has grown to almost $2 billion and employment has reached 50,000.

The East China Computer Research Institute develops the HDS 1001, a medium scale computer.

PolyMorphic Systems announces the Poly 88, an Intel 8080 machine based on the S-100 bus with 512 bytes of RAM, interfaces for video, keyboard, and cassette, and 1 kilobyte of ROM for $685 in kit form.

Computer Associates International, Inc., a leading software vendor, is founded by Charles Wang and three associates.

IMS International introduces the IMSAI 8080 microcomputer, the first computer compatible with the MITS Altair 8800 microcomputer. The compatible microcomputer phenomenon later repeats and amplifies in 1981 with the advent of the IBM PC compatibles.

Commodore International, Inc. enters the personal computer market.

Hewlett-Packard Company markets the first programmable calculators, which are essentially pocket computers.

Ohio Scientific Instruments (OSI) is founded to bring microcomputer technology to engineers, students, and hobbyists at the lowest possible cost. They start by developing three computers. The Model 300 is a Microcomputer Trainer Board that sells for $99. This primitive computer board uses the MOS Technology 6502 microprocessor, the same chip that will be used in the Apple II and PET microcomputers. The OSI Model 400 microcomputer can use one of several chips and 1,024 bytes of memory. The Model 500 has a 4K memory and 8K Microsoft BASIC in ROM. In the following year, OSI develops the Challenger family of microcomputers. OSI eventually went out of business as Apple Computer, Commodore, Radio Shack and IBM personal computers became popular.

Honeywell, Inc. acquires the interest in the failing computer company Xerox Data Systems. Honeywell agrees to assume marketing, support and maintenance for the Xerox Sigma line of mainframe computers.

CHESS 4.7, a program running on a large Control Data CYBER 176 computer, wins five games, loses none, and takes the Paul Masson American Chess Championship in California. CHESS 4.7 is developed at Northwestern University by David Slate, Larry Atkin, and William Blanchard.

The Smithsonian Institute receives the last Keuffel & Esser slide rule. K&E quits making slide rules. From now on the handy calculator will be in the form of a pocket calculator.

AT&T Corporation offers Dataphone switched digital service.

David Bunnell of MITS organizes the World Altair Computer Convention in Albuquerque, New Mexico, the first microcomputer conference. Seven hundred people attend the conference. Among the products introduced at this convention is the Cromemco TV Dazzler, the first microcomputer color graphics board.

A microcomputer for cars has been developed by General Motors Corporation. The Alpha V measures speed, fuel level and consumption, battery voltage and oil pressure, calculates journey times and keeps the engine running.

The IBM Corporation develops ink-jet, non-impact printing for addressing labels. A jet of ink, controlled by a magnetic field, is sprayed into a character form of any style and on to any surface.

In China, the chaotic years of the Cultural Revolution (1966-1976) brought computer education to a standstill with the closing of universities and many secondary schools.

Burroughs Corporation introduces the B-80 series of small computer systems. The B-80 brings the power and memory capacity of much larger computers to the small systems range.

Shugart announces its 5.25 inch "minifloppy" disk drive for $390.

JOLT is one of the first microcomputers based on the MOS Technologies 6502, a low-cost microprocessor very similar to Motorola's 6800. In the future, the Apple II microcomputer will be based on the 6502.

A computer-controlled reading machine is developed which reads aloud any printed text that is presented to it. The machine is intended to be a sensory aid for the blind.

Perkin-Elmer Corporation introduces a superminicomputer.

Cromemco Corporation introduces the Z1, the first personal computer that uses the Z-80 microprocessor.

NEC Corporation of Japan introduces System 800 and System 900 mainframe computers.

Texas Instruments, Inc. announces the TMS-9000, the first 16-bit microprocessor.

All kinds of personal computer-related gizmos and interfaces for the home and other hobbies are appearing, along with games.

Digital Equipment Corporation introduces the 36-bit DECsystem-20, the lowest priced general-purpose time sharing system on the market.

Alan Kay and Adele Goldberg's Dynabook paper sets the goals for personal computing.

After five years of preparation, the doors open on a 4,000 square foot History of Computing exhibit at London, England's Science Museum.

A beginning computer programmer's salary is $11,000.

Today's dollar will purchase 20 times more computing power than the dollar did in 1960.

The medium- and large-scale computers worldwide number 150,000. The installed value of the equipment is $60 billion.

Wayne Green publishes the first issue of *Kilobaud*, a magazine aimed at microcomputer hobbyists. At this time microcomputers are sold in kit form and a

distressing number of them don't work. Four years in the future *Kilobaud* will be renamed *Microcomputing*.

In his article "The robots are coming—or are they?" in the May *Chess Life & Review*, International Chess Master David Levy points out that interest in computer chess has been steadily increasing over the past two years, with a dramatic increase in chess programs being written in the United States and Canada.

A TQ-15 computer system is built at the Shanghai Radio Factory in China. This system is possibly modeled after the Data General Corporation's NOVA minicomputer. Inputs are paper tape, Teletype and light pen.

Digital Research, a leading independent personal computer software vendor, is founded.

Viktor Korchnoi, a Soviet grand master, defects during an IBM chess tournament.

The Data Entry Management Association (DEMA) is organized.

Willy Crowther and Don Woods at Stanford University develop the first adventure game, *Adventure*, which is based on the board game Dungeons and Dragons.

Processor Technology introduces the Sol microcomputer, designed by Lee Felsenstein, a $995 kit with walnut sides and a metal case.

RCA introduces the 1802 microprocessor. It is later used in the RCA COSMAC VIP microcomputer, which is developed by Joseph Weisbecker. The COSMAC includes 2 kilobytes of RAM, 52 bytes of ROM, a hexadecimal keypad, and interfaces for video, cassette, and audio.

On February 3, William Gates of Microsoft Corporation is the first person to raise the issue of software piracy in his "Open Letter to Hobbyists."

The National Computer Conference (NCC) is held in the New York Coliseum. The NCC, for the first time, devotes a day of the conference sessions to microcomputers.

Kenneth Appel and Wolfgang Haken resolve the four-color conjecture by using a computer.

The first major movie to use computer-aided animation is *Futureworld*.

The Institute of Computer Technology in Beijing, China develops the 013 computer which uses eight,

16-track one-inch magnetic tape units, four paper tape readers, and two printers.

The number of computer magazines grows to include *BYTE*, *Computer Graphics and Art* and *Dr. Dobb's Journal of Computer Calisthenics and Orthodontia*.

Gould SEL introduces a superminicomputer.

The first computer trade show of national scope, the Personal Computing Festival, is held in Atlantic City, New Jersey. Steven Jobs demonstrates the Apple I computer at this show.

The "Fourteenth Annual Computer Art Exposition" is published in the August issue of *Computers and People* magazine.

After the Altair 8800 microcomputer was introduced, computer clubs start springing up all over the United States.

IBM Corporation introduces the Series 1 minicomputer family of computers.

Gary Kildall invents the first operating system for microcomputers, CP/M (Control Program for Microcomputing). CP/M rose to the rank of standard operating system for 8-bit microcomputers equipped with a Zilog Z-80 microprocessor.

Before Apple Computer, Inc. is formed, the Byte Shop computer store sells the Apple I microcomputer circuit board. It is the first Apple dealer.

The Zilog Z-80, the MOS Technology 6502 and the Motorola 6800 microprocessors dominate the early years of the personal computer industry.

Technical Design Labs (TDL) in Trenton, New Jersey is one of the first microcomputer manufacturers located on the East Coast. TDL comes out with a line of computers under the product name "XITAN." TDL will later change its name to Xitan, Inc. and announce, but never build, a workable computer called "The General."

A computer store with the unlikely name of Kentucky Fried Computers (A Computer in Every Pot) opened in Berkeley, California to sell computers at discount prices. The retail business soon gave way to the manufacturing of a floating point math board. The business changed its name to North Star Computers and later becomes a successful computer manufacturing business.

The Trenton Computer Show is the first personal computer show. People all over the country come to New Jersey to see, touch, and talk about the new wonder—the microcomputer.

Vector Graphic, a company run by Lore Harp and Carol Elly, produce the Vector 1 personal computer. The Vector Graphic line will continue to expand in 1980 with the MZ System B and 1982 with the Models 2600 and 3005. Eventually Vector Graphic will go out of business.

1977

German engineer Heinz Nixdorf purchases Massahusetts-based Entrex Inc. which becomes Nixdorf Computer Company, a German manufacturer of small computers.

Jim Warren organizes the first West Coast Computer Faire in San Francisco, California. For many years this is the major trade show for the personal computer industry.

The Jet Propulsion Laboratory builds two computer-controlled Rover prototypes designed to explore Mars. The following year NASA cancels the project.

The original Altair 8800 computer, introduced in 1975, had no keyboard, no video display, and no storage device. Users would enter their programs one instruction at a time, using the switches on the front panel. The Altair 8800b, introduced in 1977, has a serial interface, which allows the connection of a video display terminal and printer.

Michael Zabinski opens one of the first computer camps outside Simsbury, Connecticut. Catching toads and tying knots in the morning, writing programs in BASIC in the afternoon. Zabinski enrolled eighty-four kids for a one-week session.

Robert McGhee develops a hexapod walking machine controlled by a digital computer. Also, in the USSR, scientists develop a hexapod walker controlled by a hybrid (analog and digital) computer.

Heathkit introduces the H-8 microcomputer kit based on an Intel 8080 microprocessor with an octal front panel keypad.

The human mind works in many different ways. Some people can use their minds to perform amazing feats of calculation without going through the usual step-by-step process. Indian mathematician Shakuntala Devi is one of them. She tries to work out the 23rd root of a 201-digit number faster than a UNIVAC computer. The answer, 546372891, takes the computer one minute and five seconds, but takes Devi only fifty seconds, pointing out that the human brain is still far more complex than any computer.

Bruce Buchanan, Edward Feigenbaum and William Von Melle develop EMYCIN, the first expert system "shell." A shell is a program that provides the framework for developing an expert system.

John McCarthy proposes a conjectural inference rule called *circumscription* to formalize the construction of educated guesses.

Paaslow, a checker playing program, developed at Duke University by Eric C. Jensen and Tom R. Truscott, beats Arthur L. Samuel's program. Paaslow examines a million potential positions every two minutes. Samuel's checker playing program had been the champion since 1967.

The Japanese car industry now employs 7,000 computer-controlled industrial robots which are used for welding, painting, controlling sheet metal pressing and assembly. Robots keep costs lower, therefore boosting foreign sales.

Bell Telephone is the first to use optical fibers to transmit TV signals. Their cable forges a link which will make data communications more efficient and economical.

Camp Retupmoc, one of the first week-long computer camps, is held in Terre Haute, Indiana.

Ohio Scientific Instruments offers the first microcomputer with floating-point Microsoft BASIC in ROM.

NorthStar Computers introduces the Horizon microcomputer, which uses a Z-80 microprocessor, 16 kilobytesof RAM, and a 5.25-inch floppy disk; and sells for $1,999.

John Backus at the IBM Corporation proposes FP, a language based on mathematical functions instead of assignments to memory.

In May, the Boston Marathon is scored by a Honeywell computer system.

Teen computer whiz Kevin Mitnik begins making a habit of tapping into data banks and destroying information, altering credit reports of perceived enemies and disconnecting the phones of celebrities. His most famous exploit—electronically breaking into the North American Defense Command in Colorado Springs—helps inspire the 1983 movie *War Games*.

Burton Smith completes the design of HEP, a machine that overcomes memory latency by switching between tasks every cycle on every processor.

The 64-key Data Encryption Standard gives users more security.

The National Computer Conference (NCC) is held in Dallas, Texas. Personal computer manufacturers are invited to the show, but they are not allowed to demonstrate their wares on the show floor. Downstairs from the show, MITS, Inc., Cromemco Corporation, and IMS International show their personal computers to curious spectators.

The DJS 050 is the first microcomputer developed in China.

Commodore International, Inc. announces the PET microcomputer. This 46-pound personal computer features 4 kilobytes of RAM and 14 kilobytes of ROM and is built around the IEEE-488 bus. The PET (Personal Electronic Translator), a MOS Technology 6502-based machine, costs $595 assembled. It is first shown in April at the West Coast Computer Faire. This is the first American-made microcomputer that you can buy, plug in and turn on.

Apple II microcomputer

Apple Computer, Inc. unveils the Apple II microcomputer, the first personal computer with color graphics, a keyboard, power supply and attractive case. It comes fully assembled and pre-tested, with 4 kilobytes of standard memory, two game paddles and a demo cassette for $1,298. Orders reach $1 million by the end of the year. The Apple II ultimately became the personal computer equivalent of the Volkswagon.

Radio Shack, a division of Tandy Corporation, announces the popular TRS-80 Model I microcomputer. The whole system which offers some graphics and can be programmed in BASIC, sells for $599.95. The TRS-80 uses a Z-80 microprocessor and has 4 kilobytes of RAM, BASIC in ROM, a keyboard, black and white display, and cassette interface. The TRS-80 is extremely successful; the company has projected annual sales of 3,000 units, but over 10,000 are sold within a month of the TRS-80's introduction.

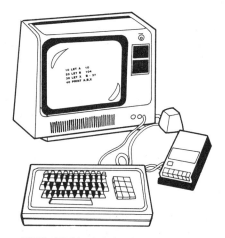

TRS-80 Model I microcomputer

The personal computer industry begins when Apple Computer, Inc., Tandy Corporation and Commodore International, Inc. introduce their off-the-shelf computers as consumer products.

Wang Laboratories, Inc. announces the VS minicomputer modeled after the IBM System/360.

The first videotex system, QUBE, appears in the United States.

The first electronic bulletin board in the United States, the Community Memory Project, is founded in Berkeley, California. Terminals are placed in retail stores and community centers and people are encouraged to speak their mind, check the city council's agenda, find toxic hot spots in the neighborhood and locate used cars and housing.

In the movie *Demon Seed* Julie Christie plays a woman who is imprisoned and impregnated by a computer.

Erwin Tomash founds the Charles Babbage Institute.

QUBE cable system is introduced by Warner Communications. It allows viewers to respond to questions and take part in polls using their cable TV.

CRTs come under suspicion when two *New York Times* copy editors are diagnosed as having cataracts. Tested for radiation, the machines are ultimately cleared. This is the first of many complaints linking eye irritations and CRTs.

Storage systems become smaller, more powerful and contain more equipment. Micropolis Corporation announces the Metafloppy, a family of 5.25-inch floppy disk systems with the storage capacity of 8-inch disks.

The Boston Computer Society (BCS) is founded by 13-year-old Jonathan Rotenberg. At its peak in the early 1990s, the group will have over 32,000 members. The first, and once premier, computer users group voted to cease operations in 1996.

MITS (Micro Instrumentation and Telemetry Systems), Inc., the developer of the Altair 8800 microcomputer, is sold to Pertec Computer Corporation for 6 million dollars. Faced with stiff emerging competition from companies such as Processor Technology, IMS International, Commodore International, and Apple Computer, Pertec is unable to retain market share and the Altair goes out of production in 1978. MITS and the Altair play a central role in the development of the U.S. personal computer market. They pioneer a whole marketing style—computer shows, computer retailing, computer company magazines, user groups and numerous add-on hardware and software options.

John V. Roach starts his Tandy career as general manager of computer services. He is basically responsible for Radio Shack coming out with the TRS-80 Model I microcomputer in 1977. In years to come he will become the chairman of Tandy Corporation.

Magnetic bubble memories are first marketed by Texas Instruments, Inc.

Datapoint Corporation announces the first local area network, the ARCnet. ARCnet transmits data at 3 million bits per second over a coaxial cable.

Digital Equipment Corporation introduces the VAX-11/780, the first member of the VAX computer family. VAX (Virtual Address eXtension) machines are a family of 32-bit computers.

William Millard founds the ComputerLand chain of computer stores. The first ComputerLand franchise store opens in Morristown, New Jersey, under the name Computer Shack. In 1984, there will be almost 800 ComputerLand franchise computer retail stores. In 1987, Millard will sell ComputerLand.

The "Fifteenth Annual Computer Art Exposition" is published in the August issue of *Computers and People* magazine.

"Ease of use" has become a popular Data Processing buzzword.

1978

Japan starts exporting mainframe computers to the United States and other countries.

Rob Barnaby and Seymour Rubenstein, formerly of IMS International (IMSAI), founds MicroPro International and commissions Barnaby to write the WordMaster word processing program, precursor to WordStar.

The Xerox Corporation introduces the Xerox 9700 laser printer. Laser printers will not become popular until Hewlett-Packard Company develops the LaserJet for use with personal computers.

Diablo Systems invents the first daisy wheel printer, which was inspired by techniques used in IBM typewriters.

Atari 800 microcomputer

Atari Corporation introduces the Atari 400 and Atari 800 microcomputers. Both microcomputers are based on the MOS Technology 6502 microprocessor. The Atari 800, which cost $1000, has a full keyboard, 8 kilobytes of RAM, two ROM cartridge slots and custom sound and graphics chips. The Atari 400 has a membrane keyboard. The machines will not be shipped until late 1979. The sound and graphics chips for the Atari 800 are designed by Jay Miner, who later designs the chips for the Commodore Amiga.

Siemens, a computer manufacturer in Germany, introduces the ND2 laser printer.

IBM Corporation announces the Model 4300 mainframe computers.

The Digital Group announces the Bytemaster, a sewing-machine-sized computer housing a display, keyboard, and disk drive.

The Epson TX-80 is the first commercially successful dot matrix printer for personal computers. It revolutionizes the low-cost printer market and becomes a runaway best seller.

The first hard disk storage drives for microcomputers are sold. These units hold up to 5 megabytes of data.

In the mid-1970s, David Levy, a Scottish chess champion made a bet that no computer could beat him at chess before August 1978. He wins the bet.

Summagraphics Corporation announces Bit Pad, the first digitizer.

Apple Computer, Inc. and Tandy Corporation (Radio Shack) announce 5.25-inch floppy disk drives for the Apple II and TRS-80 microcomputers, respectively.

AWK, a text-processing language named after the designers, Aho, Weinberger, and Kernighan, appears.

ACM Curriculum '78, a widely used model for college undergraduate computer science programs, is published.

Bill Pohlman and a team of Intel engineers develop the Intel 8086 microprocessor. It is a 16-bit microprocessor chip that is compatible with the Intel 8080.

Total computers in use in the United States exceeds 500,000 machines.

Dan Bricklin and Bob Frankston create VisiCalc, electronic spreadsheet software for the Apple II microcomputer. VisiCalc can recalculate all related numbers when one variable changes. They pool their finances and with $16,000 found Software Arts, Inc. VisiCalc is credited with taking microcomputers out of the home and making them useful in the business office.

Sales of a talking Chess Challenger, electronic dice, and other TV games are booming.

A chess playing program on a high-speed computer steals a game from San Francisco Grand Master Peter Biyasis.

The British Post Office continues trials of Prestel, its public TV information, or viewdata, service. Anyone with a TV set can gain access to computerized data and services by means of a module which links both instruments to the terminal. The system will eventually be launched in 1980 and go international in 1981.

Stanley Mark Rifkin steals $10 million from Security Pacific Bank through a banking communications network, the FEDWIRE.

Corvus Systems, Inc., announces an eight-inch hard disk using Winchester technology.

IBM Corporation introduces the System/38. Its distinctive architecture and programming allow database management and virtual storage to be used by both experienced and first-time computer users.

IBM System/38 computer

Wang Laboratories, Inc. becomes the largest world-wide supplier of CRT-based word processors.

James Martin's book, *The Wired Society*, is nominated for a Pulitzer Prize. Martin has written over thirty books.

Fifty-one thousand computer professionals gather in Anaheim, California to attend the National Computer Conference (NCC).

Texas Instruments, Inc. offers its Speak-and-Spell toy, the first widespread use of digital speech synthesis.

Exidy Sourcerer computer

The Exidy Sourcerer microcomputer sells for $895 and includes a Zilog Z-80 microprocessor. Its major innovations are the use of plug-in ROM cartridges for software and user-definable characters.

The first programmable video game system is introduced by Fairchild Electronics.

Bubble memory is first used in commercial machines.

Radio Shack is the microcomputer sales leader; selling approximately 100,000 TRS-80s. Commodore International, Inc. is second, selling 25,000 PET microcomputers, and Apple Computer, Inc. ships 20,000 Apple II microcomputers. MITS/Pertec ships 3,000 microcomputers, IMS International ships 5,000 units and all other personal computer manufacturers ship 35,000 microcomputers.

Ward Christensen and Randy Seuss create the first major microcomputer bulletin board system in Chicago, Illinois.

Cullinet Software is the first software company to go public on the New York Stock Exchange.

The "Sixteenth Annual Computer Art Exposition" is published in the August-September issue of *Computers and People* magazine.

Seymour Cray, designer of the CRAY 1 supercomputer, starts work on the CRAY 2, which is planned to be six times faster than the CRAY 1.

Start of VLSI (Very Large Scale Integration) circuit.

Canada announces *Telidon*, their version of videotex, after almost 10 years of development. By 1981 there will be 2,000 Telidon Terminals in use in several experimental projects. In 1985, Telidon will lose direct financial support and essentially disappear.

The Beijing Wire Factory in Beijing, China is producing DJA 154 computers at the rate of 60 per year. The DJS 154 is a general-purpose computer, but its primary use is in process control.

Wang Laboratories, Inc. delivers the VS minicomputer system, which becomes one of the most popular office systems, and which inaugurates the concept of *office automation*.

Harold Cohen, uses a program called Aaron and a DEC PDP-11/45 minicomputer, to produce "computer art." Linked to the computer by a wire is a small turtle-like device that does the actual drawing onto large sheets of paper. Aaron consists of three hundred subroutines that handle various aspects of producing the art.

Two-sided floppy disks begin to become popular.

Digital Equipment Corporation (DEC) and Carnegie Mellon University begin work on XCON, an expert system that configures computer systems. Within two years XCON will come into regular use, saving millions of dollars at DEC plants.

Hans Berliner's backgammon computer program wins the world championship.

The IBM Corporation introduces the "intelligent" electronic typewriter.

Raymond Kurzwell receives the 1978 Grace Hopper award for the development of the Kurzwell Reading machines, a machine that reads books aloud to the blind.

The *New York Times* switches from hot type to computerized typesetting.

IBM Corporation becomes the first company to mass produce a memory chip storing approximately 64,000 bits of data. Just eleven years earlier, the densest chip could store only 64 bits.

In February, Digital Equipment Corporation ships its 100,000th computer.

Digital Equipment Corporation is now known as DEC, and so joins IBM as one of the few in the industry recognizable by its initials.

The first Personal Computer Expo is held in New York City.

In 1971, a basic four function (add, subtract, multiply, divide) electronic calculator cost around $100 in the United States. In 1972, it cost $50. By 1975 it had dropped to $20. Two years later it was $14 and by 1978 the cost is $11.

1979

The total number of computers in the United States exceeds half a million machines.

Apple II Plus microcomputer

Apple Computer, Inc. introduces the Apple II Plus microcomputer which sells for around $1200.

Epson improves upon the TX-80 printer with another dot matrix printer, the MX-80, which soon becomes an industry standard.

TRS-80 Model II microcomputer

Radio Shack introduces the TRS-80 Model II microcomputer for business users.

The East China Institute of Computer Technology in Shanghai, China develops the HDS 801 computer. This computer (500,000 instructions per second) is a multiprocessor and is used for business processing, real-time control and engineering applications.

Adam Osborne sells his computer book publishing company to McGraw-Hill Publishing Company and founds Osborne Computer Corporation.

The first 8-bit microcomputers appear in Brazil. These computers are manufactured by Brazilian companies.

"Mighty Bee," a three-foot robot that connects via communications lines to a DEC PDP-10 computer at Carnegie Mellon University, using a software program called BKG 9.8, beats world champion Luigi Villa of Italy at the world backgammon championships in Monte Carlo.

There are sixteen major competitors developing microprocessors (Advanced Micro Devices, Data General, Fairchild, General Instrument, Intel, Intersi, MOS Technology, Mostek, Motorola, National Semiconductor, RCA, Rockwell, Signetics, Texas Instruments, Western Digital and Zilog).

Faster and more compact integrated circuits are now possible, using graphoepitaxy, M.I.T.'s new technique for growing silicon crystals by which artificial grooves are made in the crystals to control their natural growth. This breakthrough allows etched circuits to operate more quickly at reduced power and may possibly lead to 3-D circuits to provide larger programs.

The National Computer Conference (NCC) is held in New York. At this conference Sperry Rand Corporation introduces its UNIVAC 1100/60 mainframe to compete with IBM's 4300 series.

Micropad, the world's first computer terminal to accept direct handwritten data is introduced by Quest Automation.

Itel Corporation sold computers that could run IBM software. In January, to celebrate a $50 million profit, Itel flew thirteen hundred employees to Acapulco to celebrate. But IBM announces a new computer, the 4300, and suddenly Itel's computers were technologically obsolete. By the end of the year the company has disposed of all its computer business and closed its doors.

The Burroughs Corporation announces the first models of the "900" family of computer systems.

Work begins on the development of robots able to "see." They will be programmed with a "visual" coded memory and could revolutionize such industrial processes as quality control.

Bell Telephone unveils its electronic blackboard. Identical in appearance to the traditional model, it transmits each image on to a visual display unit and automatically records the information.

A computerized laser printing method is developed by the Monotype Corporation in Great Britain for publishing houses in Shanghai and Peking. The new method will change the lives of Chinese printers. Previously they had to rollerskate between rows of type to select from the 60,000 characters in the Chinese language.

MicroPro International, founded by former IMS International (IMSAI) employees Rob Barnaby and Seymour Rubenstein, introduces WordStar, the first popular word processor for microcomputers. Later word processing programs will use many of the features found in WordStar.

The Beijing Wire Factory in Beijing, China produces the DJS 220 computer, however, there are no disks units or software yet.

The cost of producing silicon is reduced by one sixth. Silicon is used in the manufacturing of integrated circuit chips.

Hewlett-Packard Company introduces the HP 41C programmable pocket calculator.

WordPerfect Corporation, a leading software vendor, is founded. The Word Perfect word processing program is an immediate success.

Allan M. Cormack and Godfrey N. Hounsfield receive the Nobel Prize in Medicine for work in computerized tomography.

Computerworld starts hosting the Ridiculous Button Contest, wherein readers submit their favorite cliches and turns of phrase in the hopes of these being chosen to become a Computerworld button. A sampling of some winners: Micros Are Thinker Toys; Garbage In, Gospel Out; Kiss My Bits; Loose Bits Sink Chips; Bugs Are Sons of Glitches; and Pardon Me, Modem.

For the first time, a bar code scanner is used to score over 5,000 runners in the Bonne Bell race in Boston, Massachusetts.

Jean Ichbiach and a team from CII-Honeywell Bull (France) develops the ADA programming language. The language is named after Augusta Ada Byron

(1815-52), who worked with Charles Babbage on the Analytical Engine and is considered the first programmer.

Hayes Microcomputer Products announces the Micromodem 100, an auto-dial, auto-answer modem. Hayes modems set the standard for modems in years to come.

George Tate launches Ashton-Tate and dBase II, the database management software for microcomputers. It makes it possible to classify, sort and select information according to numerous criteria. dBase II was developed by C. Wayne Ratliffe, who had marketed it under the name Vulcan before selling it to Ashton-Tate.

Computerized video games, such as Pac-Man, Centipede, and Space Invaders, become a huge craze.

The Source, an electronic information network service, begins offering news and stock reports to home computer owners.

Dan Fylstra founds Personal Software, Inc. to market VisiCalc, the best-selling financial spreadsheet program. Personal Software is later to become Visicorp, Inc.

Motorola, Inc. introduces the 68000, the first of a series of microprocessors that compete with those of Intel Corporation. The Motorola microprocessors will be used in the future in Apple Macintosh, Atari ST, and Commodore Amiga microcomputers.

The Burroughs Corporation announces the B-90 series of computers.

On June 18, Microsoft Corporation announces BASIC for microcomputers using Intel 8086 microprocessors.

Wealthy executives benefit from the "Tera" pocket calculator, linked to a company's computer by two-way radio.

IBM System/4 Pi: more than 5,000 of these small but rugged computers, announced in 1966, have now been used in a variety of missions in aircraft, missiles and space stations. Later models will be used aboard NASA's Space Shuttle.

At the West Coast Computer Faire in San Francisco, California, the first Apple II computer clone appears. It is called "The Orange."

The potential of expert systems in medicine becomes widely recognized when a landmark study reveals that the MYCIN expert system does at least as well as human medical experts.

CompuServe, Inc., an information service is formed on September 24.

Intel Corporation introduces the Intel 8088 microprocessor, which, in the future, will become the heart of the IBM Personal Computer.

Burrell Smith starts working on the Apple Macintosh computer in its earliest stages. The Macintosh is now just a tiny 8-bit machine based on the Apple III with a little CPU power. In 1981 the project will gather momentum when Steven Jobs gets involved. Burrell's first real prototype will be a more powerful Motorola 68000-based CPU that includes a small bit-mapped screen. Making another pass he will add more memory, performance enhancements and better communications capabilities, thus producing the first-generation Macintosh model.

The Sharp Corporation, in Japan announces a pocket computer that can be programmed in the BASIC language.

IBM Corporation sales passes the $20 billion mark.

The State Administration of Computer Industry (SACI), in China, is established to manage importing of foreign computers and to match this with the ability of China to manage and maintain them.

The first COMDEX trade show is held at the MGM Grand Hotel in Las Vegas, Nevada, with an attendance just under 4,000 people. COMDEX will become one of the dominant trade shows in the computer industry. In 1995 the attendance will be over 200,000 people.

In September, the Computer Museum starts at the Digital Equipment Corporation facility in Marlboro, Massachusetts. At this time the museum is totally sponsored by Digital Equipment Corporation. In the future, the Museum will relocate to downtown Boston, Massachusetts, and will occupy 55,000 square feet in the top two floors of a refurbished century-old wool warehouse on Boston's waterfront across the bridge from the Boston Tea Party Ship Museum. On display inside the museum are many artifacts of the fascinating history of the computer.

VisiCalc, the first electronic spreadsheet, is introduced at the West Coast Computer Faire in San Francisco, California. Written by Harvard Business School student Dan Bricklin and Bob Frankston of M.I.T. Running initially on the Apple II computer and nearly single-handedly creating the demand for the machine, VisiCalc establishes spreadsheets as a staple application, setting the stage for Lotus 1-2-3 on the IBM PC in 1982.

The East China Institute of Computer Technology in Shanghai, China develops the HDS 9 large-scale computer, a five million instructions per second computer.

Two Electronic Data Systems (EDS) employees are taken hostage in Teheran, Iran during the Iranian revolution. The employees are held hostage by the revolutionaries to convince EDS to come back and man computers it had left behind during the American evacuation. A $12,750,000 ransom is unpayable because the Iranian banking system has broken down. Receiving no support from the State Department, H. Ross Perot, founder of EDS, in February assembles a strike force of employees to storm the prison and free the prisoners. With this action, Perot, demonstrates employee benefits at a new level.

Mattel, the toy manufacturer, receives its millionth microprocessor chip for use in electronic games.

Software Arts, Inc., the company that designed and programmed VisiCalc, is incorporated.

The "Seventeenth Annual Computer Art Exposition" is published in the September-October issue of *Computers and People* magazine.

The Chinese Computer Society was founded in the early 1960s and resumed this year. It is a nationwide academic organization devoted to the development of Chinese computer science and technology.

Vulcan (which became dBase II) is the first popular database program.

1980

In 1970, microprocessors were only available with 4-bit control. Now there are 32-bit chips available.

Vector Graphic announces the MZ System B personal computer.

John Bell invents the first easy database program, the Personal Filing System, to run on Apple II personal computers.

Microsoft Corporation licenses the UNIX Operating System and starts to develop a personal computer version called XENIX.

The little Sinclair ZX-80 personal computer becomes very popular and several magazines about this machine start to appear. *Sync, The Magazine for Sinclair Owners* is the principal magazine.

John Cocke and a group of researchers at the IBM Corporation complete the IBM 801 minicomputer, the first Reduced Instruction Set Computer (RISC).

The total number of computers in the United States exceeds one million machines.

Apollo Computer, Inc., a workstation manufacturer, is founded.

Apple Computer, Inc. announces the Apple III computer. It features a new operating system and a built-in disk controller. This computer will be plagued with problems.

A FBI sting nabs an executive trying to steal the source code of the ADABAS database management system to sell to the U.S.S.R.

Shugart Associates introduces a hard disk drive for microcomputers, which stores 30 times more data than a floppy disk, and transfers the information twenty times faster.

The Sony Corporation becomes the first Japanese company to enter the word processing field with the introduction of the Series 35 word processing system.

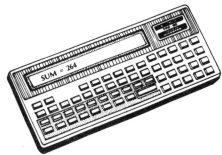

TRS-80 Pocket Computer

Radio Shack, a division of Tandy Corporation, announces the first pocket computer available in the United States—TRS-80 Pocket Computer.

Altos introduces the first microprocessor-based multi-user system, the 8000-5 microcomputer system, which can support up to four people.

The first issue of *Infoworld* is published.

Bell Laboratories develop the Bellmac-32, the first true single chip microprocessor with 32-bit architecture and a 32-bit data bus.

The Radio Shack Color Computer is the first personal computer to include music, a joystick interface, and an interface to a home TV. It is designed specifically for recreation and education.

At the World Computer Chess Championship in Linz, Austria, the program BELLE, developed by Kenneth Thompson and Joe Condon of Bell Laboratories, beats a program called CHAOS, developed at the University of Michigan.

IBM Corporation introduces a holographic scanner for use in supermarkets. The scanner reads the product code marked on packages, thereby speeding checkout.

There are 200,000 installed mailboxes on public information networks and 220,000 on private networks.

Control Data Corporation introduces the CYBER-205 supercomputer to match the performance of Cray Research's computers. The CYBER 205 and CRAY 1 operate so fast and perform so closely to each other that it is difficult to choose one over the other.

The number of mainframe and minicomputer installations number about 400,000 for a saturation ratio of about 2,000 machines per million people. This figure does not include microcomputers.

The National Computer Conference (NCC) is held in Anaheim, California. During the conference, Data General Corporation brought out its Eclipse MVS-8000 line of minicomputers.

J.C. Johnston, a graduate student at Cleveland State built his own personal computer for $592.

Mystery House, the first computer game to use graphics as well as text, is developed by Roberts and Ken Williams of Sierra On-Line, one of the nations leading computer game companies.

Robert Tarjan and Danny Sleator use a new data structure and a new analysis technique known as *amortization* to design a better network flow algorithm.

The Sinclair Research, Inc., ZX-80 is the first microcomputer to cost less than $200. Based on a Z-80 microprocessor with 1 kilobyte of RAM and 4 kilobytes of integer BASIC in ROM, it has a membrane keyboard and is the brainchild of Englishman Clive Sinclair. The successor ZX-81 will later be sold to Timex, Inc. and the price will drop to less than $100.

The IBM Corporation announces the Displaywriter word processing machine at a cost of $8,000.

The "Annual Computer Art Exposition" is published in the September-October issue of *Computers and People* magazine. This is the last year that the computer art exposition is published in this magazine.

Bjarne Stroustrup develops a set of languages, collectively referred to as "C With Classes," that serve as the breeding ground for C++.

Second-generation computer-controlled industrial robots begin to arrive with the ability to precisely effect movements with five or six degrees of freedom. They are primarily used for spray painting and industrial welding.

The Xerox Corporation introduces the Xerox 860 word processor which has a full page display.

Several video game designers from Atari, Inc. defect and start Activision, which begins designing Atari hardware-compatible, "clone" games—that is, software that plugs into Atari game machines.

Self-repairing microchip circuits, in which the functions of a damaged circuit are taken over by a neighboring circuit, are introduced by John Barker of Warwick University, England.

The fully automatic factory comes closer to actuality as computer aided manufacturing is developed in Japan, the United States and Great Britain. Computers will soon be used to design the components of machines and to control their manufacture in an automatic production system, which includes the use of robots and computer controlled machining and assembly.

It is predicted that by 1984 there will be several million general-purpose microcomputers in schools, colleges, and universities, with an even greater number available for educational use in the home.

Wang Laboratories, Inc. unable to recruit the caliber of people it needs to develop its technology, opens its own Wang Institute of Software Engineering in Lowell, Massachusetts.

Digital Equipment Corporation ships its 200,000th computer.

The first workstation is introduced by Apollo Computer, Inc. A workstation is a machine in the form of a microcomputer, designed to carry out a precise function and linked to a central system and shared peripherals.

High-performance, high-quality, and large-capacity hard disk drives are now a low-cost reality for personal computer systems.

The IBM Corporation decides it will produce a personal computer.

Ethernet is named a networking standard in a joint public announcement by Digital Equipment Corporation, Intel Corporation and Xerox Corporation. Ethernet is a new concept of processor-to-processor communications intended for an office department.

Texas Instruments 99/4 microcomputer

Texas Instruments, Inc. introduces the TI 99/4 microcomputer, one of the first 16-bit microcomputers; it is based on the TMS-9900, a Texas Instrument microprocessor. Many units are sold, but TI will still lose money on it. The TI 99/4 has a color monitor, and built-in three-voice synthesizers which make the computer ideal for music and voice applications.

The first robotic patient is designed for use as a teaching aid in universities. Next year, *Harvey*, a robot that can simulate 26 illnesses, will be developed by Michael Gordon, a professor of cardiology.

Apple Computer, Inc. goes public with an initial public offering of 4.6 million shares of common stock at a price of $22 per share. Every share is bought within minutes of the offering, making it the largest public offering since Ford Motor Company went public in 1956. Cofounders Steven Jobs and Stephen Wozniak become instant multimillionaires.

Congress passes the Computer Software Act, which allows software programs to be copyrighted.

Digital Equipment Corporation introduces the VAX-11/750, the second member of the VAX family and the industry's first Large Scale Integration (LSI) 32-bit minicomputer.

Florida becomes the first state to mandate, through legislation, that computers and related technology be used "to make instruction and learning more effective..."

Radio Shack announces the TRS-80 Model III microcomputer, a replacement for its popular Model I.

Designing a microchip which can pass through the eye of a needle is made easier by using Stereoscan,

TRS-80 Model III microcomputer

an improved scanning electron microscope installed at Great Britain's Science Research Council laboratories.

The magazine *Computers and People*, formerly *Computers and Automation*, has published computer art in one issue (usually August) from 1963 to 1980.

Sony Corporation introduces the Typecorder, a portable paperless typewriter.

In April, the Federal Communications Commission begins steps to deregulate the phone industry, paving the way for AT&T to enter the field of computer-enhanced data processing.

Commodore International, Inc. introduces the Commodore VIC-20 home computer. It uses a MOS Technology 6502A microprocessor and offers 5 kilobytes of RAM, BASIC in ROM, a color display and ROM software cartridges for $299. It becomes the first million-seller in the history of the industry.

Six thousand people attend the ACM SIGGRAPH computer graphics conference in Seattle, Washington.

1981

At ENIAC's thirty-fifth birthday celebration in Philadelphia, the ENIAC is pitted against a Radio Shack TRS-80 microcomputer and directed to square all integers from 1 to 10,000. The TRS-80 wins easily, completing the exercise in a third of a second vs. ENIACs six seconds.

Osborne Computer Corporation release the Osborne-1, the first popular, battery-operated portable computer. It contains a Zilog Z-80 microprocessor, 64K bytes of RAM memory, a full business keyboard, a built-in monitor, two floppy disk drives, and a software package of popular programs. The price tag of the Osborne-1 is $1,795. The computer weighs 23 pounds and has an operating system that can handle electronic spreadsheets and word processing. The Osborne-1 was introduced at the West Coast Computer Faire in San Francisco, California.

The Sinclair ZX-81 microcomputer is introduced in England. Sinclair now manufactures more microcomputers each month than anyone else in the world. The ZX-81 sells for $99.95.

A total of 4,360 people invest $55 million to become limited partners in Trilogy Systems' venture to build a monumental computer: an IBM-compatible supercomputer that uses Very Large Scale Integration (VLSI) circuits. Trilogy is started by Gene Amdahl, the chief engineer of the IBM System/360 family of computers, and later founder of Amdahl Corporation, a manufacturer of IBM-compatible computers. However Trilogy will never build its supercomputer.

While on a trip to China this author observes a Chinese store clerk using an abacus to total customers' bills rather than the electronic calculator that is also available to him. When asked why, the clerk replies that it is easier. This shows that technology cannot merely be injected into a culture.

Michael Gordon, a professor of cardiology in Miami, created *Harvey*, a computer-controlled robot that can simulate 26 illnesses.

The Alto microcomputer, developed by researchers at Xerox PARC, paved the way for the Macintosh. The Alto came with the Smalltalk programming language, a mouse, and Ethernet connectivity.

The last IBM STRETCH computer system is retired.

The Shanghai Computer Factory in China starts production of the DJS 185 computer. This machine is similar to a Digital Equipment Corporation PDP 11/35.

Digital Equipment Corporation (DEC) introduces a family of computer systems called DECmate, that are specialized for word processing.

Lotus Development Corporation, a leading independent software vendor, is founded by Mitch Kapor.

The Shanghai Computer Factory in China produces the 100/20 computer. This prototype machine is similar to the IBM System/360 Model 50.

The six-year-old personal computer industry passes the $1.5 billion mark.

Gallium arsenide may replace silicon as the linchpin of microelectronics.

The Nanjing Radio Factory, a major telecommunication factory in Nanjing, China, uses a DJS 130 minicomputer (Chinese copy of a Data General Corporation Nova) for business applications.

Holograms add an extra dimension to video games.

A minicomputer with the capacity of a mainframe model is introduced by Intel Corporation. The iAPX 432 uses three silicon chips, equivalent to 225,000 transistors. Much of the software is built directly into the hardware, or chips.

Burroughs Corporation acquires the Memorex Corporation, a computer storage device manufacturer. The first Memorex-built storage system specifically designed for a Burroughs computer system will appear in 1982.

China builds their first Large Scale Integration (LSI) computers.

The first French restaurant to use computers for waiters is located at Valenciennes, France. Proprietor Georges Guillaume installs computer keyboards at the tables. Customers place orders by pushing buttons that call up different menus—bar, entree, hors d'oeuvres, etc.— and then pushing the buttons for their choices.

The Xerox Corporation announces the Xerox 820, a business version of flexible home computers.

Japan holds an international conference on fifth-generation computers. Japan announces a 10-year project to develop the fifth generation computer and calls for international cooperation.

Apollo Computer, Inc. delivers its first machine, the DOMAIN, one of the new series of microcomputers designed to provide fully distributed processing.

Steve Grimm and Nikolai Weaver start Plum Software in Los Gatos, California—they are eleven years old. Their first software is a business program called Filewriter.

Apple Computer, Inc. has now become a household name. Surveys show that public awareness of Apple Computer rises from 10 percent to 80 percent this year. The Apple II microcomputer installed base exceeds 300,000 machines.

The Chinese are about 15 to 25 years behind their Western counterparts in computing. They are, however, advancing as rapidly as possible.

Zork, a second-generation computer adventure game, is introduced and made available for virtually every popular personal computer.

Steven Jobs, cofounder of Apple Computer, Inc., appears on the cover of *Inc.* magazine.

Bob Yannes is given the job of designing a low-cost sound chip for the upcoming Commodore 64 computer. He ended up creating SID (Sound Interface Device), an analog synthesizer chip that redefined the concept of sound in personal computers.

Shoppers at a large number of major supermarkets are having their purchases tallied by computer controlled checkout systems that eliminate manual keying of many items. The checkout system, which features a high-speed scanner that reads the grocery industry's Universal Product Code can make checkout faster for shoppers and easier for checkers, while it records the sales data needed to manage a modern, complex supermarket.

IBM Personal Computer

On August 12, the IBM Corporation introduces the IBM Personal Computer. In the following decade, the machine will become the most significant technology to hit the U.S. office since the telephone. The IBM Personal Computer will change the way people work and live. Microsoft Corporation's MS-DOS becomes the standard operating system for the IBM Personal Computer. Eighteen months in the future, IBM's market share will be as large as the industry leader, Apple Computer, Inc. The first IBM PC has a single disk drive, 16K of memory, and is priced at $1,565.

Epson America introduces the HX-20, an early laptop computer.

On April 12, a HP 41 calculator is used by an astronaut on the first Space Shuttle Flight.

The first computer wedding is performed by Reverend Ron Jaenisch on Valentine's Day, using an Apple II personal computer in California. The computer displays the text of the ceremony on the screen, and the bride and groom indicate their "I do's" by pressing the "Y" key.

Perkin-Elmer Corporation demonstrates the 3230 superminicomputer that runs the UNIX Operating System at the National Computer Conference (NCC).

Data General Corporation is the subject of *The Soul of a New Machine*, a Pulitzer-prize winning book that traces the development of Data General's newest, largest computer, the Eclipse. This national bestseller is written by Tracy Kidder.

A year earlier the IBM Corporation asked Microsoft Corporation to provide it with an operating system for its future microcomputer. William Gates, Microsoft owner, then bought Seattle Computer Products' Tim Patterson's 16-bit operating system SCP-DOS. Microsoft modified it, called it MS-DOS and delivered it to IBM. MS-DOS becomes a popular operating system for all IBM personal computers and IBM-compatible computers.

BBN Advanced Computers, Inc. develops the Butterfly, a parallel computer that can combine up to 256 microprocessors to achieve single program parallel processing.

Hayes Microcomputer Products, Inc. introduces the Smartmodem 300, which becomes the industry standard.

Systems Engineering Laboratories, Inc. demonstrates its most important product at the National Computer Conference (NCC) in a hotel suite and not on the show floor (SEL Concept 32/87).

The one-of-a-kind ILLIAC IV computer at NASA's Ames Research Center is dismantled. This computer was installed in 1972.

A year after its announcement, the doomed Apple III computer is delivered. The machine initially suffered a nearly 100 percent failure rate and almost dragged down the company.

The VisiCalc spreadsheet is made available for the IBM Personal Computer one week after the IBM Corporation announced the computer. During the next few years, more than 200,000 copies of VisiCalc will be sold for the IBM PC and compatible computers.

Xerox Corporation announces the Star microcomputer system. Many of today's newest computers, Apple Macintosh in particular, use concepts pioneered by the Star.

After the IBM Corporation introduces the IBM Personal Computer, Apple Computer, Inc. greets its new competitor with a full-page ad in the *Wall Street Journal* featuring a headline that reads "Welcome IBM. Seriously."

Watchmaker Timex, Inc. contracts with England's Clive Sinclair to market the Timex/Sinclair 1000, the first fully assembled under-$100 personal computer in the United States. This computer was previously named the Sinclair ZX-81.

The huge Ziff Davis publishing empire buys *Creative Computing* magazine. *Creative Computing* was started in 1974 by David Ahl. It was the first computer hobbyist publication. As the microcomputer industry grew and changed, *Creative Computing* completely lost its identity and character. When the recession hits the personal computer industry in the mid-1980s, the magazine will be terminated.

Chinese engineers design computer terminals with the goal of manufacturing them within two years.

A computer Pioneer Day celebration was held at the National Computer Conference (NCC) in Chicago. Some of the pioneers in attendance were Grace Hopper, J. Presper Eckert, Erwin Tomashi and T.H. Bonn.

Attendance at the ACM SIGGRAPH computer graphics conference in Dallas, Texas is 9,474.

The *Computer Shopper*, born as a trading paper for used computers, evolves by 1983 into a tabloid magazine devoted to direct sales of computers and related products. In 1988, Computer Shopper will bill itself as the "World's Biggest Computer Magazine."

One of the first wide area networks BITNET is founded to serve academic institutions.

Between 1975 and 1981, computer technology changed so profoundly that those few years mark a watershed not just in the history of computers but in modern culture as a whole. Thanks to the silicon chip, the once-elephantine computer shrunk in both size and cost until it was less elephant than rabbit, and it began to multiply and to expand its range accordingly.

Hewlett-Packard Company releases the Superchip, the first 32-bit microprocessor. It can add two 32-bit numbers in 55 billionths of a second.

1982

The U.S. Government charged IBM Corporation with antitrust violations in a suit that lasted 13 years until it is finally dropped in January.

In January, LOGO Computer Systems, Inc. introduces Apple LOGO, the first widely distributed commercial Logo program.

In March, the U.S. Supreme Court allows deaf lawyer Michael Chatoff to receive and answer questions via a computer placed at his desk in the courtroom.

In April, Digital Equipment Corporation introduces the VAX-11/730, the third member of Digital's 32-bit minicomputer family.

Compaq Computer Corporation is founded by Rod Canion and other ex-Texas Instrument, Inc. engineers. Compaq introduces the first portable clone of the IBM PC and becomes the IBM Corporation's biggest competitor in the personal computer market.

The FBI arrests several Hitachi employees involved in a conspiracy to steal IBM technical and product design information, in June.

In June, the International Council for Computers in Education (ICCE) is founded to serve and represent computer teachers.

In August, the first computer camp for kids with diabetes is held at the National Computer Camp.

On September 2, Stephen G. Wozniak, Apple Computer cofounder, and the U.S. Festival put on, in addition to music by many popular music artists, the first-known outdoor computer show. Wozniak sponsors the money-losing U.S. Festivals.

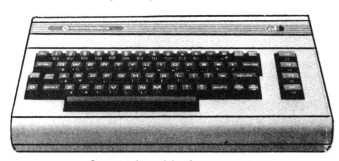

Commodore 64 microcomputer

In September, Commodore International, Inc. introduces the Commodore 64 microcomputer. It uses a 6510 microprocessor, 64K RAM, 20K ROM, and sells for $595. In the next year the price drops to $200 and the computer becomes one of the best selling computers of all time.

In September, Stevens Institute of Technology, the Hoboken, New Jersey engineering school, requires all incoming freshmen who plan to study computer science, systems planning, or management to own an Atari 800 microcomputer.

Jack Myers and Harry Pople at the University of Pittsburgh develop CADUCEUS, an expert system for internal medicine. Tested against cases from the *New England Journal of Medicine*, it proves more accurate than humans in a wide range of categories.

About forty Cray Research's CRAY 1 supercomputers have been installed. The CRAY 1 and Control Data Corporation's CYBER 205 are the fastest computers in the world, however, there are projects underway to develop computers ten times faster.

Compact disk players are marketed for the first time.

Columbia Data Products announces an IBM PC clone, the MPC.

TKISOLVER, a problem solving program by the inventors of VisiCalc, is introduced by Software Arts, Inc., in May.

The top hundred computer firms grew four times faster than the U.S. economy as a whole.

Steve Chen from Cray Research, Inc., a Taiwanese immigrant to the United States, where he did his engineering studies, designs the world's first computer featuring parallel architecture, the CRAY X-MP supercomputer. The CRAY X-MP can perform 1 billion instructions per second.

The National Computer Conference is held in Houston, Texas. Microcomputer manufacturers such as Cromemco, Lobo Drives International, Jonos, Ltd., Onyx Systems, Inc., and Morrow Decisions, Inc. display their wares.

In China, computer science departments have been established in about 100 universities.

John Warnock and Charles Geschke form Adobe Systems, Inc. to create pioneering software products for desktop publishing and electronic document technology.

Over 125,000 Osborne-1 portable computers are sold.

The Japanese electronics company, Hitachi, Ltd. announces a supercomputer that can hit a peak speed of 630 million floating point operations per second.

Rensselaer Polytechnic Institute give entering students computers to see how they will take to them. They discover that in a short time, they used them as much as students who had brought their own computers with them to school.

Sony Corporation in Japan announces compact disk technology.

Intel Corporation introduces the Intel 80286 micro-processor, which runs ten times faster than the 8086 microprocessor.

Control Data Corporation introduces the CYBER 190 series computers.

The Computer Museum

The Computer Museum relocates from a Digital Equipment Corporation facility in Marlboro, Massa-chusetts to its present home at Boston's Museum Wharf. The Computer Museum is the world's largest collection of computer industry artifacts. The mu-seum contains the relics of a machine age gone by and examples of technologies still under develop-ment.

Burroughs Corporation introduces the B-7900 main-frame computer.

System 1032, a relational database management system for DEC's VAX minicomputer, is announced by Software House.

IBM Corporation introduces the IBM 8084 and IBM 8083 mainframe computers.

Neiman-Marcus offers the ComRo household robot in its Christmas catalog. ComRo can take out the trash, clean up spills on the carpet, light cigarettes, and do a variety of other tasks.

TIME magazine names the computer its "Man of the Year." This is a graphic reflection of the importance of computer technology to all levels of our society.

Microsoft Corporation licenses MS-DOS to about 50 IBM PC clone manufacturers.

Heathkit develops HERO 1, a robot designed to initiate young people into the field of robotics.

Jimmy Carter is the first former U.S. president to use a word processor to write his memoirs.

IBM Corporation introduces the IBM 3084 supercomputer, the most powerful computer in the company's history. It features four processors run-ning under the same operating system and able to tap into the same data pool.

Over 17,000 software packages are now available to run on Apple II personal computers.

A *Fortune* article in May states that there are about two hundred Ph.D.s in artificial intelligence (AI)

The *New York Times* runs its first full page of ads for computer camps. The first computer camp had opened only five years earlier.

Tandon Company announces a two-sided floppy disk with an 875,000 character capacity.

DeVry Institute of Technology conducts a study that shows the number of women entering data process-ing jobs has increased 20 percent over the previous year.

An uncounterfeitable credit card containing a micro-computer is developed by Intelmatique, a French company.

Thomas Zimmerman and Young Harvill develop the Dataglove, a device, that when connected to a com-puter, allows the operator to move objects visualized with a head mounted display (Eyephone) by hand operation.

The Chinese did their national census with an aba-cus until this year, when they replaced the abacus with computers. China uses IBM computers and 5.1 million census takers and other workers to find out how many people live in the World's most populous nation.

The Social Security Administration admits that it will be using a computer to track draft evaders through their Social Security Numbers.

Since the first commercial electronic computer (UNIVAC I) appeared in 1951, the speed of large-scale scientific computers has doubled approximately every two years. Supercomputers, CRAY 1 from Cray Research, Inc., and CYBER 205 from Control Data Corporation, can perform over 100 million ar-ithmetical operations in a second.

Autodesk announces AutoCAD, the first CAD(Computer-Aided Design) system for personal computers.

David Bunnell starts *PC Magazine*.

Businessland opens its first computer store.

Lotus Development Corporation introduces Lotus 1-2-3, a very popular spreadsheet program for IBM compatible personal computers, VAX's, and IBM mainframes. The program is designed by Jonathan Sachs. Its particular feature is that it combines three functions in one program: spreadsheet, file management and graphics.

Franklin Computer Corporation announces the Ace 100 microcomputer, an Apple II clone.

Non-Linear Systems (later renamed Kaypro Corporation) announces the $1,795 Kaycomp II portable microcomputer, with a 9-inch screen and bundled software.

Visicorp is the first company to develop the idea of integrated software. Visi-On consists of an integrating module onto which application modules (word processing programs, spreadsheet programs, database management programs, graphics programs, etc.) can be grafted. Visi-On can only use application modules that are specifically designed for it, and it will eventually became obsolete.

A computer, in Washington, D.C., is used to help Nan Davis, a paraplegic, walk.

A total of 3800 computers (674 were imported) are installed in China.

Approximately 2.5 million personal computers are shipped worldwide. This figure will double next year.

Digital Equipment Corporation announces its first personal computer, the Rainbow.

Apple Computer, Inc. becomes the first personal computer company to have $1 billion annual sales. Apple Computer's installed base exceeds 650,000 units. 17,000 Apple II software programs are offered by more than 1,000 developers.

Pac-Man is the first computerized video game to inspire a TV-show.

The power of computer-age weapons is frighteningly revealed. In the conflict between Great Britain and Argentina over the Faulkland Islands. A single $200,000 computer guided missile, the French Exocet, demolishes the British destroyer Sheffield, a $50 million warship. The general class of weapons with microprocessors are called precision-guided munitions (PGMs).

According to a study by Professor Sanford Weinberg of St. Joseph's University, at least thirty percent of daily users of computers have some degree of "cyberphobia," or fear of computers.

Worldwide sales of personal computer systems is $6.1 billion. By 1989 this figure will soar to $37.4 billion.

A breakthrough in the application of computers to the making of films is made by Walt Disney Studios when *TRON* is released. The film contains about 5 minutes of computer generated film. The computer scenes are generated by Digital Productions, using a CRAY 1 supercomputer.

Sun Microsystems, Inc. is founded with an objective to build powerful, affordable, personal workstations for scientists and engineers. Sun's SPARC architecture becomes one of the most successful RISC designs in history.

IBM Corporation earns more than all its computer competitors combined.

General Motors Corporation introduces MAP (Manufacturing Automation Protocol), a communications protocol.

Visicorp, Inc. formerly Personal Software, Inc., announces the VisiCalc Advanced Version.

IBM Corporation introduces its first two industrial robotic systems—the 7565 and 7535 manufacturing systems—which can be programmed with an IBM developed language.

Attendance at the ACM SIGGRAPH computer graphics conference in Boston, Massachusetts is 16,557.

Susan Kare at Apple Computer, Inc. designs the first icons for the Macintosh computer (which will be formally announced in 1984). Thanks to Kare, an artist and art history Ph.D., millions of computer users will know a smiling computer terminal means their computer has been booted, a trash can lets them delete files, and a moving watch shows that a function is being executed.

Vector Graphic announces the Model 2600 and Model 3005 personal computers.

Chuck Peddle, designer of the Commodore PET and the KIM 1, becomes the president of Victor Business Products, and designs the Victor 9000 personal computer, an Intel 8088 based machine.

Bill Godbout at CompuPro develops the CompuPro personal computer based on the National Semiconductor 16-bit Pace microprocessor chip.

George Morrow at Micro Decisions produces several personal computers including the Decision I computer and the Pivot portable computer.

The installed user base for MS-DOS is 232,000.

Popular word processing programs are Magic Wand, Auto-Scribe, Easy Writer, Star Edit, and the early favorite, WordStar. In 1998, such programs as Microsoft Word deliver functionality that pioneering word processor users could only dream about.

1983

Borland International, Inc., a leading independent software vendor, is founded by Philippe Kahn.

Texas Instrument, Inc. announces MBX, a voice recognition game module developed by the Milton Bradley Company for the TI 99/4A home computer. It not only allows players to give vocal commands while playing a video game but allows the computer to respond with synthesized speech.

Microsoft Corporation announces Windows, but it doesn't ship for two years.

Microrim, founded by Wayne Erickson in 1981, introduces the first relational database for personal computers.

Borland International, Inc. announces the Turbo Pascal programming language. It instantly becomes a popular widely used language.

IBM Corporation introduces the IBM PC/XT, the first personal computer with a built-in hard disk drive, for $4,995.

The term "vaporware" is first coined to describe Ovation, an integrated software package for DOS. Announced by Ovation Technologies, but never developed or delivered.

Mattel, the toy maker, introduces the Aquarius computer at a trade show. It will not be a successful product.

There are 13 million computers in the world. Over 10 million of these machines are in use in the United States.

Hewlett-Packard Company unveils the HP 150, the first personal computer to offer a unique touch screen.

Osborne Computer Corporation declares bankruptcy and goes out of business. It was just two years ago that they introduced an inexpensive portable microcomputer (the Osborne-1).

Six million personal computers are sold in the United States.

Denning Mobile Robotics starts manufacturing computer-controlled security robots capable of guarding banks, factories and other businesses.

George Stickles and Debbie Fuhrman, who met each other via the CompuServe network, are electronically wed, with seventy-six on-line attendees cheering and throwing rice—in this case commas, semicolons, and other punctuation marks.

The number of kids attending computer camps surpasses a hundred thousand (mostly day camps).

Scholastic Inc. begins marketing *Bank Street Writer*, the first word processor designed specifically for students.

IBM Corporation introduces a 3/8-inch square memory chip that can store 288,000 bits of data.

More than 4.5 million U.S. students, mostly secondary school age, use computers in public schools.

Test versions of a biological microchip are produced by EMV Associates, a Maryland biotechnology company.

The millionth Apple II microcomputer rolls off the assembly line.

There are about 27,000 different software packages available in the United States. About a fifth of these are some type of accounting software.

NEC Corporation in Japan announces the SX-1 and SX-2 supercomputers.

The Institute of Electrical and Electronic Engineers (IEEE) agrees to a standard for carrying information over local area networks.

IBM Corporation brings out the IBM PC Jr., a home-oriented, lower-priced encore to its PC. Despite reengineering and huge marketing, the computer becomes a flop.

Software sales reach the $1 billion mark, growing at 50% a year.

Pepsi-Cola V.P. John Sculley makes the jump from soft drinks to hardware and becomes president of Apple Computer, Inc. Two turbulent years later, cofounder Steven Jobs will leave Apple Computer to form NeXT Computer, Inc.

The National Computer Conference (NCC) is held at the Anaheim (California) Convention Center. IBM unveils its System/36 and NCR Corporation releases seven models for its mainframe line. Attendance at this trade show is 97,000.

Compact Disks (CD) are introduced in the United States.

Lotus 1-2-3 takes VisiCalc's place as the popular spreadsheet program. It is marketed by the company founder Mitch Kapor.

Danny Hillis starts Thinking Machines Corporation. The Connection Machine supercomputer series will be sold around the world, primarily to scientific laboratories.

If you had bought $18,500 worth of IBM Corporation stock in 1945, it would be worth $3.8 million in 1983.

New York's Chemical Bank makes the first large-scale launch of a home banking system.

Computerized burglaries have now become popular.

Professor Hiroyasu Funakubo of Japan creates *Melkong*, a computer-controlled robotic nurse that can hold a patient in its arms, wash him or her, put the patient to bed, and tuck in the sheets.

C. Gordon Bell, computer design engineer at Digital Equipment Corporation, forms Encore Computer Corporation with Kenneth Fisher and Henry Burkhardt.

A popular movie, *War Games*, explores the possibility of how a computer system penetrated by a bright teenager (hacker) might accidentally start a nuclear holocaust.

This fall, a number of colleges and universities begin requiring incoming freshmen to purchase a personal computer along with their textbooks, handheld calculators and book bags: Clarkson College, Stevens Institute, Drexel University, Rochester Institute of Technology, Boston University, Northeastern University, and Carnegie-Mellon University.

Microsoft Corporation and a group of Japanese companies announce the MSX standard for Z-80-based computers. MSX will flop so badly that only a handful of MSX machines will ever be sold in the United States.

In August a small group of software developers at Drexel University are holed up in a secured room of a campus basement. They are engrossed in a project they can discuss with no one. The software they are developing is for a machine that is yet unannounced but will soon become "The hottest box on the block."

In 1984, that machine will finally be unveiled to the world as the Apple Macintosh.

Iomega Corporation introduces the Bernoulli Box, an innovative removable mass storage system. The name comes from the 18th century Swiss scientist, Daniel Bernoulli, whose principle of fluid dynamics is demonstrated in disk mechanism.

Apple Computer, Inc. is named to the Fortune 500—the youngest company ever to reach the list.

Texas Instruments, Inc. becomes an early casualty in the microcomputer wars; it withdraws from the home computer market and ends production of the TI 99/4A microcomputer.

Radio Shack introduces the TRS-80 Model 100 book-sized computer, which starts the whole lightweight portable computer industry. The Model 100 introduces the notion of a "laptop computer." This small machine weighs about four pounds, has built-in word processing and communications software, and costs just under $800.

Michael Zabinski runs the National Computer Camp with 135 kids (per week) from all over the world.

More than four thousand mainframes and minicomputers and seventeen thousand microcomputers are in operation in China.

Apple Computer, Inc. introduces the Lisa, a personal computer with a new graphic user interface (GUI) and a mouse. The Lisa has its own operating system, called the Lisa Operating System, that is designed to perform file management, event handling, and exception handling. The Lisa is built around the 32-bit Motorola 68000 microprocessor. The initial $10,000 offering price is prohibitive, but Lisa establishes the state of the art for personal computers. Expensive and slow, it becomes a flop. The Lisa will later be renamed the Macintosh XL.

The Intel 8080 chip, which cost $360 in 1974, sells for $3.70 in 1983.

The first implementation of C++ appears. The name is coined by Rick Mascitti.

Over twenty companies are developing IBM-compatible personal computers.

Novell, Inc., a leading independent software vendor, is founded.

Computer industry revenues reach $55 billion, $2.4 billion of it in personal computer sales.

Novell, Inc. introduces NetWare, the first file server LAN operating system.

An Apple Computer, Inc. team led by Larry Tesler develops Clascal (the first Pascal that supports object-oriented programming) and the Lisa Toolkit, the first commercial OOP application framework.

The Gavilan computer, a laptop with built-in software and a touchpad "mouse" is introduced at the COMDEX computer trade show, however it never takes off.

PC Magazine is sold to new owners; most of the staff quits to form *PC World* magazine.

IBM Corporation is doing $1 billion in sales every two weeks.

In China, 360 mainframes and minicomputers, and 5,000 microcomputers were built.

Apple Computer, Inc. introduces the Apple IIe microcomputer which runs Applesoft BASIC and sells for $1,400.

Apple Computer, Inc. introduces Apple Works, a popular integrated program for the Apple II microcomputer.

Compaq Computer Corporation goes public, and six million shares are sold in one day.

The first 16-bit PC clones appear in Brazil. These personal computers are manufactured by Brazilian companies.

Attendance at the ACM SIGGRAPH computer graphics conference in Detroit, Michigan is 14,169.

A Radio Shack TRS-80 Model I microcomputer is used to break into the military computer in the movie War Games.

NorthStar Computers comes out with its last personal computer, the Dimension. This computer will fail and the company will close its doors. Earlier NorthStar Computers was the Advantage and the Horizon.

Radio Shack, NEC and Epson all sell book-sized computers, but only Radio Shack with its Model 100 becomes popular because of its lower price ($499) and easier-to-use interface.

The Semiconductor Research Corporation (SRC) consortium is founded by thirteen computer and component firms. The consortium provides grants for new and ongoing projects, most of them at universities.

The first IBM PC-based graphics program, PC-Draw, is introduced.

1984

The U.S. market is virtually saturated with low-cost ($6.95 or so) four-function calculators. Yet Americans are still buying around 30 million replacement calculators each year. Worldwide, the calculator market is a billion dollar per year business, with sales approaching 100 million calculators per year.

Seiko in Japan introduces the first wristwatch computer.

William Gates, co-founder of Microsoft Corporation, is featured on the cover of *Time* magazine.

The 3.5-inch floppy disk debuts and eventually becomes the industry's preferred diskette size.

Tandy Corporation announces the Tandy 1000 personal computer. It becomes the best-selling IBM-compatible computer of the year.

Cirrus Logic is founded to make every kind of chip needed in personal computers except memory chips and microprocessor chips.

Fred Cohen from the University of California creates alarm when he warns the public about computer viruses.

The word "cyberspace" is first coined by William Gibson in his science fantasy novel *Neuromancer* in which the hero connects a computer directly into his brain. Cyberspace is a new word and a new world for the late 20th century, a world of information accessible via computer technology.

The Macintosh computer debuts at Apple Computer's annual shareholder's meeting. The computer receives a standing ovation.

During the Super Bowl broadcast, Apple Computer, Inc. runs a Macintosh commercial, a one-time media event that introduces the new microcomputer to several million watchers—"The computer for the rest of us."

Optical disks for the storage of computer data are introduced.

IBM Corporation introduces the IBM PC/AT with an Intel 80286 microprocessor, 256K bytes of RAM, a 16-bit bus, and a new high-density floppy disk drive.

George Orwell's *1984*, thought by many to be a prophetic indictment of the computer age, is found to contain no mention of computers.

Apple Macintosh microcomputer

Thunderscan, a low-cost high quality scanner, is introduced. By replacing the Apple ImageWriter printer ribbon cartridge, Thunderscan creates graphics files of photos, logos, and illustrations.

The Lawrence Livermore National Laboratory (LLNL) Computer Center started in 1953 with a single UNIVAC I computer. In 1984, its eight supercomputers can perform work in three minutes and seventeen seconds that would have taken the Lab's first computer a year to perform. Another way of looking at the center's growth is that one of the center's four CRAY 1 supercomputers can do the same work as 22,000 of the 1953 model UNIVAC I computers.

RACTOR, created by William Chamberlain, is the first computer program to author a book.

Mindset introduces the Mindset PC, a machine designed to bring dazzling color graphics to business users. It did not succeed, however, the Mindset did become the first computer in the New York Museum of Modern Art's permanent industrial collection.

MacPaint, a drawing program for the Apple Macintosh computer, is written by Bill Atkinson and released by Apple Computer, Inc. MacPaint aids thousands of beginner's becoming interested in computers. After its creation, the program produced countless imitators.

Aldus Corporation, leading independent software vendor, is founded.

Data General Corporation introduces the Data General One, a 10-pound laptop computer with a 12-inch LCD screen. The screen is hard to read and the computer eventually flops.

There are now 450 computer magazine titles, the largest number ever devoted to a single subject.

IBM Corporation introduces a one-megabit chip. This experimental memory chip can store more than one million bits of information. That's the equivalent of 100 pages of double-spaced typed text. This new chip has four times the memory of earlier chips.

Hewlett-Packard Company introduces the HP 110, an early laptop computer.

Lotus Development Corporation announces Jazz, which goes on to become the company's first flop.

Commodore International, Inc. buys Amiga Corporation, the developer of a multimedia microcomputer.

China announces the development of its first supercomputer, the Galaxy 100, which reportedly has a top speed of more than 100 million operations per second.

The AT&T Corporation introduces the PC 6300 microcomputer.

Satellite Software International brings out Word Perfect word processing software for the IBM PC and several other microcomputers.

We have Apple's and Orange's, now a company from Great Britain announces the Apricot PC.

The Last Starfighter film is released; it includes about 25 minutes of computer-generated film. The computer scenes are generated by Digital Productions, using a CRAY X-MP supercomputer. The movie featured a video-game whiz played by Lance Guest who helped save a real-life planet under attack.

Larry Tesler's Apple Computer software development team collaborates with Niklaus Wirth to define Object Pascal for the Macintosh computer.

Borland International, Inc. introduces Sidekick, a desktop accessory program for personal computers.

The IBM Corporation is the nation's second largest collector of patents. Ahead of IBM is the General Electric Company with 785 patents. IBM has 608, Hitachi, Ltd. is third with 596, followed by Toshiba Corporation with 539.

As competition heats up, commercial TV becomes a battleground for personal computer wars. Apple Computer, Inc. and Kaypro Corporation have frequent ads and go on to win "Cleos," the major awards of TV commercials.

Hewlett-Packard Company (HP) introduces the first desktop laser printer, called the LaserJet. This printer brings high-quality printing to personal computers.

The government breaks up AT&T's 22 Bell System companies. AT&T is reformed into seven regional holding companies. In return, AT&T is allowed to expand into previously prohibited areas including data processing, telephone and computer equipment sales, long distance, research, and computer communications devices.

The computer manufacturer Dell Computer Corporation is founded by Michael Dell. The company will later become a major mail-order computer manufacturer.

Public computer stores are new in China. Computers sold in some of the stores include the Apple II and a Chinese made Z-80 based microcomputer for about 890 yuan ($400 U.S.) or two years' earnings for most Chinese workers. The Apple II 8K-RAM is priced at 1,700 yuan (about $800 U.S.).

Wang Laboratories, Inc. introduces a stand-alone word processor, but can't compete with personal computers. The company loses more than $230 million on the product.

IBM Corporation, with revenues of $46 billion, is ranked in sixth position among the 500 leading industrial firms in America.

Motorola, Inc. introduces the Motorola 68020 microprocessor.

Apple Computer, Inc. introduces the Apple IIc computer in April at the "Apple II Forever" conference. During this year the two-millionth Apple II microcomputer is sold. Over 400,000 Apple IIc microcomputers will be sold in the products first year.

Electric Dreams, a movie directed by Steve Barron, portrays a love triangle involving a boy, a girl, and a computer.

We like to poke fun at the old-time bookkeeper who sat on a high stool and recorded his figures slowly and meticulously with a quill. Today, bookkeepers use computers and electronic spreadsheets. But, in the old days, you never heard the excuse, "Our computer is down."

Digital Equipment Corporation introduces the VAX-11/785 computer.

The European Community proposes the European Strategic Programme for Research and Developemnt in Information Technology. It has five components: microelectronics, software technology, advanced information processing, office systems, and computer integrated manufacturing. Its aim is to develop the technologies needed for the European information technology to be competitive in the 1990s.

IBM Corporation and Sears Roebuck, team up to form Trintex, which becomes the Prodigy, Inc. information service in 1988.

Congress passed the Semiconductor Chip Protection Act to protect the technology embodied in chips and the associated masks. Congress is concerned that chips and masks, representing one of the major achievements of American ingenuity, are vulnerable to copying and decides to explicitly create a new form of intellectual property protection to help stimulate continued investment in new chip design.

ADA becomes a trademark of the United States Department of Defense. Four years earlier, the programming language ADA was named in honor of Augusta Ada Byron.

When addressing an audience of Chinese faculty and students assembled at a university in Shanghai, President Ronald Reagan said "New satellites can be launched for use in... computer technology.... We hope to see the day when a Chinese scientist working out an engineering problem in Fudan University will be able to hook into the help of a scientist at a computer at MIT. And the scientist in Boston will be able to call on the expertise of the scientist in Shanghai, and all of it in a matter of seconds. My young friends, this is the way of the future."

The Lawrence Livermore National Laboratory (LLNL) Octopus Networking System is one of the most powerful in the world and a pacesetter for the computer industry. The System which began 20 years ago as a single CDC 6600 supercomputer with 12 Teletypes attached, is in 1984, one of the largest and most sophisticated local area networks ever developed. The system now uses eight big computers—four CRAY 1 supercomputers, three CDC 7600 supercomputers and one CRAY X-MP supercomputer. It runs 24 hours a day, every day of the year. Some 2,400 employees at the Laboratory are users of the system.

Tandy Corporation introduces *DeskMate* the graphic interface.

The Gallup Poll finds that 68 percent of parents of high school students believe that computer training should be required for both college-bound and non-college bound students.

Former Commodore International, Inc. president Jack Tramiel buys Atari Corporation from Warner Communications.

IBM Corporation introduces the *Writing to Read* educational system.

Sales of home computers priced below $1,000 fall 30% from 1983 levels.

In April, Timex/Sinclair scrubs its microcomputer line.

The Counterfeit Access Device and Computer Fraud and Abuse Act is signed into law by President Ronald Reagan as part of the Comprehensive Crime Control Act of 1984. In 1986, it will be amended with the Computer Fraud and Abuse Act.

Coleco introduces ADAM, a Z-80 microprocessor-based home computer with tape drive, printer and software for $599. A lot of computer for the money, however, Adam is so poorly designed that it sometimes erases its own tapes during boot-up. It is nicknamed the "Adam bomb."

The National Computer Conference (NCC) is held at the Las Vegas, Nevada Convention Center.

President Ronald Reagan signs legislation to permit the formation of the Microelectronics and Computer Corporation (MCC), a consortium of 21 companies whose purpose is to develop intelligent computers.

Attendance at the ACM SIGGRAPH conference in Minneapolis, Minnesota is 20,390.

1985

Chip manufacturers produce more chips than are needed. Result—the world chip industry loses an estimated $6 billion.

The Nintendo Entertainment System makes its debut.

China expects to produce 1,000 medium systems, mainframes and minicomputers this year.

In February, Apple cofounder Stephen Wozniak leaves Apple Computer, Inc. to form a new company.

Amiga 1000 microcomputer

Commodore International, Inc. introduces the Amiga 1000, the world's first multimedia computer. This computer is powered by an advanced three chip set: Agnes, Denise and Paula. These three chips can do tricks that personal computers a decade later still won't be able to do—such as display multiple screens with independent pixel resolutions and bit depths on a single monitor. The Amiga 1000 will prove to be a classic example of a product ahead of its time.

IBM Corporation, which does business in 130 countries is one of the largest nonunion companies in America.

Aldus Corporation releases PageMaker software for the Apple Macintosh computer. This revolutionary software is the first to enable a single individual to write, layout, paginate and print a book or article, including illustrations, using only a microcomputer and a laser printer. Desktop publishing provides writers, publishers, and artists an inexpensive and efficient way to compose and print large documents. A few years later PageMaker will be developed for IBM compatible microcomputers.

Adobe Systems Inc. develops the page description language PostScript which is first used in Apple Computer's Laserwriter printer. It functions as an interface between the software and the laser printer, allowing the user to print directly onto the page.

After the release of Aldus PageMaker, Apple Computer, Inc. relaunches the Macintosh computer with the LaserWriter printer as a desktop publishing system. This combination starts the desktop publishing era.

Microsoft Corporation ships the Windows operating system for IBM-compatible computers.

National Cash Register announces the 50 pound NCR Personal Computer Model 4 with two vertical disk drives. The keyboard alone weighs 4.5 pounds.

An authentic IBM PC-XT personal computer sells for over $20,000 in China.

The CD-ROM is invented by Philips and promoted throughout the world with Sony Corporation. This data storage device can contain a thousand times more data than a floppy disk.

The number of personal computers used in offices in the United States rises to nine million, with an estimated 15.6 personal computers for every 100 office workers.

The vanilla SNOBOL 4 programming language for microcomputers is released.

IBM Japan is the employer of choice for female college graduates looking for their first job.

Apple Computer, Inc. ships MacApp, its object-oriented application framework for the Macintosh computer.

IBM Corporation has 792,506 stockholders—more people than live in the cities of San Francisco, California, Washington, D.C., or Stockholm, Sweden.

A Japanese mechanic is killed by a malfunctioning Kawasaki computer-controlled robot.

Atari Corporation releases the Atari 520ST microcomputer.

David Deutsch of Oxford University in England provides the first theoretical description of how a quantum computer might work.

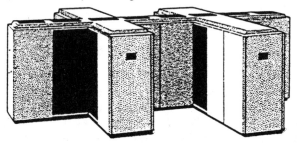

IBM 3090 mainframe

The IBM Corporation's most expensive product is the $9.3 million 3090 Model 400 mainframe. IBM's least expensive item is a plastic diskette holder for 65 cents. For $9.3 million you could buy 14,307,692 diskette holders. Tax not included.

Al Rogers, of freeware fame, creates FrEDWriter, a popular word processing package.

The Chinese Computer Federation is founded to develop and promote computer science and technology in China.

Gateway 2000, an IBM-compatible microcomputer manufacturer, opens for business on a farm outside Sioux City, Iowa. A year later, Gateway will ship its first PC. The company later becomes a major force in mail-order computer sales.

Apple Computer, Inc. now employees 5,700 people.

Digital Equipment Corporation introduces the DEC Microvax II, a compact version of their VAX minicomputer system.

The movie *Weird Science* is about two nerdy teenagers who use a computer to conjure up the woman of their dreams.

First Comics, Inc. publishes *Shatter*, the first comic book written, illustrated and lettered entirely on a computer. Shatter is the name of a free-lance policeman in a futuristic city with a seedy atmosphere. The computer used to create *Shatter* is an Apple Macintosh Computer.

Five national supercomputer centers are formed in San Diego, California; Pittsburgh, Pennsylvania; Princeton, New Jersey; Ithaca, New York; and Champaign-Urbana, Illinois, where the center is called the National Center for Supercomputing Applications (NCSA). The mission of these centers is to give peer-reviewed researchers access to advanced computational resources, and to train scientists of all fields to better attack the unanswered questions in their disciplines.

In September, Apple Computer, Inc. cofounder Steven Jobs resigns to start the new company, NeXT Computer, Inc., to develop workstations for the college market.

Intel Corporation releases the 80386 microprocessor, which is at least 50 percent faster than the Intel 80286 microprocessor.

Cray Research, Inc. introduces the CRAY 2 supercomputer. This compact machine breaks the gigaflop barrier—it can execute in excess of one billion floating point operations per second. The CRAY 2 uses 240,000 chips and weighs 5,500 pounds.

Apple Computer's Japanese-language version of the Macintosh, called the DynaMac, makes its debut in Japan. It features 412 kilobytes of RAM and Kanji installed in ROM. The Kanji MAC will become a very popular computer.

Martha Poppe designs Brazil's new definitive series of eleven stamps which feature the value as a large dot matrix print across the centers.

There are about fifty million "computer-like things" in the world. Twenty-five years earlier there were only about five thousand.

A computer program written in the FORTH programming language controls the submersible sled that locates the wreck of the sunken Titanic. Image processing helps discover this wreck.

Third generation robots arrive with limited intelligence and some vision and tactile sensing.

The Tandy Corporation introduces the Tandy 1000 personal computer which immediately becomes a popular IBM PC compatible machine.

Bank Street's *Voyage of the Mimi*, pioneering multimedia package combines computer, video, and text.

Since 1958, China has developed approximately 200 different computer models, but only 10 of these have reached serial production of a few hundred units.

The Tandy Corporation announces the Model 200 laptop computer.

Zenith Corporation introduces a touch sensitive display screen, based on surface acoustic wave technology.

In September, after losing over $60 million on the Apple III computer, it is quietly removed from Apple Computer's product line.

Japanese computer companies hope to introduce personal computers that use the MSX operating system (developed by Microsoft Corporation) to the U.S. market. They were unsuccessful.

The Media Laboratory at the Massachusetts Institute of Technology creates the first three-dimensional holographic image to be generated entirely by computer.

Intel Corporation introduces the 32-bit microprocessor, the i386, which offers microcomputers performance at the level of yesterday's minicomputers.

Digital Equipment Corporation stops making the Rainbow personal computer.

IBM, Toshiba, NEC, Fujitsu, Hitachi and Mitsubishi all report I-MB DRAM chips at an annual ISSCC convention.

he Japanese electronic firm Hitachi, Ltd. announces the S-810 supercomputer, which can process 600 million operations per second.

The IBM Corporation developed token-ring technology in the early 1980s, and releases the first commercial products during this year. Token Ring is based on the concept of using a token, which is passed around a network, to give a device access to the network.

An IRS computer error results in 27,000 companies receiving warning notices to pay employee federal withholding taxes that they had, in fact, already paid.

Toshiba Corporation introduces the successful T1100 laptop computer.

Apple Computer, Inc. introduces AppleTalk, a local area networking environment.

AT&T Corporation announces the UNIX PC, a 68000-based, $5,600 machine that fails to establish UNIX as a PC standard.

The one million bit RAM chip is invented.

Since 1958, the Institute of Computing Technology at the Academia Sinica in China has developed 16 computer systems including 103,104,119 (vacuum tube computers), 109B, 109C (transistor computers), and 111,013,150-AP, 757 (integrated circuit computers).

Japan leads the world in robotics development, production, and application.

Steven Jobs and Stephen Wozniak, cofounders of Apple Computer, Inc., receive the National Technology Metal from Presidend Ronald Reagan at the White House.

Intel Corporation introduces the iPSC microprocessor, a commercial version of a "hypercube" topology machine developed by the Caltech group of Charles Seitz and Geoffrey Fox.

There are about 4,000 mainframes and minicomputers in operation in China. This is about the same number as are currently in Baltimore, Maryland. In addition, China has about 30,000 microcomputers, mostly in schools, and mostly obsolete units purchased from manufacturers in Hong Kong.

Apple Computer, Inc. discontinues the Lisa microcomputer. The Lisa is renamed the Macintosh XL.

Attendance at the ACM SIGGRAPH computer graphics conference in San Francisco, California is 27,400.

1986

In February, Digital Equipment Corporation hosts DECWORLD '86, the world's largest single-company computer exposition held to date.

Compaq Computer Corporation releases the Deskpro 386, the first personal computer to use Intel Corporation's 80386 microprocessor chip.

Texas Instruments, Inc. develops the 34010 graphics processor, a microchip designed to ease the burden of the microcomputer's main microprocessor.

There are now over 30 million computers in use in the United States.

Robert Birge, Albert Lawrence and Alan Schick of Carnegie-Mellon University conduct research focused on the effort to develop a theory of molecular computing.

Computers in education

The Saddleback Valley Unified School District in Orange County, California requires its more than 6,000 students to be computer literate. Juniors and seniors have to take a semester-long computer course as a requirement for graduation.

IBM introduces the PC Convertible, IBM's entry into the portable laptop market. It is a 12- to 16-pound battery-powered laptop that sells for $2,000. It will be unsuccessful.

Over 200,000 AppleTalk networks are now in place, making it one of the world's most preferred local area computer networks.

Gordon Bell, who while at Digital Equipment Corporation, engineered the PDP-5, PDP-8 and PDP-11 minicomputers and helped set the standards for interactive computing, becomes assistant director of computing and information sciences and engineering directorate at the National Science Foundations in Washington, D.C.

Borland International, Inc. releases the Turbo Prolog programming language.

Grace Murray Hopper, the grand lady of programming languages, serves as grand marshal in the Orange Bowl Parade, in Miami, Florida.

Apple Computer, Inc. purchases a CRAY X-MP/48 supercomputer for use in simulating future hardware and software products.

Compaq Computer Corporation makes the Fortune 500 list of American companies.

Sperry Corporation and Burroughs Corporation, two major manufacturers of computer equipment, merge to create Unisys Corporation. The Unisys computer products include three mainframe lines, a UNIX server family, minicomputers, proprietary networked workstations and DOS-based personal computers. Unisys Corporation is second only to the IBM Corporation in computer revenues.

Apple Computer, Inc. now sells microcomputers in more than eight countries.

Silicon Beach Software releases SuperPaint, the first graphics program to combine draw and paint functions.

A survey shows that 91 percent of the nation's schools use microcomputers for instruction.

The IBM Corporation introduces the RT PC, the first commercial Reduced Instruction Set Computer (RISC) from a major computer vendor.

Hewlett-Packard Corporation introduces the 32-bit PA-RISC microprocessor chip. Practically all PA-RISC chips go into HP's 9000 series workstations.

Floating Point Systems announces a hypercube supercomputer.

SIMM (Single In-line Memory Module) starts to become the preferred method for housing RAM.

The Smalltalk/V programming language appears. This is the first widely available version of Smalltalk for microcomputers.

Joint ventures with Honeywell, Inc. and Groupe Bull enable NEC Corporation to become the world's third largest computer company.

Digital Equipment Corporation introduces the VAX 8200, VAX 8310, VAX 8500, VAX 8550, VAX 8700, and VAX 8800 systems.

PictureBase, a graphics database, is released by Symmetry Corporation. It allows users to create an easily-accessed graphics library.

Propelled by Aldus Pagemaker, the Macintosh Plus and the LaserWriter laser printer, the desktop publishing market takes off in earnest, creating a new niche for Apple Computer, Inc. and revolutionizing the printing process.

Hewlett-Packard Company introduces the Spectrum line of Reduced Instruction Set Computers (RISC).

Tandy Corporation has over 7,300 retail outlets including almost 5,000 company-owned Radio Shack stores in the United States. All of these stores sell personal computers and related items.

Centram, Inc. releases TOPS, the first Local Area Network (LAN) that allows Apple Macintosh computers to share files with IBM Personal Computer's via a file server.

The Apple Macintosh Plus is introduced at the Boston Macworld Expo. It begins to establish the Macintosh computer as a powerful business machine.

Analytics, Inc. develops a prototype computer that obeys sound and the eye.

Fortune magazine declares Digital Equipment Corporation founder and president Kenneth H. Olsen "arguably the most successful entrepreneur in the history of American business."

Syracuse University begins a teacher education class taught entirely by computer.

Intel Corporation releases the Intel 82786 graphics processor, a microchip designed to ease the burden of the microcomputer's main microprocessor.

Apple Computer, Inc. introduces the Apple IIGS computer.

The first conference on object-oriented systems (OOPSLA 86) is held.

Heathkit introduces the HERO 2000 robot, designed to be used as an educational tool in schools and universities.

Digital Equipment Corporation acquires the technology and other assets of Trilogy Technology Corporation.

On November 3, Computerworld, the computer industry's weekly newspaper, publishes its one-thousandth issue.

Logo Computer Systems, Inc. introduces *LogoWriter*.

The Mips R2000 is introduced, a 32-bit microprocessor with 110,000 transistors. It was used in the first generation of RISC workstations and servers.

Researchers at Illinois State University announce a transistor capable of switching 230 billion times per second.

Apple Computer, Inc. releases the Object Pascal programming language for the Apple Macintosh.

CompuServe, Inc. starts providing online service in Japan.

Twenty-two thousand people attend the ACM SIGGRAPH computer graphics conference in Dallas, Texas.

The IBM Corporation employs over 400,000 people worldwide. In 1994, this number will be reduced to 215,000 people to adjust to changes in the demand for mainframe computer systems and services.

Microsoft Corporation is listed on the New York Stock Exchange. It sells shares to the public at $21 each, making William Gates, Microsoft's chairman, the world's youngest billionaire.

1987

A share of stock in Microsoft Corporation now sells for $100.

David Hillis, of Thinking Machines Corporation, develops the Connection Machine, a supercomputer that contains 64,000 microprocessors that can process more than 2 billion operations per second.

IBM Personal System/2

In April, IBM Corporation introduces its PS/2 family of microcomputers and ships over one million units by year end.

The IBM Corporation announces 4 megabyte DRAM chips.

SIGGRAPH 87, the ACM conference on Computer Graphics and Interactive Techniques, is held in Anaheim, California, drawing a total attendance of 30,541.

ETA Systems introduces its ETA-10 family of supercomputers.

Motorola, Inc. announces the 68030 microprocessor.

In May, Apple Computer, Inc. spins off a software subsidiary, Claris Corporation.

The IBM Corporation helps the National Science Foundation establish the backbone of the Internet.

Sun Microsystems, Inc. introduces its first workstation based on a RISC (Reduced Instruction Set Computer) microprocessor.

computer fraud

The FBI estimates average computer fraud at $650K, for a total of $3-5 billion per year.

Apple Computer, Inc. introduces HyperCard, a flexible courseware authoring tool that revolutionizes software development. The development team of HyperCard is led by Bill Atkinson.

Business Week magazine ranks Digital Equipment Corporation eighth among "America's Most Valuable Companies."

Workstations using RISC (Reduced Instruction Set Computer) architecture are announced by several computer manufacturers.

Over one million Apple Macintosh computers have been sold worldwide.

OOPSLA 87, the conference on Object Oriented Programming Systems, Languages and Applications, is held in Orlando, Florida.

The last National Computer Conference is held in Las Vegas, Nevada.

There are 5.2 million installed mailboxes on public and private information networks.

The Eighteenth ACM North American Computer Chess Championship, held at the Fall Joint Computer Conference is won by CHIPTEST-M developed by graduate students at Carnegie-Mellon University. Designed around a VLSI chip that searches chess moves at a rate of approximately 500,000 positions per second, CHIPTEST-M attains a perfect 4-0 performance in a field that includes current and former chess champions.

Hitachi, Ltd. in Japan introduces the S820/80 supercomputer.

There are now almost 2,000 working expert systems. The most popular area of application is finance, followed by fault diagnosis and manufacturing control.

Compaq Computer Corporation reaches a billion dollar in sales in its fifth year of operation.

IBM started using the mouse as an input device on their personal computers.

Bell Laboratories physicist David Miller replaces silicon transistors on a microchip with infinitesimal mirrors.

Digital Equipment Corporation introduces the VAX 8978 and VAX 8974 systems, and the VAX 6200 series of compact, high-performance network computer systems.

Coral Software introduces Allegro Common LISP with Object LISP for the Macintosh computer.

Apple Computer, Inc. introduces a new generation of Macintosh computers—the expandable Macintosh SE, and the Macintosh II, which brings color and peripheral interface slots to the Macintosh for the first time.

Thirty years after its inception, Digital Equipment Corporation has 110,500 employees, occupies 33.6 million square feet in 1,057 buildings, and does business in 64 countries.

Tandy Corporation introduces two personal computers: Tandy 1000 HX and Tandy 1000 TX.

1988

The IBM Corporation introduces the mid-range AS/400 mainframe computer.

The Computer Security Act, a first step in improving the security and privacy of information contained in federal computer systems is signed January 8th by President Ronald Reagan.

Apple Computer, Inc. reports net sales of over $4 billion for this fiscal year.

Unisys Corporation introduces the 2200/400 computer family to replace its mid-range 1100 series computers.

Computer viruses have now become a commonplace, unpleasant and sometimes costly fact of life for computer users.

A gang of hackers who call themselves the Legion of Doom begin to cruise electronic bulletin boards. Gang members reportedly "borrow" phone company technical documents and distribute them on bulletin boards.

In April, National Assessment of Educational Progress publishes *Computer Competence: The First National Assessment*. The study concludes, in general, that students do not know a lot about computers or how to use them.

There are 6.9 million installed mailboxes on public and private information networks.

Apple Computer, Inc. releases the Macintosh IIx, the first Mac to use high-density floppy disk drives that can read PC disks. It is also the first Macintosh computer that uses the Motorola 68030 microprocessor.

4,700,000 microcomputers, 120,000 minicomputers, and 11,500 mainframes are sold this year.

Texas is the first state to require public school children to complete at least one computer course before graduating from high school.

The Design Automation Conference celebrates its 25th year as the key event in the design automation community.

Burton Smith becomes the chief designer of Tera Computers and begins the design of a trillion-operations-per-second computer.

Fujitsu, Ltd. pays the IBM Corporation $237 million to settle the suit alleging it copied IBM system software.

In the early 1970s, the Rand Corporation predicted that computer-controlled robots would be widely used for collecting garbage, inspecting sewers, and as household slaves by 1988. This prediction turns out to be a little off course.

The population of computer-controlled industrial robots has increased from a few hundred in 1970 to several hundred thousand, most of them in Japan.

Cray Research, Inc. introduces the CRAY Y-MP supercomputer. It is capable of performing 2 billion operations per second and costs $20 million.

Apple Computer, Inc. announces its own font technology for the Macintosh—TrueType. It will be released in three years.

Sandia National Laboratory announces a massively parallel hypercube computer with 1,024 parallel processors, which, by breaking down problems into parts for simultaneous solution, proves to be over 1,000 times faster than a conventional mainframe computer.

The IBM Corporation introduces the ES/3090 S series mainframe computer.

There are 72,500 ATMs (Automated Teller Machines) installed across the country. They have proven to be convenient, easy to use, and extremely popular because they provide 24-hour banking services.

In 1984, IBM Corporation and Sears Roebuck teamed up in a joint venture called Trintex. In 1987, *Fortune* magazine asked, "Are IBM and Sears crazy? Or Canny?" By the time they had invested about $250 million in what came to be called Prodigy, Inc., a major information service was formed. Initial service began in the summer of 1988 in San Francisco, Atlanta, and Hartford and has since spread across the country.

Several microcomputer manufacturers are now cloning IBM PS/2 personal computers.

Color laser printers come on the market.

Seven leading computer companies announce the formation of the Open Software Foundation, intended to develop and provide an open software environment.

Computer networking is well established.

Computer memory today costs only .000 000 001 of what it did in 1950.

A study shows that 2 million microcomputers are used in U.S. schools.

Claris Corporation re-labels many former Apple Computer, Inc. software products and announces several new Claris software products: MacPaint 2.0, MacDraw II, Claris CAD and Filemaker II.

Niklaus Wirth finishes the Oberon programming language, his follow-up to the Modula-2 programming language.

First computer bowl is held.

In October, Steven Jobs unveils the NeXT computer which is the first computer that uses erasable optical disks as the primary mass storage device.

Cray Research, Inc. dominates the supercomputer market with 60 percent of the supercomputers in service.

Sun Microsystems, Inc. surpasses the $1 billion sales mark.

NEC of Japan replaces Texas Instruments, Inc. as the No. 1 manufacturer of computer chips.

Around 45 million personal computers are in use in the United States.

The installed base for MS-DOS is 29,550,000.

In November, a computer "virus" spread through many university, military and corporate computers. A set of instructions is designed to copy itself and spread from computer to computer through networks of shared disks. The virus is called the "Internet Worm" and creates an estimated $40 million to $90 million worth of damage before it is stopped.

Motorola, Inc. unveils the 88000 line, its RISC (Reduced Instruction Set Computing) microprocessor chip set.

The 10th International Conference on Software Engineering takes place in Singapore.

There are 5 known distinct strains of computer viruses. Four years later there will be over 1,000 viruses.

Twenty-five thousand people attend the ACM SIGGRAPH computer graphics conference in Atlanta, Georgia.

1989

The San Francisco earthquake reminds us how vulnerable we are. Two MacUser (a popular Macintosh publication) editors are killed by a crumbling brick facade. Apple Computer, Inc. loses a major Research and Development building.

Apple Computer, Inc. introduces the portable Macintosh. It will later be called the World's most intelligent boat anchor.

The trend from analog to digital continues to revolutionize a growing number of industries.

Intel Corporation introduces the i860, a 64-bit RISC microprocessor. This is the first microprocessor chip that contains over one million transistors.

Deep Thought, a chess playing computer defeats grandmaster Bent Larson of Denmark, a former contender for the world chess title. The computer achieves the distinction of being the first computer to defeat a grandmaster. The hardware "heart" of this computer fits on a circuit board the size of a large pizza. It has two processors which can search about 750,000 positions per second. Deep Thought is developed at Carnegie Mellon University by five graduate students. Subsequently, Deep Thought will be defeated by world champions Gary Kasparov and Anatoly Karpov.

Apple Computer, Inc. unveils the System 7 Operating System for the Macintosh computer to software developers.

Fujitsu, Ltd. of Japan announces the VP2600 supercomputer.

PC World USSR, the Soviet Union's first computer magazine, sold out on newsstands within hours. The first issue carries articles on the history of the IBM PC and computer productivity in the United States.

The Japanese electronics firm NEC Corporation announces the SX-X supercomputer with an expected speed of 20 billion calculations per second.

Control Data Corporation discontinues its ETA-10 supercomputer subsidiary and gets out of the supercomputer business.

Publication of Cliff Stoll's "The Cuckoo's Egg," a best-selling tale of international computer espionage. Stoll, an astronomer at an Internet lab, recounts how he electronically tracked down German hackers who were breaking into computers at American and European military and defense industry-related sites to steal information for the KGB.

There are over 100 million computers in use throughout the world. Over half of these machines are used in the United States.

Supercomputing legend Seymour Cray announces the formation of Cray Computer Corporation, a spin-off from supercomputer market leader Cray Research, Inc. Seymour Cray will concentrate on developing gallium arsenide-based supercomputers: CRAY 3 and CRAY 4.

Intel Corporation releases the Intel 80486 microprocessor, which is at least 50 percent faster than the 80386 microprocessor. The 80486 has over a million transistors.

There are 8.6 million installed mailboxes on public and private information networks.

The World Wide Web is born at the CERN physics laboratory in Geneva, Switzerland to help physicists around the world collaborate on research projects.

The *Softletter newsletter* ranks the following top ten software companies by revenue: Microsoft, Lotus, Ashton Tate, Wordperfect, Autodesk, Borland, Adobe, Aldus, Logitech and Software Publishing.

The computer is now recognized as a powerful tool for artistic expression.

Kazuo Kyuma at Mitsubishi Electric in Japan, develops a prototype optical neural network chip.

Corel Systems Corporation introduces Corel DRAW, a Windows-based illustration program for IBM compatible personal computers.

Computational power per unit of cost has roughly doubled every 18 to 24 months for the past 40 years.

The Microframe contains a microprocessor called SCAMP (Single Chip A Mainframe Processor) that contains as many circuits as a minicomputer, over 10 million transistors in four square inches. The Microframe is a microcomputer with the power of a minicomputer.

This year the world's scientific journals publish about 100 articles with the words "supercomputer" or "supercomputers" in the title.

The total number of computers in public schools is estimated to be 2.5 million, or about 1 for every 20 students.

Tin Toys, a computer-animated short subject by John Lasseter from Pixar, Inc. wins an Oscar.

Seymour Cray

World chess champion Gary Kasparov defeats the Deep Thought computer program with relative ease. Seven years in the future he will also defeat Deep Blue, an updated version of Deep Thought.

Japan controls 77 percent of the world market in the production of DRAM memory chips.

Worldwide sales of personal computers exceed $37 billion and associated sales of peripherals, including printers, terminals, and storage devices is $56 billion.

Digital Equipment Corporation introduces DECsystem 3100, their first RISC-based UNIX general-purpose computer system.

Jaron Lanier, an artist and mathematician, is the first person to realize the potential of virtual reality systems beyond military applications. He forms VPL Research, Inc. and markets virtual reality systems for a variety of applications.

Solbourne Computer introduces the first Sun 4 compatible computer.

Starent Corporation begins to ship computers that combine RISC architecture with vector processing.

Two Japanese scientists announce that they have succeeded in using superconductive materials (materials based on the Josephson effect) to make microprocessors and memories (which must be kept at a temperature of -452° F).

Digital Equipment Corporation extends the VAX-family of computers into the mainframe arena with the VAX 9000 computer.

NEA publishes a Report of the Special Committee on Educational Technology, which recommends that there be a computer on every teacher's desk by 1991.

The International Council for Computers in Education (ICCE) and the International Association for Computing in Education (IACE) merge to form the International Society for Technology in Education (ISTE).

Electronic music "controllers" emulate the playing techniques of many other acoustic instruments including many wind and string instruments, drums, and others.

Poqet Computer Corporation announces a one pound DOS Personal Computer for $1995. This is the first pocket-sized MS-DOS-compatible computer.

Between 1983 and now the South Korean output of computer chips are up from $500,000 worth a year to $1.5 billion—an unprecedented surge in output.

Compuserve, Inc. starts providing online service in Germany and Great Britain.

Twenty-six thousand people attend the ACM SIGGRAPH computer graphics conference in Boston, Massachusetts.

A research team from Amdahl Corporation find a prime number that contains 65,087 decimal digits. An Amdahl mainframe computer was used to compute this large prime number.

1990

The Internet has made it possible for computer users in different countries to participate simultaneously in playing games, passing messages, etc.

Personal computers in domestic use have more processing power than the one that first put men on the Moon.

A compact, cylindrical computer, called the Aladdin processor, is announced in the February edition of SIGNAL, the official publication of the Armed Forces Communication and Electronic Association. This soda-can-sized computer is intended to achieve one billion floating point operations per second processing speed in a cylindrical volume only 4 inches in diameter and 6 inches long.

China expects to produce 2,000 mainframes and minicomputers this year.

Apple Computer, Inc. introduces several low-end Macintosh computers: Macintosh LC, Macintosh Classic, and Macintosh IIsi.

Bell Laboratories develops SAM (Speech Activated Manipulator), a computer-controlled talking robot that has a vocabulary of 127 English words. SAM combines the functions of several machines and can see, understand, touch and speak.

Inc. magazine names Steven Jobs, cofounder of Apple Computer, Inc., as Entrepreneur of the Decade for the eighties.

More than 125,000 people from 100 countries attend the COMDEX trade show in Las Vegas, Nevada.

The IBM Corporation and Sears Roebuck launches the Prodigy online service.

There are 12.75 million installed mailboxes on public and private information networks.

The second major version of Hypercard is released by Claris Corporation, a subsidiary of Apple Computer, Inc.

Continuous speech systems can handle large vocabularies for specific tasks.

Beyond The Limits, an exhibit installed at the Smithsonian Air and Space Museum, deals with the history of computers in aviation.

Intel Corporation introduces the iPSC/860, the first in a series of parallel supercomputers based on the i860 RISC microprocessor. The iPSC/860 uses 128 microprocessors to deliver a 7.6 gigaflop performance.

Fiscal year revenues for Apple Computer, Inc. surpass $5.5 billion.

In July, several pioneers of the PC industry, including Apple Computer, Inc. cofounder Stephen Wozniak; Lotus Development Corporation founder Mitch Kapor; and Sun Microsystems, Inc. cofounder John Gilmore; form the Electronic Frontier Foundation (EFF) to protect the First and Fourth Amendment rights in computer technology.

Digital Equipment Corporation introduces a fault-tolerant VAX computer.

Nearly fifty universities around the world have acquired supercomputers.

On July 17, the U.S. Patent Office recognizes Gilbert Hyatt as the inventor of the microprocessor. His patent (No. 4,942,516) is the first to refer to a unique integrated circuit that contains all the necessary elements of the computer. Prior to the courts decision, the invention had been attributed to Marcian E. Hoff, Federico Faggin and Stanley Mazor of Intel Corporation. These engineers did create the first commercial microchip in 1971 (the Intel 4004).

Bell Laboratories scientist Michael Price produces a microchip with 128 optical transistors. Price uses four arrays of 32 optical transistors—each array small enough to fit into the typed letter O.

IBM Corporation announces the ES/9000 (Enterprise System/9000) family of mainframes.

Jeff Hawkins at Grid Systems Corporation invents the Gridpad, the first pen-based computer. The computer recognizes handwriting and translates it into characters, functions and shapes.

The IBM Corporation introduces the System 390 family of mainframe computers.

NEC Corporation announces the development of the first erasable and programmable 16 megabit memory chip.

Bell Laboratories engineer Alan Huang and a team uses photons (light particles) to carry data, a technique that makes it possible to achieve calculation speeds a thousand times greater than that of usual electronic transport, without wasting energy. This is the first optical digital processor that uses, not electrons, but, laser beams to carry information. This machine may lead to computers in which the only limit to computing power will be the speed of light. This is a research process that may be made usable in the 21st century.

John Hait of the Rocky Mountain Research Center invents an optical transistor. His invention is capable of performing logic functions and information processing from laser beams.

World Chess Champion Anatoly Karpov was the first human to lose a chess game to a computer (MEPHISTO).

Several Japanese companies announce the development of a new generation of 4-bit SRAMs (Static Random Access Memory). Unlike a DRAM, a SRAM does not need constant reactivating to save the information in its million of cells.

Apple Computer, Inc. introduces AppleEvents and AppleScript, giving users access to application objects, laying the foundation for component software.

Bernard and Andre Jonas of Tekodex in France, develop the first computer-controlled robotic vacuum cleaner.

Fujitsu, Ltd. in Japan introduces the VP2600 supercomputer.

The IBM Corporation replaces MS-DOS with the OS/2 operating system, which is designed to facilitate multi-tasking and client/server computing. OS/2 uses a graphical user interface (GUI).

Computers are still inaccessible to many people. But several companies try to fix that by looking at adaptive technology that make personal computers useful for people with sensory or physical disabilities.

Motorola, Inc. introduces the 68040 microprocessor.

Digital Equipment Corporation marks the 20th anniversary of the first PDP-11 minicomputer by introducing two new PDP-11 systems: MicroPDP-11/93 and PDP-11/94. The longest lived family of minicomputers has more than 20 members. More than 600,000 PDP-11 systems have been installed.

The number of personal computers used by U.S. businesses is over 24 million.

Kirk MacKenzie invents a mouse equipped with a keyboard.

Apple Computer, Inc. announces Claris Corporation will become a wholly owned, independent subsidiary of Apple Computer, Inc.

The IBM Corporation introduces the RS/6000 family of RISC (Reduced Instruction Set Computer) workstations.

There are more than 756 computer virus occurrences.

The first major international art exhibition, "Monet in the '90s: The Series Paintings," opens in Boston and travels to Chicago and London.

IBM Corporation introduces the PS/1 home computer.

Microsoft Corporation releases Windows 3.0, a windowing environment for IBM compatible personal computers. Two million copies of this operating system sell the first year.

Intel Corporation introduces a parallel supercomputer with over five hundred i860 RISC microprocessors.

The Computer Professionals for Social Responsibility file a Freedom of Information Act request for FBI records on secret monitoring of bulletin boards across the country.

The IBM Corporation develops the world's smallest logo. It built its logo 13 atoms high—a mere five-billionth of a meter from top to bottom. As an exercise in nanotechnology, the "I" is composed of nine atoms of xenon. The "B" and "M" are bigger. Each uses 13 atoms. But the letters are still only five nanometers or five-billionths of a meter tall. When the temperature rose above -243° C (-380° F), "IBM" fell apart.

Bellcore, the research arm of the seven regional Bell operating companies (with a role comparable to the original Bell Laboratories) announces a neural chip that can perform 100 million synapse connections per second, thus evaluating about 100,000 patterns in that same interval.

Gordon Moore, one of the founding fathers of the microelectronics industry, receives the National Medal of Technology from President George Bush.

Twenty-five thousand people attend the ACM SIGGRAPH computer graphics conference in Dallas, Texas.

There are 313,000 computers on the Internet. Six years in the future there will be close to 10 million.

Microsoft Corporation exceeds $1 billion in annual sales, the first computer software company to do so.

The first issue of *PC Novice* magazine is published.

Microsoft Corporation releases its first product for the Russian market—Russian DOS 4.01.

1991

Sales of IBM personal computers surpass 60 million units.

Each memory chip in the IBM PC of 1981 could hold 64,000 bits of information—enough for a three-page letter. Ten years later, in 1991, a memory chip can hold four million bits of information—enough to store 180 typewritten pages. In the 1981 chip, the transistors measured three millionths of a meter across; in the 1991 chip the transistors measure only eight-tenths of a millionth of a meter across. This is why six chips in 1991 can do what 200 chips did in 1981.

The chip that defines how fast the computer works is the microprocessor chip. Between 1981 and 1991 the speed of microprocessors increased 100 times.

The World Wide Web (WWW) is launched. Tim Berners-Lu, a scientist at the European Particle Physics Laboratory (CERN) in Geneva, Switzerland, develops the Web as a research tool.

Apple Computer, Inc. introduces System 7.0, a powerful operating system for the Macintosh computer.

Rear Admiral Grace Murray Hopper (USN Ret.), a Digital Equipment Corporation employee and programming language pioneer, is awarded The National Medal of Technology by President George Bush.

Federico Faggin develops the first chip endowed with a synaptic internal logic system. The chip is intended for OCR (Optical Character Recognition) and is able to read up to 20,000 characters per second without error.

Go Corporation introduces PenPoint, an operating system for pen-based computers.

Digital Equipment Corporation unveils a set of personal computers, all optimized for network personal computing: the Intel 80386-based DECpc 333 portable and DECpc 320sx notebook computer, the

Intel 80486-based DECpc 433 workstation, and the DECpc 433T deskside system.

There are more than 2,500 computer virus occurrences.

Apple Computer, Inc. announces QuickTime, giving software developers greater access to multimedia tools.

The IBM Corporation announces their first loss in seven decades as mainframe business suffers declining sales.

There is a total of 605,000 computer systems analysts and scientists—65% of them are men; 34.5% of them are women. There are also a total of 212,000 operations and systems researchers and analysts—58.5% of them are men; 41.5% of them are women.

AT&T Corporation purchases the NCR Corporation, a major computer manufacturer.

In France, CNRS patents a procedure for an optical computer. The principle behind this computer is to replace electricity by light in order to convey information.

The Bell companies receive permission to enter the on-line information services market.

The first general-purpose pen-based notebook computer is introduced.

Insite Peripherals develops the floptical disk drive which can store 20.8 megabytes on standard 3.5-inch diskettes.

Digital Equipment Corporation ranks number 30 in *Fortune* magazine's annual survey of the largest U.S. industrial corporations.

LAN-based E-mail software is on the rise—5,400,000 mailboxes are in use.

The ACM SIGGRAPH Traveling Exhibition opens at the Computer Museum in Boston, Massachusetts. The exhibit includes many computer-generated illustrations.

Microsoft Corporation introduces DOS 5.0, a major upgrade to the MS-DOS operating system.

More than 125,000 people attend the COMDEX trade show at the Sands Expo and Convention Center in Las Vegas, Nevada. More than 1,900 companies exhibit their wares at this show.

The following states have the most computer companies: California, Massachusetts, New York, and Texas. The following states have the least computer companies: Pennsylvania, Connecticut, Virginia, and Ohio.

Hewlett-Packard Company introduces its RISC-based HP 9000 Series 700 workstations.

Donald Eiger and a development team at the IBM Corporation demonstrates a switch that depends on the motion of a single atom. In theory, this switch would be 1,000 times smaller than today's electronic switches used in computer chips.

Countries ranked by computers in use per 1,000 people: (1) United States, (2) England, (3) Canada, (4) Norway, (5) Japan, (6) Ireland, (7) Singapore, (8) Switzerland, (9) Denmark and (10) Sweden.

Purchasers of personal computers can get five times the clock speed, 62 times the RAM (Random Access Memory) and four times the floppy disk storage that the same dollars would have bought in 1981.

Convex Corporation introduces the first supercomputer that uses gallium arsenide chips instead of silicon. Its main advantage is that gallium arsenide generates less heat than silicon, thus allowing the computer to be air cooled. The Convex C3 supercomputer also allows for a large shared memory—up to 4 gigabytes.

Advanced Micro Devices, Inc. introduces the AMD 386 microprocessor to compete with Intel's 80386 microprocessor chips.

Peter Fromherz and Andreas Offenhausser of the University of Ulm, Germany, graft neurons from leeches onto silicon oxide, creating an electronic component controlled by the neuron. Researchers begin to envision bioelectric prostheses to enable the blind to recover sight and direct brain/computer transactions.

Digital Equipment Corporation develops a computer-controlled "armored" robot to be used in airlines, banks, and police stations.

A working version of the original Charles Babbage Difference Engine is displayed at the Science Museum in London, England.

Deep Thought II triumphs over 11 other computer chess programs at ACM's 22nd International Computer Chess Championship in Albuquerque, New Mexico. Deep Thought II runs on an IBM RS/6000 computer and has 24 custom chess processors.

A consortium of universities led by CalTech purchases a "Delta" supercomputer containing 528 i860

RISC microprocessors. The peak speed of this machine is 32 gigaflops.

There are 2,702 computer science professors teaching in U.S. universities and colleges.

IBM Corporation introduces a thin film multichip module for workstations and personal computers. The module holds nine computer chips and 100 feet of connecting wire in a 2-inch square package.

GCC Technologies becomes the first company to offer laser printers for less than $1,000 and PostScript laser printers for less than $2,000.

The viruses "Stoned" and "Jerusalem" account for the majority of virus incidences.

Frank Wanlass is awarded the IEEE Solid State Circuits Award for his invention of complementary MOS (CMOS) transistors he built in the mid-1960s. His invention was patented on December 5, 1967.

Apple Computer, Inc. introduces the Quadra Macintosh computer and the PowerBook notebook.

During the first month of Desert Storm, the U.S. communicates with Saudi Arabia via modems running at 9,600 bps.

On October 21, the historic alliance becomes official when Apple Computer, Inc. and IBM Corporation sign the papers during a press conference at the Fairmont Hotel in San Francisco, California. The two companies agree to work on computers based upon the PowerPC chip manufactured by Motorola, Inc.

The National Semiconductor Corporation introduces a poker chip-sized microprocessor that will let people operate new digital answering machines and other devices by simply speaking.

Unisys Corporation announces the 2200/900 mainframe. This computer system can handle a throughput of up to 5,000 transactions per second.

Ten years ago, the IBM Corporation unveiled the IBM Personal Computer, a machine that has transformed the way millions of people work, spawned new industries and made computer technology less mysterious. Though IBM's personal computer was not the first, it legitimized the machines in the computer market. IBM's PC went on to set the worldwide personal computer standard. Today, every nation from Hong Kong to Hungary has a local industry cranking out inexpensive clones of IBM's personal computer.

There are 19 million installed mailboxes on public and private information networks.

IBM Corporation and Germany's Siemens AG unveil a joint venture to make advanced computer memory chips. The 16 megabit dynamic random access memory (DRAM) chips are to be manufactured in France.

ACM/IEEE-CS Curriculum '91, which includes computer engineering and liberal arts programs, is published.

Borland International, Inc. buys Ashton-Tate Corporation.

Over 900 computer viruses have been identified.

Thinking Machines Corporation, Cambridge, Massachusetts develops the CM-200 supercomputer, a machine that can read a year's worth of newspapers in the blink of an eye. The supercomputer can whiz through more than 9 billion calculations a second, and can be used by as many as 100 engineers and scientists at a time. At roughly $10 million each, it will be used mostly by government and industry for applications ranging from global weather prediction to oil exploration. It broke the supercomputer speed record by doing 9.03 billion mathematical calculations a second.

The IBM Corporation is the top U.S. company in terms of stock market value, the fourth leading company in sales at $69 billion, and first in profits at $6.02 billion.

Apple Computer, Inc. releases TrueType, its own font technology.

Texas Instruments, Inc. announces the development of a computer chip that uses light instead of electrons and wire to transmit information. The chip is called an optoelectronic integrated circuit, or OEIC. Its high-speed optical connections use less power and can be packed on a circuit board more densely than the copper wires and traces that carry signals from chips.

Unisys Corporation announces the A19 computer. It is 51,000 times faster than the UNIVAC I computer. In fact, it is one of the fastest single-processor commercial mainframes.

Apple Computer, Inc. and IBM Corporation form technology alliance. The four areas of general understanding for the two companies include the following: (1) to create object-oriented systems software, (2) to work on two fronts that will make it easier to integrate Macintosh computers into IBM's client/server enterprise systems, (3) Apple's use of IBM's RS/6000 RISC architecture in future Macintosh RISC-based computers, and (4) a commitment to work together to develop a common multimedia platform.

Computer bulletin board services (BBSs) begin in Brazil.

Twenty-eight thousand people attend the ACM SIGGRAPH computer graphics conference in Las Vegas, Nevada.

1992

In January, the Michelangelo virus became a major problem among computer users.

Semiretired mathematician Marion Tinsley, won the World Checkers Championships for the 19th straight year, this time against the computer program Chinook, devised by computer scientist Jonathan Schaeffer of the University of Alberta, Canada.

The IBM Corporation introduces the world's tiniest transistor.

Motorola, Inc. announces the first product of its joint venture with the IBM Corporation and Apple Computer, Inc. The Power PC 601 is a 32-bit RISC microprocessor that stuffs 28 million transistors onto a chip.

In New York, five young men are charged with breaking into computer systems at several regional phone companies, large firms such as Martin Marietta, universities and credit-reporting concerns such as TRW. The case marks the government's first investigative use of court-authorized wiretaps to obtain conversation and data transmission of hackers.

Ncumb Corporation announces plans to make a supercomputer by 1994 that will be capable of crunching 6.5 trillion numbers a second. The machine will cost around $200 million.

Dylan (named for Dylan Thomas), an object-oriented programming language resembling Scheme, is released by Apple Computer, Inc.

Japanese supercomputer manufactures start delivering vector supercomputers: the NEC SX-4 which attains a peak speed of 22 gigaflops; and the Hitachi S-3800-480, which has a peak speed of 32 gigaflops—as well as general-purpose mainframes, such as the Fujitsu 2600.

The IBM Corporation delivers the IBM 3030-9000 mainframe with a peak speed of 2.7 gigaflops.

Microsoft Corporation releases the Windows 3.1 operating system for IBM-compatible personal computers.

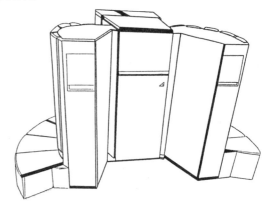

CRAY Y-MP supercomputer

Cray Research, Inc. introduces the CRAY Y-MP C90 supercomputer. The C90 is 100 times faster than the CRAY 1, which was introduced in 1976. Even more spectacular has been the growth in memory size, by a factor of 500. The CRAY C90 has 2 gigabytes of central memory and with 16 central processing units (CPUs) it gives a combined peak performance of 16 billion floating point operations per second.

The number of computers in the world has doubled since 1991; between 1992 and 1993 they will double again.

Digital Equipment Corporation releases Alpha which encompasses a 64-bit RISC architecture, a single-chip microprocessor, and a family of systems, technologies, and services.

Over 1500 DOS computer viruses are known. Last year there were only 900 known computer virus strains. In 1988 there were only three known computer viruses.

Apple Computer, Inc. launches the Macintosh Performa line, designed especially for the consumer market, and available through 2,000 retail outlets in the U.S.

Francis Carruboaur, John Cocke, Norman Kreitzer, and George Radin of the IBM Corporation are named Inventors of the Year for their work with Reduced Instruction Set Computer (RISC).

Robin Milner won the ACM Turing Award for his development of the ML language.

The Thinking Machines Corporation delivers a CM-5 supercomputer to Los Alamos National Laboratory. This supercomputer has 1,024 microprocessors containing more than 500 million transistors altogether.

Intel Corporation develops the "flash card," which holds 20 chips with 20 megabytes of memory on a board the size of a credit card.

IBM Corporation, Siemens AG, and Toshiba Corporation join forces to build a 256-megabit Dynamic Random Access Memory (DRAM) chip.

There are 19.1 million installed mailboxes on public and private information networks.

Hewlett-Packard Company unveils what it calls the world's smallest disk drive, a matchbox-sized device that can supply portable memory to machines like hand held computers. The 1.3-inch disk drive can hold 21.4 megabytes of memory.

Polish President Lech Walesa plays host to Dell Computer's staff in Warsaw during the launch of Dell Poland in May.

A typical supercomputer facility holds over one million user files, containing many millions of megabytes of information.

Roland Moreno of the Innovatron Group invents the microchip card, a diskette that contains a dedicated microprocessor and other integrated circuits.

Apple Computer, Inc. introduces 12 new Macintosh computers.

Digital Equipment Corporation introduces a Reduced Instruction Set Computer (RISC) chip, the 21064 microprocessor. It is a 150 MHz microprocessor that is designed to perform at up to 300 million instructions per second.

The IBM Corporation unveils several low-end UNIX workstations.

The Microsoft Windows 3.1 operating system ships with TrueType built in. The market for TrueType fonts finally takes off.

The number of people suffering computer related injuries has risen dramatically with the popularity of desktop computers. The Bureau of Labor Statistics surveys show that in 1981 when the desktop computer was just being introduced, cumulative trauma disorders affected 23,000 workers, accounting for 18 percent of all workplace illnesses in the United States. By 1992, when there are over 50 million desktop computers in use, the number has risen to 281,000 or 62 percent.

Almost five million laptop computers are purchased this year.

Attendance at the ACM SIGGRAPH computer graphics conference in Chicago, Illinois is 30,000.

Intel Corporation overtook NEC Corp. of Japan to become the world's largest manufacturer of chips.

There are over 1 million host computers on the Internet.

1993

Prototype 256 megabit chips appear in laboratories.

Sharp Corporation is the world's largest producer of flat panel screens for computers.

Mosaic, the first graphical Web browser, is released by the National Center for Supercomputer Applications (NCSA) at the University of Illinois.

Gateway 2000 sells its millionth personal computer.

President Bill Clinton puts the White House online with a World Wide Web page and E-mail addresses for the president, vice-president, and first lady.

Between 1968 and 1993 the cost of making one transistor on a chip fell from 2 cents to 0.0003 cents and the number of transistors can be put on a commercial chip goes from 1,000 to 16 million.

Over five and a half million laptop computers are purchased this year.

CompuServe, Inc. starts providing online service in France.

Apple Computer, Inc. introduces the Newton, a pocket-sized, pen-based computer. Newton combines electronic calendar, card index, note-taking and telecommunications functions.

Cray Computer Corporation introduces the CRAY 3 supercomputer series. Seymour Cray formed Cray Computer in May 1989 after splitting off from Cray Research, Inc. Starting with a single-processor, $3 million system with 64 Megawords of memory, the CRAY 3 scales up to a 16-processor system with 1 Gigaword of memory and is priced at a little more than $30 million.

The Hammond Atlas of the World is the first atlas to be created entirely from a digital database.

The IBM Corporation is issued the most U.S. patents.

Ten years ago John Sculley took a risk by quitting PepsiCo and joining an upstart Silicon Valley firm (Apple Computer, Inc.) locked in mortal combat with the IBM Corporation. After a decade under Sculley, Apple Computer, Inc. has become a powerhouse in the personal computer industry. It is now allied with the IBM Corporation.

Cray Research, Inc. introduces the Alpha-based T3D supercomputer.

Scientists at the IBM Corporation develop a short wave-length blue-laser technique to store information at a density of 2.5 billion bits per square inch. The scientists predict that by using the new technology it will be possible to develop optical disks that can store several billion bytes of information.

Engineering school deans rate Massachucetts Institute of Technology as the highest graduate school in computer engineering as reported in *U.S. News & World Report.*

There are over 25 million users of the Windows operating system on IBM-compatible personal computers.

Intel Corporation, the world's largest maker of computer chips, releases the Pentium microprocessor, representing the fifth generation of a chip family that dates back to 1979 and is the main component of personal computers. The Pentium chip contains some 3 million transistors and is capable of processing speeds of up to 300 MIPS at 100 MHz. It sells for $878.

President Bill Clinton announces plans to create the National Information Intrastructure, popularly referred to as the data superhighway.

Oliver Stone's TV miniseries *Wild Palms* is set in the near future and uses virtual reality to simulate alternate environments.

An art exhibit titled *Genetic Images* at the Centre Georges Pompidou in Paris, France uses a Thinking Machines Corporation CM-2 Connecting Machine (a supercomputer) to generate real-time images that "evolved" with audience interaction.

Consumers spent $2 billion on computer software.

Leonid Levin proposes a method to check, by computation, the correctness of mathematical proofs.

The IBM Corporation ships Power PC 601 workstations.

In February, Steven Jobs, NeXT, Inc.'s chairman and Apple Computer, Inc.'s cofounder, acknowledges that he can not make lightning strike twice. Jobs announces plans to scrap his slow-selling NeXT workstations and focus solely on software.

The Academy of Motion Picture Arts and Sciences give Tom Brigham a technical achievement award for his work in developing morphing.

Approximately 2,000 employees of Microsoft Corporation own more than $1 million apiece of Microsoft stock.

The *Guinness Book of World Records* states that the Alpha microprocessor from Digital Equipment Corporation is the world's fastest microprocessor.

The Alaska public school system provides the highest number of microcomputers per student (one computer for every nine students).

Cray Computer Corporation installs a CRAY 3 demonstration supercomputer at the National Center for Atmospheric Research (NCAR). The machine will be turned off in two years when Cray Computer files for Chapter 11 bankruptcy.

Michael Spindler replaces John Sculley as CEO of Apple Computer, Inc.

1994

Commodore International, Inc., the innovative computer manufacturer that gave the world the PET, the VIC-20, the Commodore-64, the Commodore-128, and the Amiga, close their doors. Commodore was founded by Jack Tramiel in 1954. Around twenty million users will remember the Commodore-64 as it was one of the best selling computers of all time. The Amiga personal computer was a machine ahead of its time.

There are now almost 55 million personal computers with DOS-only operating systems.

Apple Computer, Inc. announces plans to license the Mac OS to other personal computer vendors.

The 13th IFIP World Computer Congress is held in Hamburg, Germany.

Eighty-five percent of America's school teachers use computers in the classroom. The survey is based on 1,000 telephone interviews of elementary and secondary teachers, media coordinators and administrators.

In April, Netscape Communications Corporation, developer of a popular Internet browser, is formed.

Apple Computer, Inc., AT&T, IBM Corporation, and Siemens announce the formation of Versit, a group dedicated to creating specifications for interoperability between telephones and computers.

In March, Apple Computer, Inc. ships the first Power Macintosh computers.

There are over four million host computers on the Internet, the network of networks.

Convex Computer Corporation introduces the Exemplar Scalable Parallel Processor, a parallel-processing supercomputer that employs as many as 128 of Hewlett-Packard's CMOS-based PA-RISC processors, with up to 32 gigabytes of globally shared memory.

Thinking Machines Corporation, with an installed base of 112 supercomputers, files for Chapter 11 bankruptcy. It has not had a profitable year since 1990.

IBM Corporation introduces the Model 9X2, a top-of-the-line water-cooled mainframe computer that uses CMOS microprocessors for bipolar circuits.

The use of CD-ROM's have grown tremendously. Most of the product lines offered by major personal computer vendors for homes and consumers include built-in CD-ROM drives. Proliferating information and software products on CD-ROMs are beginning to strut their stuff. They will become still more eye-catching in the next few years.

Andrew Grove, CEO of Intel Corporation, predicts that, by the end of this decade, personal computer sales will surpass 100 million units worldwide—more than sales of cars or televisions.

In June, Apple Computer, Inc. announces eWorld, its new on-line computer service. Users can get news, information and other services from about 100 concerns. Two years in the future, Apple Computer will cancel this service.

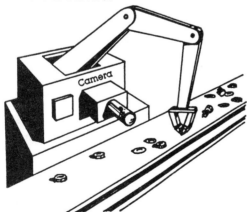

computer controlled robot

There are about 53,000 computer controlled robots in use in the United States, second only to Japan who has a command lead with seven times as many robots in their workforce.

A mathematical proof that quantum computation can greatly speed factoring focuses attention on the feasibility of building computers based on quantum mechanical principles.

Researchers develop a computer "superchip" that they say will rapidly speed up deciphering of the human genetic code and could eventually help doctors treat congenital diseases before they develop.

Chinese semiconductor companies produce 250 million integrated circuit chips and import 2.5 billion chips during 1994.

Hewlett-Packard Company ranks as the top seller of Personal Digital Assistant's (PDA) selling 106,000 units; Fujitsu, Ltd. ranks second, selling 64,000 units; and Apple Computer, Inc. ranks third, selling 60,000 units.

In 1943, IBM Chairman Thomas Watson, Sr. predicted that there would be a need for 5 computers. The installed base of PCs worldwide is now 200 million.

The annual cost for generating the electrical power to run all the world's personal computers is $4.6 billion.

Japan produces $32 billion worth of integrated circuit chips. North America produces $40 billion worth.

According to a *New York Times* article, computer memory chips are even hotter than illegal drugs on the black market.

College professor Thomas Nicely found an error in the Intel Pentium microprocessor. On June 13, in the midst of running several billions of calculations on his Pentium-based microcomputer, Nicely, to his amazement, discovered an error. Where 4,195,835 divided by 3,145,727 should have yielded 1.333820449, the computer instead read 1.333739068. The Intel Corporation eventually admitted that there was a flaw in the chip and that they would replace all of the Pentium chips.

Mosaic establishes itself as the de facto graphical user-interface standard for the Internet.

Cray Research, Inc. unveils the J90 family of supercomputers targeted for industrial users.

The computer industry is rapidly moving to the high-performance RISC (Reduced Instruction Set Computer) architecture—an architecture that until now has been used primarily in workstations. RISC is fundamentally more powerful and efficient than CISC (Complex Instruction Set Computing) technology.

The installed base of personal computers exceed 80 million in the United States and 200 million worldwide (0.3 and 0.035 unit per person, respectively).

The most widely installed operating system for personal computers is DOS (or MS-DOS).

More than 10 million people in the United States suffer from computer-related injuries and health problems.

Seven and a half million laptop computers are purchased this year.

The speed of microprocessors has been increasing exponentially in the last ten years or so, and the rate of performance increase in microprocessors has been dramatic—by over 100 times between 1982 and 1994—with no end in sight.

The annual sales of the personal computer industry went from zero to $50 billion in 17 years.

The Internet celebrates its 25th anniversary.

Three South Korean companies, Samsung, Goldstar, and Hyundai, have sizable and advanced microelectronic capabilities and are large manufacturers of computer chips.

In 1970, the chip industry could sell you a chip with 1,000 components on it. Today, it can sell you a chip with 16 million components on it for a comparable price.

1995

Apple Computer, Inc. finally allows other businesses to clone the Macintosh computer.

Chip design at the largest chip manufacturing companies is done using supercomputers, so complicated is the task.

Five hundred thousand visitors attend the CeBIT Computer Show in Hanover, Germany.

The installed base of personal computers in Brazil is 2.8 million units.

A small demonstration piece of Charles Babbage's Difference Engine is auctioned at Christies (London). The piece is sold to the Powerhouse Museum in Sydney, Australia for 160,000 pounds. The device is one of several similar demonstration pieces assembled in the late 1870s by Henry Prevost Babbage, Charles Babbage's son, after his father's death in 1871.

Over nine million laptop computers are purchased this year.

In July, more than 800,000 visitors pass through the gates of the Fenasoft Computer Show in São Paulo, Brazil. To date, this is the largest computer exhibition ever held in the world (2400 exhibitors). In comparison, 500,000 people attended the CeBIT Computer Show in Hanover, Germany, in March 1995, and 225,000 visitors attended the 1995 COMDEX computer show in Las Vegas, Nevada (the largest computer show in the United States). Brazil is one of the world's ten fastest growing markets for computer software products and services, and is the fastest growing market for computer imports from the United States.

When a devastating earthquake hit the port city of Kobe, Japan, in January, the earth was still shaking when Japanese students started using the Internet to share information about the disaster with a worldwide audience. Even though telephone lines failed and roads were impassable, the Net remained up and running, and became a vital link to the outside world.

Walt Disney Pictures releases *Toy Story*, the world's first completely computer-animated film. *Toy Story* is created on Silicon Graphics, Inc. desktops and rendered on Sun Microsystems, Inc. workstations linked by Pixar, Inc. Marionette software. The *Toy Story* film crew consists of about 110 people, far fewer than the 600 people it typically takes to do a hand-drawn animation film.

Motorola, Inc. introduces the Power PC 602, a 64-bit microprocessor chip.

Philippe Kahn, former CEO of Borland International, Inc.—the company he founded, starts a new company. The company, called Starfish Software, sells Sidekick, a personal information manager and Dashboard, a Windows utility.

Mips introduces the R10000 microprocessor chip. The R10000 inherits its superscalar design from the R8000, which was created for the scientific supercomputing market.

More than 206,000 people descend on the gambler's paradise, Las Vegas, to attend COMDEX, the United States' largest computer trade conference.

Timex develops a watch with a computer that holds 64 kilobytes of data. You can use a personal computer to send data to the watch.

Cray Research, Inc. introduces the next generation of its flagship high-end supercomputers. The T90 family of supercomputers can perform from 1.8 billion to 60 billion calculations per second and sell from $2.5 million to $25 million.

Intel Corporation, the world's largest maker of computer chips, starts selling the Pentium Pro microprocessor, representing the sixth-generation of a chip family that dates back to 1979 and is the main component of personal computers.

In February, America OnLine, Inc., with two million subscribers, overtakes CompuServe, Inc. and Prodigy, Inc., to become the largest consumer information service in the United States.

Sports International Ltd., a sports book provider on the Caribbean Island of Antigua, launches an online Internet casino service. *Global Casino* offers customers a "virtual" walk through a casino where they can gamble real money on computer-simulated blackjack, craps, roulette, mini-baccarat, poker, and slots.

Softbank Corporation, a Japanese software distributor and publisher of computer magazines, purchases the Ziff-Davis Publishing Company, publisher of *PC Magazine, PC Week, MacUser, Computer Shopper*, and a variety of other computer magazines.

NexGen Corporation previews its next generation microprocessor, the Nx686, which will be 1.3 to 2 times the speed of Intel Corporation's Pentium and Pentium Pro chips.

The home computer market is projected to be the largest computer market in the United States.

There are about 40 million Internet users in North America.

Several software publishers are now offering free "try-before-you-buy" CD-ROMs. When you are ready to buy the full version, you call an 800 number to purchase the "key" to unlock it.

At the NGO (Non-Governmental Organizations) Forum in Beijing, China, Apple Computer, Inc. provides nearly 30,000 attendees with access to the latest technology, including the Internet and e-mail, in 27 languages using WorldScript software.

Peter Fromherz and Alfred Stett, physicists at the Max Palnck Institute of Biochemistry in Munich, Germany, made a silicon chip that can directly stimulate a nerve cell. Their so called silicon-to-neuron junction triggers a single nerve cell in a leech without killing the cell.

The National Science Foundation decides to scrap its present supercomputer centers program. In its place, the agency introduced an initiative that fo-

cuses on taking advantage of newly emerging computer technology and on broadening participation in computational science and engineering.

A National Research Council report cites Stanford University, M.I.T., the University of California at Berkeley, Carnegie Mellon University and Cornell University as having the top computer science doctoral programs.

Prodigy, Inc. becomes the first consumer online service to provide access to the World Wide Web.

Computers cost jobs, at least according to the city of Brussels. The city council approves a 1,000 Belgian franc (U.S. $34) tax per year on all computer screens used by companies. The tax, which took effect January 1, replaces a tax the city fathers had levied on motors at the turn of the century. They had believed all motors would cost jobs. The city expects to raise $900,000 per year from the tax.

William Hewlett and David Packard, cofounders of the Hewlett-Packard Company, are awarded the Price Waterhouse Information Technology Leadership Award for Lifetime Achievement.

Gigabit chips are now in the laboratory. Within the next decade, the semiconductor industry plans to be selling these chips.

Salaries in the Information Systems area have increased an average of 4.5%, while other professions average 3%. But, women are still vastly outnumbered in upper management jobs.

Intel Corporation is now assembling personal desktop computers to be sold in Japan under the Toshiba name.

Digital Equipment Corporation demonstrates an array of 12 eight-way AlphaServer 8400s to handle large scientific computing tasks. The 96-microprocessor array can churn up to 57.6 billion floating-point operations per second. This supercomputer has a price tag of $4.5 million.

BYTE magazine reports the top twenty companies that got the computer industry to where it is today: Adobe Systems, Apple Computer, AT&T, Autodesk, Borland International, Commodore International, Compaq Computer, CompuServe, Inc., Digital Equipment Corporation, IBM Corporation, Intel Corporation, Lotus Development Corporation, Microsoft Corporation, Motorola, Novell, Shugart/Seagate, Sun Microsystems, Tandy Corporation, Word Perfect and Xerox PARC.

In July, U.S. House Speaker Newt Gingrich said he envisions a world in which people "self-apply technology" in their daily lives, using expert systems software, for example, to do their own wills and diagnose medical problems. He predicted that information technology will "change the whole fabric of government."

personal computer

Sixteen million personal computers are sold in the United States; 34 million worldwide. Workstation's sales add a million units more. To put this in perspective, PCs' and automobiles' yearly unit sales are now in the same ballpark.

In *Copycat*, a serial-killer movie, an agoraphobic expert on serial murders relies on the Internet to talk to the outside world. And it is through the Internet, which she calls "an open window," that the killer contacts her. Copycat's computer is used as a way of seeing and communicating. Maybe the best computer movies in the future will be those that don't view technology as heroic or villainous, but accept it as part of everyday life.

Sun Microsystems, Inc. introduces the Java programming language. Java, a language for creating lively World Wide Web sites on the Internet was named during a trip to a local coffee shop after the development team decided the original project name, Oak, wasn't a suitable marketing title.

In 1959, the first planar transistor measured 764 microns in diameter and could be seen with the naked eye. In 1995, a contemporary transistor measures about two microns across and has elements as small as 0.4 microns.

The Microsoft Network (MSN) goes online in August. Microsoft Corporation offers MSN automatically to every Windows 95 user.

The major commercial online services—America Online, CompuServe, and Prodigy—increasingly are becoming Internet providers and bringing millions of new users onto the Net.

NeXT Computer, Inc., the company Steven Jobs founded after leaving Apple Computer, Inc., unveils software tools to cut the time it takes to develop software for the World Wide Web.

At the IEEE International Solid-State Circuits Conference, engineers present papers that describe a memory chip that can hold a billion bits of information and a microprocessor that performs in excess of a billion instructions per second, a 1,000-fold increase in capacity and processing power since the early 1980s. Engineers at this conference also expect the progression of semiconductor technology to continue: they contend that terachips (capable of handling a trillion bits or instructions) will arrive by the end of the next decade.

The global market for information technology reaches $164 billion.

Two years ago, the debut of Apple Computer, Inc.'s Newton technology was heralded as a major milestone of the information age. The Newton was soon joined by several other hand-held communication devices, or personal digital assistants (PDA). Last year, PDA shipments reached 390,000 units, far short of early predictions. It now looks like the PDA may not live up to its original expectations.

Most personal computers are beige machines. Acer, a Taiwanese company, for years made PCs designed by other companies. In September, it starts making charcoal black machines. In past years other black personal computers have appeared: Bell & Howell produced a black Apple II microcomputer for the educational market, and the NeXT microcomputer from Steven Jobs company was black.

A Billion Channel Extraterrestrial Assay (BETA) will search the heavens for signs of intelligent life in outer space.

J. Andrew McCammon, Professor of Pharmacology, UCSD, is awarded the Cray Research Information Technology Leadership Award for Breakthrough Computational Science.

Storage Technology Corporation introduces the 1.3 terabyte Kodiak mainframe disk array. Kodiak has nearly twice the capacity of Iceberg, the companies first storage device, and is based on RAI technology.

Texas Instruments announces the Extensa 450 and Extensa 550 portable computers.

On August 24, Microsoft Corporation, after two years of unprecedented hype and anticipation, releases Windows 95. Windows 95 is a new version of Microsoft's Windows operating system, for IBM-compatible personal computers, the software that creates the on-screen look of a computer and manages other programs from behind the scenes. It is designed to provide millions of users of Window systems the ability to run their programs more easily, faster, and better.

Silicon Graphics' first claim to fame is as a workstation vendor whose snazzy boxes serve up rich graphics and make scientific visualization popular. During the past two years the company has been making forays into supercomputer territory. Arrays of its own R8000 RISC microprocessors provide ample processing power for its Power Challenge supercomputer.

Hewlett-Packard Company acquires Convex Computer Corporation, a company that had succeeded in fabricating high-speed gallium arsenide CPU's—the same technology that had done in Cray Computer Corporation.

Cyrix Corporation introduces the 6x86-100 and M1rx-120 microprocessor chips.

Interactive Media Corporation introduces KanguruDisk, a removable plug-and-play storage device that stores up to 1.6 gigabytes. It functions as a portable hard disk that lets users transport and plug in applications and files to the computer they are working on.

The electronic marketplace makes its debut on the World Wide Web.

The computer horror game, Phantasmagoria, is released by Sierra On-Line. Involving more than 200 people, two years of work, and $4 million in development costs.

Three months after Microsoft Corporation announces its Microsoft Network, it has signed up 525,000 subscribers.

At COMDEX, the United States' largest computer show, Hunter Digital demonstrates a "no hands" mouse. It replaces the traditional pointing device attached to a computer with a tail-like cord with two foot pedals.

In September, the U.S. Department of Energy's Accelerated Strategic Computing Initiative (ASCI) awards a $45 million contract of the development of a supercomputer capable of sustained 1 TFLOPS processing.

The world's worst computer viruses include SATAN, a polymorphic bug that prevents log-in and access to the file server; NATAS, another polymorphic virus (NATAS is SATAN spelled backward) that infects the boot area of the disk and is difficult to detect; GREEN CATERPILLAR, a bug that infects a directory upon viewing or when a file is copied; JUNKIE, a virus that infects the boot sector and files; MONKEY, a stealth boot virus that encrypts the master boot sector codes so the hard disk is unrecognizable when a user boots up from a floppy disk; WORD FOR WINDOWS MACRO, a virus which attacks operating systems; MICHELANGELO, designed to infect computers in mid-March to commemorate Michelangelo's birthday; and JERUSALEM, an older virus that has more than 250 existing strains.

Sun Microsystems, Inc. begins shipping 64-bit workstations based on its UltraSPARC microprocessors.

Microsoft Corporation and DreamWorks SKG announce a joint venture to produce interactive and multimedia technology. Steven Spielberg is one of the principals.

Advanced Micro Devices, Inc. (AMD) acquires NexGen Corporation and renames the Nx686 microprocessor as the AMD K6. The K6 microprocessor is the first x86 chip with special multimedia instructions and is expected to run about twice as fast as an Intel Pentium Pro.

In November, Apple Computer, Inc. surpassed the IBM Corporation to regain its ranking as the second largest personal computer maker behind Compaq Computer Corporation.

Several movies and television programs convey a suspicious attitude toward computers. Five films depict computers as the embodiment of evil, threatening to take over everything that makes us civilized: intelligence, emotions, Social Security numbers. Some even kill, In *Virtuosity*, Sid 6.7, a computer-generated serial murderer, moves from virtual reality into plain old reality. In *Johnny Mnemonic*, a high-tech messenger has a computer chip implanted in his brain, about to explode. The futuristic action film *Strange Days* sells black market disks that send data rushing to your brain to re-create torture and murder. *Hackers* has a computer literate thief who threatens to turn someone into a stranger with a police record. In *The Net* computers steal Sandra Bullock's Social Security number and do turn her into a stranger with a police record. Most of these movies flopped.

Twenty-four million people in the United States and Canada now use the Internet. Almost a third of users access the Internet everyday, and two thirds of users access the Internet from work. Internet user are affluent, young and primarily male.

Like the famed marble lions that stand guard at the New York Public Library's main branch in Manhattan, LEO is up and ready to roar. LEO, which stands for Library Entrance Online, is an on-line public Library information system that promises to revolutionize how patrons gather information from the library's 50 million items. LEO is a fully integrated system that links users in each of the library's 82 branches to thousands of periodical listings and an extensive assortment of databases—and beyond that to the World Wide Web on the Internet.

Forty-one percent of all computer users—27 million in the United States—use computers at work and at home (*TODAY/IntelliQuest* survey).

Digital Equipment Corporation announces the AlphaServer 8400 computer which is based on Digital's powerful Alpha microprocessor. Oracle Corporation has designed software for the machine. The AlphaServer is the first computer based on the UNIX operating system that is faster and more reliable than a mainframe. Digital also unveils a less costly AlphaServer 8200 that uses a slower version of the Alpha microprocessor chip.

America OnLine, Inc. acquires Global Network Navigator, a subsidiary of O'Reilly & Associates that provides online news and information.

CompuServe, Inc., an H & R Block company, acquires Internet In A Box maker, Spry.

Macintosh clones make their appearance; Macintosh clone maker Radius, Inc. shows its System 100 at the Seybold Seminars '95 in Boston, Massachusetts. The System 100 is based on Apple Computer's 8100 Power Macintosh and runs on the PowerPC 601 microprocessor chip.

In December the sixth *Harvard Cup Human-Versus-Computer Chess Challenge* is held at the Manhattan Conference Center in New York City. Six American grandmasters, all among the best chess players in the world, slug it out with leading computer programs. The Harvard Cup event is specifically designed to measure the progress of computer chess research over time.

Welcome to the World's Largest Casino! blares the sign in garish colors. But this isn't Las Vegas; its cyberspace. And the sign is really only a handful of bytes on a server located on the Dutch side of St. Maarten, an island in the Caribbean. The offshore Internet Casino, Inc. went online with blackjack, poker, slot machines and other gambling games.

The Digital Equipment Corporation's Alpha 2164 is the current fastest single-chip microprocessor in the world, with three times the integer performance of an Intel Pentium/100 and faster floating point unit performance than Mips' R8000 supercomputer chip set.

C. Gordon Bell, director of the Bell-Mason Group, is awarded the MCI Information Technology Leadership Award for Innovation.

Full commercial Internet service is now available in Buenos Aires and other major cities in Argentina.

Advanced Micro Devices, Inc. introduces the K5 microprocessor chip.

In principle, a computer obeying the laws of quantum mechanics can efficiently solve a number of complex problems that a conventional computer can't handle. This striking capability has stimulated a wide-range exploration of the possibility of building such a computer.

Popular computer magazines are *PC Magazine, Computer Shopper, BYTE, Windows, Multimedia World, Macworld, Home Office Computing, Home PC, PC Novice, Computer Gaming World, Dr. Dobb's Journal, Visual Developer Magazine, Microsoft Systems Journal, C/C++ Users Journal, LAN, Database Programming and Design, Game Developer, WEB Techniques, Net Guide, Web Developer, Internet World, MacUser,* and *Desktop Publishers.*

Forty percent of all households have personal computers, and sixty-two percent of these PCs are equipped with modems.

Power Computing ships cheaper, faster Macintosh clone microcomputers.

In June, Fritz3 won the World Computer Chess Championship in Hong Kong. In December, world champion Gary Kasparov defeated Fritz4 in a two-game match in London. Fritz4, an improved version of Fritz3, analyzes 172,000 positions per second and executes 203 million instructions per second.

1996

In January the Public Broadcasting Service (PBS) began broadcasting *21st Century Jet: The Building of the 777.* This five-part special shows how the first 100% digitally designed airplane is built. The Boeing 777's software includes 5 million lines of code, including 2 million lines unique to the 777. There are 1,700 computers, totaling 60% of the 777's computing power, running the passenger entertainment systems. The other 40% is used for flying and navigating the plane. Engineers at the Boeing Company used 2,400 computer-aided design and manufacturing workstations on eight IBM mainframes to design the Boeing 777.

The prices of notebook computers will fall throughout the year as vendors flood the market with new releases that sport faster microprocessor chips.

Kids can literally climb on a 20-times-life-sized trackball that operates the world's largest personal computer at The Computer Museum in Boston, Massachusetts.

In January, Microsoft Corporation and Compaq Computer Corporation co-sponsor an educational sitcom series that is shown to hundreds of millions of viewers in China. In the first episode of this comedy, the father goes to America and blows the family's entire savings on a personal computer.

Gilbert Amelio (from National Semiconductor Corporation) replaces Michael Spindler as CEO and A.C. "Mike" Markkula as chairman at Apple Computer, Inc.

China has ordered that all users of the Internet and other information networks register with its Ministry of National Security, its national police agency. Internet users who do not register can be punished. The Chinese government regulations forbid transmission of information considered harmful to state security or "public order."

Packard Bell Electronics, Inc. purchases Zenith Data Systems, Inc.

Countries with the most computers per 1,000 people: United States (319), Australia (225), Canada (220), Norway (218) and Japan (117).

Shakespeare has given way to computer literacy in today's classroom. A survey of over 1,400 public school teachers reports that at least 70 percent of the teachers rank the three Rs, the value of hard work, citizenship, computer skills, U.S. history and geography as essential components of public school curriculum. Less than 25 percent list classic works from Shakespeare and Plato, or writings by American authors such as Ernest Hemingway or John Steinbeck, as "absolutely essential."

IBM Corporation closes the door on an era of mainframe disk storage by stopping production of the once-dominant IBM 3390 disk subsystem. The 3390 used 10.8-inch disk drives.

Of the public libraries serving populations of 100,000 or more, 23 percent provide direct public access to the Internet and 70 percent provide commercial database searches with staff assistance.

On February 14 at the University of Pennsylvania, School of Engineering and Applied Science, a celebration is held commemorating the 50th anniversary of ENIAC, the world's first large-scale electronic digital computer.

All of the 38,706 registered runners in the 100th Boston Marathon wear a Champion Chip, a tiny radio-frequency chip laced on to their shoes. The chip transmits data on the runners performance to a custom information system set up by Digital Equipment Corporation for the Boston Athletic Association. The runners step on an electronic pad at the finish line that triggers an RF signal from the chip. The signal input is tabulated and made available just moments later on the World Wide Web.

The industry's 800-pound gorilla, AT&T Corporation, is evolving into three independent primates—a long distance carrier, an equipment and a computer maker.

Microsoft Corporation introduces the blueprints for a low-maintenance personal computer (PC) that can sit as the centerpiece of home computing and entertainment centers. The Simple Interactive Personal Computer (SIPC) essentially calls for PC manufacturers to build systems that are simple to use and easy to integrate with other consumer electronic equipment, such as televisions, VCRs or home stereos.

Hewlett-Packard Corporation introduces the PA-8000, a 64-bit microprocessor chip.

On April 19, CompuServe, Inc. is spun off by H & R Block, Inc. and is now traded on the New York Stock Exchange. It is the second online service to become publicily-owned.

Cray Research, Inc. introduces a second generation of its massive parallel processor (MPP) with scaled-down and air-cooled models. The T3E parallel processors are priced between 1 and 40 million dollars and use powerful versions of Digital Equipment Corporation's Alpha microprocessor.

Toshiba Corporation in Japan begins marketing a computer-controlled washing machine. It has an LCD panel that tells users how much water is in the tub, which button to press next and how to fix malfunctions.

In May, the IBM PC Company, the personal computer division of the IBM Corporation, announces an ultra-slim notebook computer. The ThinkPad 560 weighs 4 pounds, is 1.2 inches thick, can have up to 40 megabytes of memory, has a hard disk and is powered by an Intel Pentium microprocessor.

Packard Bell Electronics, Inc. acquires the personal computer operations of NEC Corporation outside of Japan. The combined firm is called Packard Bell

NEC and is now the fourth largest PC maker after IBM Corporation, Apple Computer, Inc., and Compaq Computer Corporation.

Interactive exhibits at the Motorola Museum of Electronics in Schaumburg, Illinois, give kids hands-on experience with models of logic and mathematics used by integrated circuit (IC) designers.

Apple Computer's year-old eWorld online service ceases to exist in its present form and becomes a World Wide Web site instead.

Software saboteurs create the first computer virus specifically targeted at Microsoft Corporation's Windows 95 Operating System. The virus can corrupt programs so that they no longer function, and then spread to other users' machines. Analysts have named the virus Boza after a Bulgarian liquor "so powerful that just looking at it will give you a headache."

The U.S. Navy launches an Arleigh Burke Class Aegis Destroyer named the USS Hopper (DDG-70) in honor of Grace Murray Hopper. Admiral Hopper was the grand lady of software and made many contributions in the development of programming languages. She died four years ago at the age of 85.

The U.S. Postal Service unveils the first postage stamp to honor the computer during ceremonies in Philadelphia, Pennsylvania that mark the 50th anniversary of the Electronic Numeric Integrator and Calculator (ENIAC).

World chess champion Gary Kasparov faces the chess computer Deep Blue in a six-game match. By the end of the match, Kasparov has outmaneuvered Deep Blue's developers—Chung-Jen Tan and his team at the IBM Thomas J. Watson Research Center in Yorktown Heights, New York—to win. But it is a tough battle. Kasparov predicts that both chess players and scientists will find great value in studying the games of this match for what they reveal about chess and about the way machines reason. Deep Blue can evaluate about 200 million positions per second. Kasparov's key advantage over Deep Blue was that he could learn, both as a game progressed and between games. In fact, the machine made the world champion player even tougher.

The IEEE Computer Society is now 50 years old.

China is fast becoming a major producer and exporter of consumer electronics and is determined to expand its integrated circuit (IC) industry. China has 330 semiconductor plants of which 25 produce ICs; the rest produce discrete devices.

Sun Microsystems, Inc. releases the Sun UltraSPARC-II microprocessor chip.

The IBM Corporation set up the first official Olympic site on the World Wide Web. The site plugs into the Olympic's computer systems and brings records and scores to anyone who has a computer and software to access the web.

Intel Corporation's latest microprocessor technology requires each transistor to be 100 times thinner than a human hair.

portable computer

Portable computers are getting faster, lighter and feature-rich.

In Turkey over 800 high schools have computer labs and courses on computer literacy and general computing are being introduced. Over 5,000 teachers have taken inservice training from universities and there are about 100,000 computer literate teachers in Turkey.

Mips Technologies, Inc. introduces a family of microprocessor chips designed to accelerate development of graphics-based content. The R5000 provides a high level of 3D graphics processing for applications such as Internet content creation.

India has about 130,000 highly skilled programmers, and some 20,000 new ones enter the workforce every year. A programmer in India is paid the equivalent of about $4,500 per year.

Silicon Graphics, Inc. buys the supercomputer maker Cray Research, Inc.

China occupies the world's third largest territory, behind only Russia and Canada. Its land area is occupied by 1.2 billion people, 22 percent of the world's population. The People's Republic of China is now a huge market for electronic products from cellular phones to personal computers. Information technology is now essential to Chinese industry.

Taiwan computer giant Acer Inc. launches a $500 network computer, becoming the first big maker to market an inexpensive personal computer in developing countries for logging on to the Internet.

Apple Computer, Inc. announces Harmony, an interim version of its Copland operating system for the Macintosh computer.

The World Wide Web has surpassed newspaper classified ads and auction houses as the best source for tracking down and trading collectibles.

Texas Instruments, Inc. is working on a way to make chips that can hold as many as 125 million transistors on them, allowing computers to process information significantly faster than current models. However, the technology won't be on the market until next year.

Samsung Electronics Company in South Korea is currently the world's largest manufacturer of computer memory chips.

America OnLine, Inc. starts providing online service in France, Germany, and Great Britain.

The PC Expo is held in New York. At this year's convention, networking, mobile computing, and wireless communications grabbed the spotlight.

There are about 35 million worldwide users of the Internet.

Markets are developing for Internet products and services in almost all regions of the world.

IBM Corporation and the Justice Department reach an agreement in July to eliminate the last remaining terms of a 1956 antitrust decree that was designed to keep IBM from monopolizing the computer industry. Citing increased competition in the computer industry, the Justice Department says the restrictions are no longer needed. The latest agreement phases out, over five years, business restrictions on IBM's midframe and mainframe computers.

Brazil has more computers (31,000) on the Internet than all the rest of Latin America. Brazil's National Research Network, whose acronym is RNP in Portuguese, serves as the nation's interstate backbone for the Internet.

On July 15, MSNBC, a 24-hour, all-news cable network created by Microsoft Corporation and NBC, lights up for the first time. MSNBC is a convergence of TV and the computer.

Compaq Computer Corporation introduces its line of Presario personal computers, a series of models that combines home computing with multimedia entertainment.

There are over 2.5 million personal computers in use in China.

Sony Corporation in Japan unveils its first personal computers, multimedia machines with violet-gray cases.

Attendance at the ACM SIGGRAPH computer graphics conference in New Orleans is 25,000.

Timex, in Middlebury, Connecticut, upgrades the Timex Data Link watch, which uses wireless technology to download info-nuggets such as telephone numbers and appointment dates from a personal computer to the watch.

Intel Corporation's first microprocessor, the Intel 4004, had about 2,200 transistors on it and had about 10 people designing it. Today, the chips that Intel engineers are working on, instead of 2,200 transistors, have about 10 million transistors, or about a 5,000-fold increase in the complexity of the chips if you measure it by the number of transistors. The size of the design team has gone from 10 people to 400 or 500 people, and the costs have gone up at least proportionally.

Thirty-six percent of all homes in America have a personal computer.

Back in 1964, when preparing an article, Gordon Moore, then the 36-year old R&D director at Fairchild Semiconductor (now Chairman of the Board, Intel Corporation), plotted the relationship between the number of transistors on a memory chip and time. The trend, he discovered, was that every 18 to 24 months, chip density doubled. Thirty-two years later, the relationship still holds.

In July, more than 700 hackers attended the Defcon IV annual computer hackers conference in Las Vegas, Nevada. The average age of attendees was 27 and females comprised 8 percent of the attendees.

All the on-line chess brains in the world couldn't beat Russian world champion Anatoly Karpov in August in the first open chess game on the Internet.

Sixteen million users access the Internet daily.

Susan Kare, sometimes called the Betsy Ross of the personal computer, designed the signature icons of the Apple Macintosh operating system (the moving watch, paintbrush, trash can, etc.) and most of the icons in Microsoft's Windows 3.0 operating systems.

The IBM Corporation employs about 225,000 people worldwide and 110,000 people in the United States.

The COMDEX Hispano America Confrence is held in Miami Beach, Florida in December. One of the main objectives of this conference is to feature information products (programs in Spanish and/or Portuguese) and services from Latin America countries.

America OnLine, Inc. has over 6 million online subscribers.

Very small personal computers are the major topic at a Wearable Computers Conference sponsored by the Boeing Company. The U.S. Army describes a computer the size of a pill that can be swallowed to track the core body temperatures of soldiers on training missions.

Internet traffic is doubling every year.

Digital Ocean in Kansas introduces the Seahorse, a rugged version of the Apple Newton. This personal digital assistant has a protective yellow rubber boot.

In September, the first, and once premier, computer user group, the Boston Computer Society (BCS) votes to cease operations. BCS was founded in 1973 by 13-year-old Jonathan Rotenberg. At its peak in the early 1990s, the group had 32,000 members worldwide. In late 1996 the membership was down to 18,000.

In September, Apple Computer, Inc. decides to kill its plans for the Copland Operating System for the Macintosh computer. The Copland OS had been planned to replace System 7 in mid-1997.

Sixty-five percent of U.S. households with income over $60,000 have personal computers.

IBM Corporation and Sears Roebuck sell the Prodigy online service to a group of investors called Internet Wireless.

The Java team leaves Sun Microsystems, Inc. and starts Marimba Inc. to create a Java technology to automatically distribute software over the Internet.

Silicon Valley's smoothest salesman closes another deal. Steven Jobs persuades Apple Computer, Inc., his old stomping grounds, to spend $400 million to purchase his NeXT Software Inc. Apple Computer plans to modify the NeXT operating system (OS) as a future OS for the Macintosh computer.

The 16 million bit DRAMs of 1993 had transistors half of a millionth of a meter in size. Today, the 64 million bit DRAMs on the commercial market reduce that size to 0.35 of a millionth of a meter.

A National Research Council report calls for greatly increased use of cryptography to protect electronic information and highlights shortcomings of current government policies on the availability of cryptographic technology.

Scotland produces nearly 40 percent of the branded personal computers sold in Europe and supplies 7 percent of the world's total PC output. Scotland also produces 12 percent of the semiconductors manufactured in Europe and has the highest concentration of semiconductor fabricators in Europe.

According to a national survey, the personal computer ties with aspirin as the fourth "most important invention."

Motorola, Inc. unveils the StarMax line of PowerPC-based Macintosh clone computer systems.

The California Highway Patrol is spotting motorists using laptop computers as they zip down the highways of Silicon Valley. One person reports that he does his E-mail while driving 80 miles an hour.

In 1976 the government of Taiwan decided it needed microelectronics technology to support its ambitions in the electronics industry. In 1976 they bought from RCA the technology to set up a microelectronics laboratory. During the 1970s the lab was making transistors seven-millionths of a meter across. Today it is making transistors as small as a quarter-millionth of a meter across, which is as advanced as any commercial process in the world today.

It requires 16 million bits to store 700 typed pages or a copy of *Gone With The Wind*. This information can be sent from one computer to another or from a computer to a fax or printer in less than one second. The cost of transmitting digitized data is heading toward becoming free.

Microsoft Corporation annnounces NetPC, a network personal computer. This machine is essentially a PC without a floppy drive. It includes a locked-down operating system to prevent theft of data configuration problems and the introduction of viruses. The operating system will automatically update when the computer is booted, and install applications and updates when invoked.

Automakers are worried about runaway growth in the software needed for today's microprocessor-run cars, *Electronic Engineering Times* noted. An engine controller has 100,000 lines of code.

EMC Corporation and NCR Corporation unveiled what is believed to be the world's largest data warehouse, containing 11 terabytes, or 11 trillion bytes, of information. This robust database consists of about 2.75 billion pages of text.

One of the world's oldest counting machines is now also one of the newest. Scientists at the IBM Zurich Research Laboratory have constructed a tiny abacus that substitutes carbon-60 buckyballs for the traditional beads. This nanoscale abacus is the first room-temperature device that can store and manipulate numbers at the molecular level.

IBM Corporation introduces a network computer (NC) featuring a built-in reader for smart cards that allows users to download their "computing personalities" from any remote location. The idea is to enable users to turn any remote system into their own personalized PC, eliminating the need for users to carry around portable systems.

The microprocessor is now 25 years old. Intel Corporation made memory chips to store data back in the late 1960s and early 1970s. It developed the microprocessor—in effect a tiny computer—for Busicom, a Japanese company that wanted an all-purpose chip for electronic calculators. Since then, the microprocessor has become powerful and commonplace. It serves as the brain of millions of personal computers and is found in automobiles, airplanes, appliances and other consumer electronics products.

For the first time, a robot has programmed another robot without human intervention. Via the Internet, a robot in Great Britain taught a tricycle-like robot in the United States to navigate using its ultrasound sensors, like a bat.

Sun Microsystems Inc. unveils the JavaStation network computer. This $742 computer includes a keyboard and mouse but no monitor. JavaStation uses Sun's Java chip and the Java language. This computer introduces a new form of computing based on software resident on central servers.

Andrew Grove, president and CEO of Intel Corporation, speaking to an assemblage of 7,000 computer people at the COMDEX Show, predicted what a microprocessor will look like 15 years from now, in the year 2011. Grove describes a processor with 1 billion transistors; a die size of 1.8 inches, about the size of a half-dollar; a performance of 10 gigahertz;

and running 100,000 millions of instructions per second.

IBM Corporation demonstrates technology that uses the natural salinity in the human body as a conductor to send and receive data electronically. However, IBM does not expect to produce a commercial product that uses this technology for at least a few more years.

In October, at a California Microprocessor Forum Conference, Motorola, Inc. and IBM Corporation as well as start-up Exponential Technologies, Inc. announce new PowerPC chips. Exponential's X704 chip, a 500-MHz PowerPC chip will be used in next year's Macintosh and Macintosh clone computers. Motorola and IBM are expected to have a 500-MHz PowerPC chip sometime in 1999.

In November some 225,000 computer users attend the COMDEX Computer Convention in Las Vegas, Nevada.

The Boeing Company now designs new jetliners completely by computer. Engineers at Boeing use IBM RS/6000 workstations during the jetliner design stage. In the next five years, Boeing plans to install 10,000 RS/6000 workstations that can carry the processing burden previously handled by mainframe systems.

In December, Intel Corporation announces the "ultra supercomputer," a breakthrough device which is about 2.5 times faster than any supercomputer. In a single second, it can perform as many calculations as the entire United States population can do working on hand calculators for 125 years. The initial ultra supercomputer will contain 9,200 PentiumPro processors operating in tandem at a cost of $55 million.

In December, scientists at the IBM Corporation announce that they achieved a new milestone in storing information on a hard disk, developing a disk drive that can hold five billion bits of data in a square inch. The drive can store the text of 625 novels on a single square inch of disk surface. That is between five and ten times the capacity of the disk drives currently used in typical personal computers.

The American chip market is the world's largest, representing more than a third of all chip sales— $154 billion.

1997

The Association for Computing Machinery (ACM) is now 50 years old.

Sun Microsystems, Inc. is scheduled to release a line of low-cost microprocessors geared solely to running applications based on the Java language.

Eighty thousand Apple Macintosh computers users attend the Macworld Expo at the Moscone Convention Center in San Francisco, California.

Intel Corporation introduces the P55C microprocessor, a Pentium with multimedia extensions for both desktop and notebook systems. Several computer manufacturers release personal computers that use the MMX-enabled Pentium chip.

The efficiency of information technology has increased 100 octillion times (100,000,000,000,000, 000,000,000,000,000,000) since ENIAC was introduced. Today's microprocessor works 10,000 times faster than the microprocessor used in the first IBM PC.

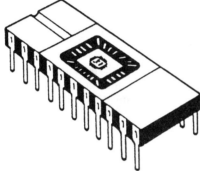

computer chip

There are now 200 billion chips in the world, 10 billion of them are microprocessors. They are found in clocks, TV's, game machines, appliances, automobiles, etc.

Intel Corporation announces a new approach to boost the storage capacity of "flash memory" chips, the circuitry that lets computers and other devices hold information even when they're turned off.

There are approximately 1.25 million independent computer consultants in the United States.

Gateway 2000, Inc., a popular direct-sell computer manufacturer, announces that it will start using resellers to market its computers to the high-end corporate market.

Motorola, Inc. developed a technique that replaces aluminum wiring with copper interconnects in integrated circuits which will result in smaller, faster computer chips. The process takes advantage of copper's greater resistance to electromigration.

The IBM Corporation received 1,724 U.S. patents, more than any other company. About 50 patents related to the use of copper in computer chips.

IBM Corporation announces that within the next five years it will build all its microprocessors using a new manufacturing process that depends on copper instead of aluminum to build transistors. This process results in smaller, faster computer chips.

Tandy Corporation now operates a 6,800-store Radio Shack chain and a 113-store Computer City chain.

In the final game of a six-game match in New York, world chess champion Gary Kasparov resigns after just 19 moves, giving IBM chess computer, Deep Blue, the win. It is the first tournament that Kasparov has ever lost to any opponent, human, or computer, since he became champion.

There are approximately 200,000 COBOL programmers in the current workforce.

Andrew Grove, a Hungarian immigrant, and holocaust survivor who became president and chief executive officer of Intel Corporation is Time magazine's "Man of the Year." Grove's aggressive drive and reputation as a briliant design engineer proved crucial to Intel's development of progressively more powerful computer chips, which set the pace for technology and are today the brains in more than 85 percent of the world's personal computers.

Two companies announce 56,000 (56K) bit/sec modems which are designed to speed up Internet communications.

A supercomputer, Teraflops, at Sandia National Laboratories in New Mexico, breaks the trillion-calculations-per-second barrier. The $55 million supercomputer shattered the computing speed record by performing 1.34 trillion calculations a second, about 22,750 times as fast as a Pentium 100 desktop personal computer. The supercomputer has 76 cabinets, which house 9,072 Intel Pentium Pro microprocessors.

COMDEX Conferences are held in Las Vegas (November) and Miami Beach (December).

"The Robot Zoo," an interactive exhibit opens at the Tech Museum of Innovation in San Jose, California. It features eight giant robot animals and computer workstations.

French neuroscientist Patrick Pirim invents a Generic Visual Perception Processor that reproduces several aspects of human vision on a chip.

In September, Apple Computer, Inc. bought Power Computing's Macintosh business in an effort to eliminate Macintosh clones.

Gateway 2000, Inc., a two-person start-up microcomputer manufacturing operation in 1985 is now a multi-billion dollar company.

Computer chip giant Intel Corporation introduces a new version of its Pentium II microprocessor that operates at 450 megahertz.

America OnLine Inc. worldwide membership now tops 10 million.

1998

A small business in Lima, Peru uses the Internet to sell tropical fish and other products from the Amazon jungle. This is but one of many businesses in poor countries that use the Internet as an electronic pathway to doing business in wealthy countries.

Seventy thousand E-mail messages are sent by fans to Olympic athletes in Nagano, Japan.

At the Livermore Science Laboratory in California, computers are humming along at up to 3 trillion calculations per second. That is the equivalent of 20,000 high-end personal computers working in parallel. Eventually they will top 100 trillion calculations per second (100 teraflops).

Compaq Computer Corporation buys Digital Equipment Corporation for roughly $9.6 billion. This merger puts Compaq into the No. 2 position among U.S. computer vendors.

Apple Computer, Inc. introduces the ultra modern iMAC network Macintosh computer.

Around the world the pressure is on for public schools to gain Internet acess.

In 1979, Intel's 8088 microprocessor chip held 29,000 transistors. Today engineers can pack over 5 million onto the same silicon slab.

Japan's Seiko Instruments, Inc. unveils a wristwatch computer called the Rupeter. The terminal can down load data including pictures and text from other personal computers.

The world's premier computer graphics conference, SIGGRAPH, is held in Orlando, Florida.

Radio Shack's Computer City superstores become part of the CompUSA computer superstore chain.

In August, Dell Computer Corporation edged out Compaq Computer Corporation as the No. 1 U. S. seller of desktop computers. Dell Computer is the world's biggest direct seller of personal computers. Michael Dell, CEO of Dell Computer, is the youngest and longest-serving CEO of a major computer company, and at 33, the 13th richest man in the world.

Microsoft Corporation releases the Windows 98 operating system.

Estimates in the late spring held that the Internet has ballooned to more than 320,000,000 pages. There are approximately 1,900 different search sites.

In September, the Internet came into its own as a communications medium when the Starr Report was put on the World Wide Web for downloading. Millions of people used the Internet to get the report of the investigation of allegations about President Clinton's extramarital affair. The fact that so many people could do this at one time, and do it successfully, marked a milestone in the worldwide computer network's usefulness as a means of reaching masses of people in one fell swoop. The Internet has become a counterpart of radio, telephone, TV, fax, conversation, the Postal Service, and one of the most useful tools in business.

In September, Motorola, Inc. becomes the fourth major chip manufacturer to stop the production of computer memory chips because of a worldwide slump in the sale of chips. Memory chip prices have fallen more than 70 percent over the past year.

PICTURE CREDITS

All illustrations are from the picture archives of the Camelot Publishing Company except as noted below: Apple Computer, Inc. 93, 115; Atari Corporation, 99; Bendix Aviation Corporation 39; Burroughs Corporation, 149, 152, 154; Commodore International, Inc. 109, 117; Control Data Corporation 49, 59, 147, 152; Cray Research, Inc., 131; Digital Equipment Corporation, 67, 151; General Electric Company, 154; Hewlett-Packard Company, 153; Honeywell, Inc., 149, 151, 152, 153; IBM Corporation 35, 36, 37, 42, 46, 47, 50, 62, 82, 107, 122, 147; Lawrence Livermore National Laboratory, 77; Moore School of Electrical Engineering, University of Pennsylvania, 27; Motorola, Inc., 150; National Cash Register Corporation, 150; Radio Corporation of America, 45, 67, 149; Siemens, 151; Sperry Rand Corporation 33, 49, 55, 147, 152, 153; Systems Engineering Laboratories, 148; Tandy Corporation, 101, 106; Texas Instruments, Inc. 105; Varian Data Systems, 148; Wang Laboratories, 148, 150; and Xerox Corporation, 79.

PORTFOLIO

Computers have rapidly become an important force in almost every segment of our society. No matter what size or type, all computer systems perform four basic tasks: input, processing, output, and storage. Computers come in many sizes and shapes—ranging from mammouth supercomputers to small hand-held computers. This *portfolio* illustrates some of the computers that have been used during the past five decades.

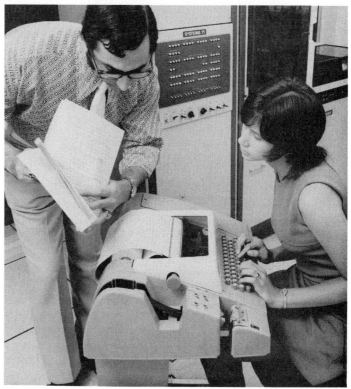

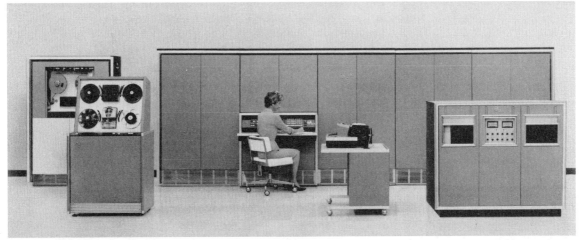

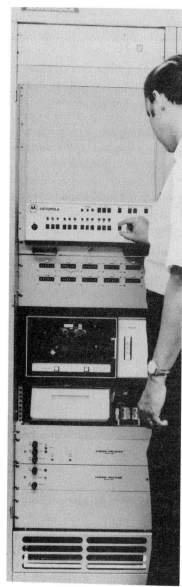

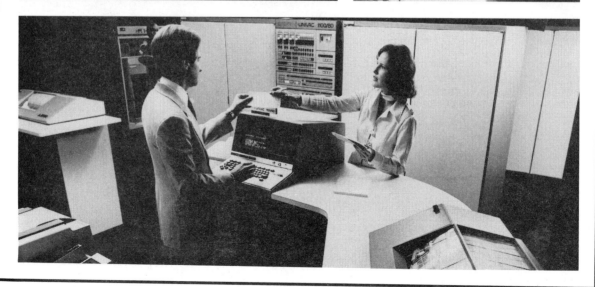

PORTFOLIO CAPTION: **PAGE 147**: IBM STRETCH computer system (*top left*); Sperry Univac 1100/90 computer system (*top right*); Control Data Corporation CDC 6600 supercomputer system (*bottom*); **Page 148**: Wang computer system (*top*); Varian Data Systems 620i minicomputer system (*bottom left*); Systems Engineering Laboratories Systems 71 minicomputer system (*bottom right*); **Page 149**: Honeywell H-1200 computer system (*top*); RCA 301 computer system (*center*); Burroughs B-5500 computer system (*bottom*); **Page 150**: NCR Century 200 computer system (*top*); Motorola MDP-1000 minicomputer system (*bottom left*); Wang professional computer system (*bottom right*); **Page 151**: Siemens (Germany) System 4004 computer system (*top*); Honeywell DPS-88 computer system (*center*); DECsystem-10 minicomputer system (*bottom*); **Page 152**: Control Data Corporation CDC 6400 supercomputer system (*top*); Honeywell 6/10 minicomputer system (*center left*); Burroughs B-1900 computer system (center right); Sperry Univac 1100/80 computer system (*bottom*); **Page 153**: Honeywell H-2200 computer system (*top*); Hewlett-Packard HP 3000 Series business computer system (*bottom left*); Sperry Univac 9400 computer system (bottom right*)*; **Page 154***:* Burroughs B-6500 computer system (*top*); General Electric Company GE-435 medium-scale computer system (*bottom*).

SELECTED BIBLIOGRAPHY

The following bibliography represents only a partial listing of the sources used for this study. It does not include primary materials such as computer manufacturers journals and brochures, oral computer history conservations, computer site visits, foreign language publications or daily newspapers.

I started working with computers (IBM 650 and IBM 704 machines) in the late 1950s and started collecting material for historical computer books in 1960. Most of the entries in this study were generated from computer publications, on-site computer visits and from first hand experiences during the past forty years. Some of the entries were extracted from some of my previously published college textbooks and reference books.

COMPUTER-RELATED NEWSPAPERS AND LARGE-FORMAT PUBLICATIONS

Automation News, Computer Grapics News, Computer Graphics Today, Computer Shopper, Computerworld, EDP Weekly, EDP News, Electronic News, Florida Business Journal, Information Week, Lawrence Livermore National Laboratory Weekly Bulletin, Microtimes, and *Robot X News.*

COMPUTER-RELATED PERIODICALS

ACM Computing Surveys, ACM Journal, ACM SIGGRAPH Newsletter, AFIPS Annuals of the History of Computing, AmigaWorld, A+ Magazine, Bell Laboratories Record, Business Automation, Business Week, Byte, Classroom Computer Learning, Communications of the ACM, Computer Artist, Computer Dealer, Computer Decisions, Computer Design, Computer Graphics World, Computer Graphics Review, Computer Museum Report, Computer Pictures, Computer Using Educators, Computers and Automation, Computers and People, Control Engineering, Creative Computing, Data Management, Datamation, Data Processing, Discover, Electromechanical Design, Electronic Design, Electronic Education, Electronic Engineer, Electronic Industries, Electronics, Family Computing, Forbes, Fortune, Hardcopy, Hewlett-Packard Journal, High Technolgy, Home and Educational Computing, Home PC, IEEE Annals of the History of Computing, IEEE Computer Graphics and Applications, IEEE Spectrum, Infosystems, Insight, Invention & Technology, International Science and Technology, Journal of Computers in Mathematics and Science Teaching, Journal of Data Education, Journal of Data Management, MacArtist, MacUSER, MacWorld, Manufacturing Systems, Mathematics Teacher, Microcomputing, Money, Newsweek, Online Today, PC Computing, PC Magazine, PC Novice, PC Today, PC World, Personal Computing, Perspectives in Computing, Pico, Popular Electronics, Popular Computing, Portable Computer, Robotics Age, Robitics Today, Robotics World, Scientific American, Science Digest, Science & Technology, The Computer Shopper, The Computing Teacher, The Futurist, The Institute, The Journal, The MACazine, Upside, U.S. News & World Report, Word Processing.

BOOKS

Aspray, William, Editor. *Computing Before Computers.* Ames: Iowa State University Press, 1990.

Augarten, Stan. *BIT by BIT: An Illustrated History of Computers.* New York: Ticknor & Fields, 1984.

Austrian, Geoffrey D. *HERMAN HOLLERITH: Forgotten Giant of Information Processing.* New York: Columbia University Press, 1982.

Baxandall, D. and Jane Pugh. *Calculating Machines and Instruments.* Science Museum, 1975.

Bernstein, Jeremy. *The Analytical Engine: Computers—Past, Present + Future.* New York: Vintage Books, 1964.

Bernstein, Jeremy. *Three Degrees Above Zero: Bell Labs in the Information Age.* New York: Charles Scribner's Sons, 1984.

Billings, Charlene W. *Grace Hopper: Navy Admiral and Computer Pioneer.* Hillside, New Jersey: Enslow Publishers, Inc., 1989.

Blohm, Hans, Stafford Beer, and David Suzuki. *PEBBLES TO COMPUTERS: The Thread.* Toronto, Canada: Oxford University Press, 1986.

Bowden, B.V. *Faster Than Thought.* London: Sir Isaac Pitman & Sons, Ltd., 1953.

Braun, Ernest and Stuart Macdonald. *Revolution in Miniature*. New York: Cambridge University Press, 1978.

Campbell-Kelly, Martin and William Aspray. *COMPUTER: A History of the Information Machine*. New York: BasicBooks, 1996.

Cheney, Margaret. *Tesla: Man Out of Time*. New York: Barnes & Noble Books, 1993.

Computers and Their Future. Llandudno, North Wales: The World Computer Pioneer Conference, 1970.

de Beauclair, W. *Rechnen mit Maschinen*. Braunschusig, Germany: Friedr, Vieweg & Sohn, 1968.

Dilson, Jesse. *The Abacus: A Pocket Computer*. New York: St. Martin's Press, 1968.

Dvorak, John C. *Dvorak Predicts: An Insider's Look at the Computer Industry*. New York: Osborne McGraw-Hill, 1994.

Eames, Charles and Ray., *A Computer Perspictive*. Cambridge, Massachusetts, Harvard University Press, 1973.

Eckert, W. J. and Rebecca Jones. *Faster, Faster*. New York: IBM Corporation, 1955.

Engineering Research Associates Staff. *High-Speed Computing Devices*. New York: McGraw-Hill Book Company, 1950.

Evans, Christopher. *The Making of the MICRO: A History of the Computer*. London: Victor Gollancz, Ltd., 1981.

Fang, Irving E. *The Computer Story*. St. Paul, Minnesota: Rada Press. 1988.

Fernbach, S. and A. Taub. *Computers and Their Role in the Physical Sciences*. New York: Gordon and Breach Science Publishers, 1970.

Fishman, Katharine Davis. *The Computer Establishment*. New York: Harper & Row, Publishers, 1981.

Flynn, Jennifer. *20th Century Computers and How They Worked: The Official Starfleet History of Computers*. Carmel, Indiana: Alpha Books/Prentice-Hall Computer Publishing, 1993.

Freed, Les. *The History of Computers*. Emeryville, California: Ziff-Davis Press, 1995.

Gibilisco, Stan, Editor. *McGraw-Hill Encyclopedia of Personal Computing*. New York: McGraw-Hill, Inc., 1995.

Glass, Robert L. *Computing Catastrophes*. State College, Pennsylvania: Computing Trends, 1983.

Glass, Robert L. *The Universal Elixir and other Computing Projects which Failed*. Seattle, Washington: Computing Trends, 1977.

Goldstine, Herman H. *The Computer from Pascal to von Neumann*. Princeton, New Jersey: Princeton University Press, 1972.

Greene, Laura. *Computer Pioneers*. New York: Franklin Watts, 1985.

Halacy, Dan. *Charles Babbage: Father of the Computer*. New York: The Macmillan Company, 1970.

Harmon, Margaret. *Stretching Man's Mind: A History of Data Processing*. New York: Mason/Charter Publishers, 1975.

Hartree, Douglas R. *Calculating Instruments And Machines*. Urbana: The University of Illinois Press, 1953.

Hawkins, Gerald S. *Stonehenge Decoded*. New York, Dell Publishing Company, 1965.

Heims, Steve J. *John Von Neumann and Norbert Wiener*. Cambridge, Massachusetts: The MIT Press, 1980

Helms, Harry. *The McGraw-Hill Computer Handbook*. New York: McGraw-Hill Book Company, 1983.

Hoover's Guide To Computer Companies. Austin, Texas: The Reference Press, Inc., 1995.

Hyman, Anthony. *CHARLES BABBAGE: Pioneer of the Computer*. Princeton, New Jersey: Princeton University Press, 1982.

IBM authors. *Time to know: a brief history of IBM*. New York: IBM Corporation, 1967.

Jespersen, James and Jane Fitz-Randolph. *RAMS, ROMS & Robots: The Inside Story of Computers*. New York: Atheneum, 1984.

Juluissen, Egil and Karen Petska-Juliussen. *Computer Industry Almanac*. Incline Village, Nevada: Computer Industry Almanac, Inc., 1994.

Kaufmann, William J., III and Larry L. Smarr. *Supercomputing and the Transformation of Science*. New York: Scientific American Library, 1993.

Kean, David W. *The Author of the ANALYTIC ENGINE*. Washington, D.C.: Thompson Book Company, 1966.

Kidwell, Peggy A. and Paul E. Ceruzzi. *Landmarks in Digital Computing.* Washington, D.C.: Smithsonian Institution Press.

Lammers, Susan. *Programmers at Work.* Redmond, Washington: Microsoft Press, 1986.

Lavington, Simon H. *Early British Computers.* Bedford, Massachusetts: Digital Press, 1980.

Lee, J.A.N. *Computer Pioneers.* Los Alamitos, California: IEEE Computer Society Press, 1995.

Levering, Robert, Michael Katz, and Milton Moskowitz. *The Computer Entrepreneurs: Who's Making It Big and How in America's Upstart Industry.* New York: NAL Books, 1984.

Lias, Edward J. *A History of General Purpose Computer Uses in the United States 1934 to 1977 and Likely Future Trends.* New York: New York University, 1978.

Littman, Jonathan. *Once Upon A Time in Computerland.* Los Angeles, California: Price Stern Sloan, 1987.

Livesley, R.K. *An Introduction to Automatic Digital Computers.* London: Cambridge University Press, 1960.

Lukoff, Herman. *From Dits to Bits...: A personal history of the electronic computer.* Portland, Oregon: Robotics Press, 1979.

Lundstrom, David E. *A Few Good Men from Univac.* Cambridge, Massachusetts: The MIT Press, 1987.

Macrae, Norman. *John von Neumann: The Scientific Genius Who Pioneered the Modern Computer, Game Theory, Nuclear Deterrence, and Much More.* New York: Pantheon Books, 1992.

Malone, Michael S. *The Microprocessor: A Biography.* New York: Springer-Verlag, 1995.

Manes, Stephen and Paul Andrews. *GATES: How Microsoft's Mogul Reinvented an Industry—and Made Himself the Richest Man in America.* New York: Doubleday, 1993.

Manners, David and Tsugio Makimoto, *Living with the CHIP.* London: Chapman & Hall, 1995.

Metropolis, N., J. Howlett, and Gian-Carlo Rota, Editors. *A History of Computing in the Twentieth Century.* New York: Academic Press, 1980.

More About Computers. Armonk, New York: IBM Corporation, 1971.

Moreau, R. *The Computer Comes of Age: The People, the Hardware, and the Software.* Cambridge, Massachusetts: The MIT Press, 1984.

Morrison, Philip and Emily Morrison, Editors. *Charles Babbage and his Calculating Engines.* New York: Dover Publications, 1961.

Newall, R.S. *Stonehenge.* London: Her Majesty's Stationery Office, 1959.

Oldfield, Homer R. *King of the Seven Dwarfs.* Los Alamitos, California: IEEE Computer Society Press, 1996.

Palfreman, Jon and Doron Swade. *The DREAM MACHINE: Exploring The Computer Age.* London: BBC Books, 1991.

Parker, Sybil P., Editor. *Encyclopedia of Electronics and Computers.* New York: McGraw-Hill Book Company, 1982.

Peak, Martha H., Editor. *REFLECTIONS: An Oral History of The Computer Industry.* Manhasset, New York: Computer Systems News, 1987.

Pearson, Jamie Parker. *DIGITAL AT WORK: Snapshots from the first thirty-five years.* Burlington, Massachusetts: Digital Press, 1992.

Pfeiffer, John. *The Thinking Machine.* New York: J.B. Lippincott Company, 1962.

Pullan, J.M. *The History of the ABACUS.* New York: Frederick A. Praeger, Publishers, 1968.

Ralston, Anthony and Edwin D. Reilly. *Encyclopedia of Computer Science, Third Edition.* New York: Van Nostrand Reinhold, 1993.

Ranade, Jay and Alan Nash. *The Best of BYTE.* New York: McGraw-Hill, Inc., 1994.

Randell, Brian, Editor. *The Origins of Digital Computers.* New York: Springer-Verlag, 1973.

Redmond, Kent C. and Thomas M. Smith. *Project WHIRLWIND: The History of a Pioneer Computer.* Bedford, Massachusetts: Digital Press, 1980.

Reid, T.R. *The Chip: How Two Americans Invented the Microchip and Launched a Revolution.* New York: Simon and Schuster, 1984.

Rodgers, William. *THINK: A Biography of the Watsons and IBM.* New York: Stein and Day, Publishers, 1969.

Roop, Peter and Connie Roop. *Stonehenge: Opposing Viewpoints.* San Diego, California: Greenhaven Press, 1989.

Rosen, Saul. *ACM 71: A Quarter Century View.* New York: Association for Computing Machinery, 1971.

Rutland, David. *Why Computers Are Computers: The SWAC and the PC.* Philomath, Oregon: Wren Publishers, 1995.

Seidman, Arthur H. and Ivan Flores. *The Handbook of Computers and Computing.* New York: Van Nostrand Reinhold Company, 1984.

Shasha, Dennis and Cathy Lazere. *OUT OF THEIR MINDS: The Lives and Discoveries of 15 Great Computer Scientists.* Copernicus/Springer-Verlag, 1995.

Shurkin, Joel. *Engines of the Mind: A History of the Computer.* New York: W.W. Norton & Company, 1984.

Slater, Robert. *Portraits in Silicon.* Cambridge, Massachusetts: The MIT Press, 1989.

Sobel, Robert, *IBM: Colossus In Transition.* New York: Times Books, 1981.

Sobel, Robert. *IBM vs. JAPAN: The Struggle for the Future.* New York: Stein and Day, Publishers, 1986.

Spencer, Donald D. *Computers: An Introduction.* Columbus, Ohio: Merrill Publishing Company, 1986.

Spencer, Donald D. *Great Men and Women of Computing.* Ormond Beach, Florida: Camelot Publishing Company, 1996.

Spencer, Donald D. *Introduction to Information Processing, Third Edition.* Columbus, Ohio: Charles E. Merrill Publishing Company, 1981.

Stein, Dorothy. *ADA: A Life and a Legacy.* Cambridge, Massachusetts: The MIT Press, 1985.

Stibitz, George R. and Jules A. Larrivee. *Mathematics and Computers.* New York: McGraw-Hill Book Company, 1957.

Time-Life Book Editors. *Understanding Computers: Computer Basics.* Alexandria, Virginia: Time-Life Books, 1985.

Toole, Betty Alexandria. *ADA, the Enchantress of Numbers.* Mill Valley, California: Strawberry Press, 1992.

Trask, Maurice. *The story of CYBERNETICS.* London: Studio Vista Limited, 1971.

Turck, J.A. *Origin of Modern Calculating Machines.* Chicago: The Western Society of Engineers, 1921.

Veit, Stan. *Stan Veit's History of the Personal Computer.* Asheville, North Carolina: WorldComm, 1993.

Von Neumann, John. *The Computer and the Brain.* New Haven: Yale University Press, 1958.

Wilkes, Maurice V. *Computer Perspectives.* San Francisco, California: Morgan Kaufmann Publishers, 1995.

Williams, Michael R. *A History of Computing Technology.* Englewood Cliffs, N.J.: Prentice-Hall, Inc. 1985.

Watson, Thomas J., Jr. *Father, Son & Co.: My Life at IBM and Beyond.* New York: Bantam Books, 1990.

Wulforst, Harry. *Breakthrough to the Computer Age.* New York: Charles Scribner's Sons, 1982.

Zientara, Marguerite. *The History of COMPUTING.* Framingham, Massachusetts: CW Communications, 1981.

INDEX